THE HOUND OF T[...]

SIR ARTHUR IGNATIUS CONAN DOYLE was born in Edinburgh in 1859, to the Irish-born Mary Doyle, née Foley, and Charles Altamont Doyle, an artist and draughtsman who was the grandson of the famous Irish political caricaturist, John Doyle ('H.B.'), and brother of Richard 'Dicky' Doyle, the illustrator. Conan Doyle studied at the Jesuit school, Stonyhurst, before taking a degree in medicine at Edinburgh. He helped to pay for his degree by signing on as a ship's surgeon on board a Greenland whaler, and after graduation worked on an African steamer, before practising medicine in first Bristol, and then Southsea. He married Louisa Hawkins in 1885. In his spare time the young doctor wrote magazine stories, with some degree of success, but he struggled to place his first attempt at a detective novel, *A Study in Scarlet*, which was published in *Beeton's Christmas Annual* for 1887 to a lukewarm reception. However, after his 'consulting detective', Sherlock Holmes, and his sidekick, John Watson, MD, appeared again in *The Sign of the Four* (1890), in a series of *Strand* magazine stories, they became a publishing phenomenon. Conan Doyle quit medicine for a career as a full-time writer, in which he achieved extraordinary international success. He went on to write two more Holmes novels, and fifty-six short stories, as well as the historical novels he regarded as his best work, his 'Professor Challenger' novels, and tales of the supernatural. In 1902, following the publication of his defence of Britain's role in the Anglo-Boer war, he was knighted. Louisa died in 1906, and the following year Conan Doyle married Jean Leckie, whom he had known for some years. Having devoted much of the time and energy of his later years to the cause of Spiritualism, he died in 1930. But it is for his contribution to detective fiction, and international popular culture more generally, that he is remembered. His widely translated work has inspired radio, stage, film, and television treatments, countless commercial spin-offs, and been the subject of academic books and articles. Many international societies celebrate the Holmes stories, including the Baker Street Irregulars, who publish the *Baker Street Journal*.

DARRYL JONES is the general editor of the Oxford Sherlock Holmes and Professor of Modern British Literature and Culture at Trinity College Dublin. He is the author or editor of thirteen books, including the Oxford World's Classics editions of M. R. James's *Collected Ghost Stories* and Arthur Conan Doyle's *The Hound of the Baskervilles* and *Gothic Tales*.

THE OXFORD SHERLOCK HOLMES

OXFORD WORLD'S CLASSICS

ARTHUR CONAN DOYLE

The Hound of the Baskervilles

Edited with an Introduction and Notes by
DARRYL JONES

OXFORD
UNIVERSITY PRESS

OXFORD
UNIVERSITY PRESS

Great Clarendon Street, Oxford, OX2 6DP,
United Kingdom

Oxford University Press is a department of the University of Oxford.
It furthers the University's objective of excellence in research, scholarship,
and education by publishing worldwide. Oxford is a registered trade mark of
Oxford University Press in the UK and in certain other countries

First published as an Oxford World's Classics paperback 2023

Impression: 1

Published in the United States of America by Oxford University Press
198 Madison Avenue, New York, NY 10016, United States of America

British Library Cataloguing in Publication Data

Data available

Library of Congress Control Number: 2022943953

ISBN 978-0-19-883522-6

Printed and bound in the UK by
Clays Ltd, Elcograf S.p.A.

ACKNOWLEDGEMENTS

No scholarship is ever done alone, and I am just the latest in a very long line of editors of Sherlock Holmes in general, and *The Hound of the Baskervilles* in particular. I owe a lot to all of them, but would particularly want to mention Christopher Frayling, Francis O'Gorman, and W. W. Robson, whose work on *Baskervilles*, though sometimes very different from mine, has helped me enormously.

At OUP, I would like to thank Luciana O'Flaherty for her enthusiasm for this edition, and all the new Oxford World's Classics Sherlock Holmes editions. She set me off down a long and fascinating road into the heart of the Great Grimpen Mire.

For many discussions about Arthur Conan Doyle and Sherlock Holmes down the years, and more generally for intellectual companionship and good cheer, I would like to thank Ailise Bulfin, Clare Clarke, Nick Daly, Bernice Murphy, Eve Patten, Deaglán Ó Donghaile, and Kevin Smith. Jarlath Killeen and I have been disagreeing for almost thirty years—so here's to the next thirty!

This book is for my wife, Margaret Robson, and my daughter, Morgan Jones, who make my time worthwhile.

CONTENTS

GENERAL EDITOR'S PREFACE
TO THE SERIES

As Arthur Conan Doyle knew better than anyone, death is never the end. Sherlock Holmes did not die when he and Professor Moriarty plunged over the Reichenbach Falls at the end of 'The Adventure of the Final Problem' in 1893, nor did he die after being put out to pasture by Conan Doyle in what is chronologically the latest of his adventures, 'His Last Bow' (published in 1917, but set in 1914), which left him in retirement on the Sussex Downs, keeping bees. Not even the death of his creator on 7 July 1930 would spell the end of Holmes, who has continued to live an increasingly vivid and complex afterlife, in stage, cinema, and television adaptations, in print and online in fictional sequels, spin-offs, and continuations, and fan fictions, and in a rich repository of academic scholarship and 'Sherlockian' research.

Between them, Arthur Conan Doyle and Sherlock Holmes changed the face of literature. The modern history of genre fiction is almost inconceivable without them, and Holmes himself is certainly the most celebrated literary detective, and perhaps the most famous literary character, ever created. The twenty-first century has been a time of volcanic activity in the worlds of Sherlock Holmes and Conan Doyle. Important critical works such as Catherine Wynne's *The Colonial Conan Doyle* (2002), Douglas Kerr's *Conan Doyle: Writing, Profession, and Practice* (2013), and Clare Clarke's *Late Victorian Crime Fiction in the Shadows of Sherlock* (2014), are just a few of the books to have changed the way we think about Holmes. In addition, Lellenberg, Stashower, and Foley's *Arthur Conan Doyle: A Life in Letters* (2007) and Andrew Lycett's biography *Conan Doyle: The Man who Created Sherlock Holmes* (2007) have greatly enriched the store of our knowledge. Across a variety of media, Holmes has found new lives, and ever larger audiences.

These new editions of the collected Sherlock Holmes bring to bear the best of modern criticism and scholarship on the residents of 221B Baker Street and their many adventures and problems. The editors of each of the volumes are themselves the latest in a long line of often extraordinary textual and literary scholarship, to which we are all greatly indebted, and which our work continues and develops. These editions comprise scrupulously edited texts, full textual annotations, and readable, informative, and provocative introductions. Once again, the game is afoot!

Darryl Jones
Trinity College Dublin

INTRODUCTION

Readers who are unfamiliar with the novel may prefer to treat the Introduction as an Afterword.

ON 25 March 1902, a parcel arrived at the Porter's Lodge of King's College Cambridge. As per his express instructions, the parcel was immediately taken to the rooms of the Tutor, Montague Rhodes James, who was awaiting its arrival along with his colleague, the University Registrary John Willis Clark. The 25th of March is Lady Day, the Feast of the Annunciation, and so the pair were supposed to be at a service in the College Chapel. But the parcel contained a book—Arthur Conan Doyle's long-anticipated *The Hound of the Baskervilles*, in which the great detective Sherlock Holmes had returned after a long silence of almost nine years.

Though he was two years away from publishing *Ghost Stories of an Antiquary*, the volume which would forge his reputation as the greatest of all English ghost story writers, M. R. James was an avid and highly knowledgeable reader of genre fiction, and he and Clark had been reading *Baskervilles* to each other as it came out in 'tantalizing monthly instalments' in *The Strand Magazine*. 'Sir Arthur Conan Doyle should be gratified if he knew how many evenings were devoted to speculation by undergraduates and others gathered in my rooms, and knew that the numerous false leads he laid down were eagerly followed', he wrote in his memoirs.[1] James was, according to his friend and former student, the Irish diplomat Sir Shane Leslie, 'deeply awed' by *The Hound of the Baskervilles*, which reminded him of a legend he knew about King Henry VIII's body bursting in his coffin, and the liquid being licked by a large black dog, in accordance with the prophecy of a friar whom the king had tortured.[2]

The publication of *Baskervilles* in book form, by George Newnes and Company, was deliberately timed for maximum sales—it came out before the last instalment of the novel appeared in *The Strand*,

[1] M. R. James, *Eton and King's: Recollections, Mostly Trivial 1875–1925* (1926; Ashcroft: British Columbia, 2005), 116.

[2] Shane Leslie, unpublished memoir of M. R. James, Leslie papers, King's College Cambridge MS. SJRL 1/2.

so readers who had been following the story could find out what happened without having to wait another few weeks. M. R. James was one such reader, and he and Clark bunked off the sermon to read the end of the story. The publication of *Baskervilles*, in fact, was designed to cause a sensation—and it did.

Sherlock Holmes was dead, to begin with. 'Killed Holmes', Conan Doyle wrote in his diary in December 1893, on the publication of 'The Final Problem'.[3] When the great detective plunged to his death over the Reichenbach Falls, wrestling with his nemesis Professor Moriarty, this was the cause of national shock and bereavement. 'You brute!', one appalled correspondent wrote to Conan Doyle.[4] In the City of London, it was claimed, clerks donned black armbands in mourning.[5]

Just two years earlier, in 1891, Dr Arthur Conan Doyle, author and ophthalmologist, had sent a pair of Sherlock Holmes stories, 'A Scandal in Bohemia' and 'The Red-Headed League', to Herbert Greenhough Smith, the editor of *The Strand Magazine*. This event was to change the lives of Conan Doyle, Greenhough Smith, and the magazine's publisher George Newnes. Writing long after the fact, Greenhough Smith recalled that 'I at once realized that here was the greatest short-story writer since Edgar Allan Poe. I remember rushing into Mr. Newnes's room and thrusting the stories before his eyes.'[6] There may be some hindsight involved here, but the judgement wasn't wrong. When 'A Scandal in Bohemia' was published in *The Strand* in June 1891, it marked the beginning of a phenomenal relationship, the making of both the author and the magazine. Together, as the literary historian Mike Ashley writes, these three men, Conan Doyle, Newnes, and Greenhough Smith, started 'a revolution . . . [which] changed the face of popular fiction in Britain and the English-speaking world'.[7] The first appearance of Holmes marked the beginning of a major boom in periodical publication, and of one

[3] Andrew Lycett, *Conan Doyle, The Man Who Created Sherlock Holmes* (London: Phoenix, 2007), 207.

[4] Reginald Pound, *The Strand Magazine 1891–1950* (London: Heinemann, 1966), 45.

[5] Lycett, 207.   [6] Pound, 41.

[7] Mike Ashley, *Adventures in The Strand: Arthur Conan Doyle and The Strand Magazine* (London: British Library, 2016), 9. For an analysis of the way in which the author and the magazine's interests tracked one another and eventually diverged, see Jonathan Cranfield, *Twentieth-Century Victorian: Arthur Conan Doyle and the Strand Magazine, 1891–1930* (Edinburgh: Edinburgh University Press, 2017).

of the great periods of popular genre fiction in English.[8] Such was their success that Conan Doyle wrote to Greenhough Smith claiming that 'Foreigners used to recognize English by their check suits. I think they will soon learn to do it by their *Strand Magazines*. Everybody on the Channel boat, except the man at the wheel, was clutching one.'[9]

But while Holmes was the making of Conan Doyle, he was also, the author began to feel, his undoing. Right up to the end of his life, Doyle felt that his real talents lay as a historical novelist: he maintained that *The White Company* (1891) and *Sir Nigel* (1906) were 'the most complete, satisfying thing that I have ever done. All things find their level, but I believe that if I had never touched Holmes, who has tended to obscure my higher work, my position in literature would at the present moment be a more commanding one.'[10] Sherlock Holmes 'had become a sort of nightmare—an old man of the sea about my neck', Doyle reportedly said to the Rev. Silas K. Hocking, in whose company he first visited the Reichenbach Falls in the Swiss Alps in August 1893. 'If I don't kill him soon he'll kill me.'[11] And so, off the Reichenbach Falls Holmes and Moriarty plunged, 'reeling over, locked in each other's arms . . . deep down in[to] that dreadful cauldron of swirling water and seething foam', there to lie 'for all time'.[12] He wasn't coming back. 'Poor Holmes is dead and damned', Conan Doyle wrote to the novelist David Christie Murray. 'I couldn't revive him if I would (at least not for years), for I have had such an overdose of him that I feel towards him as I do towards *pâté de foie gras*, of which I once ate too much.'[13] The very idea of Sherlock Holmes made Arthur Conan Doyle feel sick.

Conan Doyle's parenthetical remark, '(at least not for years)', left the door open, just a tiny crack, for the return of Sherlock Holmes

[8] For the history of this, see, for example, Peter Keating, *The Haunted Study: A Social History of the English Novel 1875–1914* (London, 1989), 9–91

[9] H. Greenhough Smith, 'Some Letters of Conan Doyle, with Notes and Comments', *The Strand Magazine* (October 1930), 395.

[10] Arthur Conan Doyle, *The Crowborough Edition*, vol. XXIV: *Memories and Adventures* (Garden City, New York, 1930), 86.

[11] Richard Lancelyn Green, 'Introduction' to ACD, *The Uncollected Sherlock Holmes*, ed. Richard Lancelyn Green (London: Penguin, 1983), 65. This is a later account, from G. B. Burgin's *Memoirs of a Clubman* (1921), though as Lancelyn Green notes, Hocking and several others had written accounts in a similar vein in the mid-1890s.

[12] ACD, 'The Final Problem', in *Sherlock Holmes: The Complete Short Stories* (London: John Murray, 1928), 556.

[13] Pound, 45.

somewhere down the line. And, down there in the deeps, the corpse did twitch a couple of times in the years to come. In July and August 1898, *The Strand* published a pair of semi-Holmes stories, 'The Man with the Watches' and 'The Lost Special', in which an unnamed detective or 'amateur reasoner of some celebrity' proposes solutions to fiendishly difficult crimes: 'It is one of the elementary principles of practical reasoning', the amateur reasoner claims, sounding for all the world like Holmes, 'that when the impossible has been eliminated the residuum, *however improbable*, must contain the truth'.[14] 'The Man with the Watches' and 'The Lost Special' simultaneously were and were not Holmes stories, but they at least allowed for the possibility of the great detective's return.

Such a return would have been enormously lucrative for all concerned. And, by the Spring of 1901, the time was definitely right. In November 1899, the American actor William Gillette's play *Sherlock Holmes* began a spectacularly successful theatrical run in the Garrick Theatre, New York. It was due to start its West End run in London in September 1901 (there had been a single London performance in the Duke of York's Theatre on 12 June 1899). In Ashley's words, this 'provided an ideal opportunity for cross-promotion'.[15] And so Conan Doyle wrote to Greenhough Smith, proposing either a non-Holmes novel for his regular fee of £50 per 1000 words or else a new Holmes novel for double that amount. There was no doubt as to what the decision would be. The precise figures are a little cloudy, but it has been suggested that *The Hound of the Baskervilles* in serial form added between 30,000 and 150,000 to *The Strand*'s sales.[16] For the first and only time in its history, issues of the magazine went through a seventh printing, to meet the unprecedented demand.[17] *The Strand* had always paid its authors well. Doyle got 30 guineas each for the first set of Holmes stories—not bad for an effective unknown—and 50 guineas each for the second set. For *Baskervilles*, he earned between £480 and £620 per instalment—some £6000 in total, about the same as it

[14] ACD, 'The Lost Special', in *The Conan Doyle Stories* (London: John Murray, 1929), 559.

[15] Ashley, 129.

[16] For the figure of 30,000, see Pound, 74; for 150,000, see Philip Weller, *The Hound of the Baskervilles: Hunting the Dartmoor Legend* (Tiverton: Devon Books, 2001), 17. Ashley suggests an increase of 100,000 (38).

[17] Richard Lancelyn Green and John Michael Gibson, *A Bibliography of A. Conan Doyle* (Oxford: Clarendon Press, 1983), 130.

had just cost him to build his opulent new house, Undershaw, a fourteen-bedroom mansion on four acres near Hindhead, Surrey.[18] For a professional writer like Arthur Conan Doyle, the pull of Holmes was always ultimately irresistible: 'You will be amused to hear that I am at work upon a Sherlock Holmes story', he once wrote to Greenhough Smith. 'So the old dog returns to his vomit.'[19] He still felt sick—but think of the money!

The story of *The Hound of the Baskervilles* begins with three men returning to England from South Africa. The first of these is Arthur Conan Doyle himself. Always a committed imperialist and militarist, when the Second Boer War broke out in 1899, Doyle went to the headquarters of the Middlesex Yeomanry in Hounslow to enlist in the army. 'What I feel', he wrote to his mother, 'is that I have perhaps the strongest influence over young men, especially young athletic sporting men, of anyone in England (bar Kipling). That being so it is really important that I give them a lead.'[20] He was a man of forty, with no military training or experience, and so, he recalled, 'the colonel would only put me on his waiting list, took my name, still without recognizing me, and passed on to the next case. I departed somewhat crestfallen and unsettled'.[21] Shortly afterwards, he took up the opportunity to go to South Africa as a military doctor, based in a field hospital set up on a cricket pitch in Bloemfontein, where he treated an outbreak of enteric fever (typhoid) amongst the troops, which he believed was caused by the Boers cutting off the water supply to the town, and which cost 5000 lives.[22]

Conan Doyle's South African experience gave his imperialism, always highly pronounced, a decidedly reactionary turn. A man of forthright views, he was a keen writer of letters to the press, and across the course of the Boer War, these letters took a very hard line about the best way to deal with 'Brother Boer', advocating the use of 'Boer irreconcilables' as human shields, of explosive 'dum dum' bullets, and most notoriously of concentration camps.[23] On returning

[18] Pound, 74; Weller, 17.   [19] Greenhough Smith, 393.
[20] ACD, *A Life in Letters*, ed. Jon Lellenberg, Daniel Stashower, and Charles Foley (London: Harper Perennial, 2008), 434.
[21] ACD, *Memories and Adventures*, 169.   [22] Ibid., 178.
[23] Ibid., 194; ACD, *The Unknown Conan Doyle Letters to the Press*, ed. John Michael Gibson and Roger Lancelyn Green (London: Secker and Warburg, 1986), 82, 84, 85.

from South Africa, Conan Doyle's first major endeavour was a gargantuan 700-plus-page account of the conflict, *The Great Boer War* (1900), which expressed his belief that the Boer was 'the most formidable antagonist who ever crossed the path of Imperial Britain. . . . Napoleon and all his veterans have never treated us so roughly as these hard-bitten farmers with their ancient theology and their inconveniently modern rifles.'[24] Doyle was particularly struck by the sheer physical hardiness of the Boers, 'one of the most rugged, virile, unconquerable races ever seen upon earth'—compared with whom, he worried, the British were in danger of looking like weak and unmanly specimens.[25] The book was criticized in some quarters for its bullish imperialism, and one piece of criticism hit home so hard that he remembered it twenty years later: 'Doyle's book makes the impression that it was ordered or influenced by the English Jingo party.'[26] Doyle was not a man much given to reflection or self-doubt, and so, characteristically, his response to this criticism was to double down. In 1902, he published a short, propagandistic tract, *The War in South Africa: Its Causes and Conflicts*, and poured his vast energies into a subscription campaign to translate it into as many languages as he could think of. This book contained a long chapter vigorously defending the British use of concentration camps in South Africa: 'We have pushed our humanity in the matter of refugees so far that we have looked after our enemies better than our friends', he claimed.[27] For the rest of his life, he saw no cause to change his mind about the Boer War. In his autobiography, he recalled advocating for the genocide of the Boers: 'It would be very awkward for us to have a colony which was full of dangerous men. . . . Our only chance is to kill them now, and that's what we will do if we have the time.'[28] It was for *The War in South Africa*, and its accompanying propaganda campaign, that Arthur Conan Doyle was knighted by King Edward VII in 1902.

On the voyage back from South Africa, Conan Doyle became friendly with another man returning from the conflict, the journalist Bertram Fletcher Robinson. He was very much the kind of masculine

[24] ACD, *The Great Boer War* (1900; London: Smith, Elder, & Co., 1902), 2.

[25] Ibid., 1. For an excellent analysis of this, see Cranfield, 43–62.

[26] ACD, *Memories and Adventures*, 215.

[27] ACD, *The War in South Africa: Its Causes and Conduct* (New York: McClure, Phillips, & Co., 1902), 85.

[28] ACD, Memories and Adventures, 204.

type that Arthur Conan Doyle liked and admired, a six-foot-three Cambridge rugby blue and College rower: 'Bertram Fletcher Robinson was an immense figure of a man', his friend the novelist Max Pemberton recalled, 'a magnificent Rugby forward and a fine rider to hounds.'[29] Fletcher Robinson came from a family with a strong background in colonial adventures—his father was a friend of Giuseppe Garibaldi, alongside whom he fought in Argentina against the dictator Juan Manuel de Rosas in the 1840s, before going on to help map the west coast of South America in the 1850s, and then undertaking a 700-mile trek across the Andes on horseback.[30] After Cambridge, Fletcher Robinson began to make a name for himself as a military journalist, writing the series 'Famous Regiments' for *Cassell's Magazine*. This attracted the attention of Arthur Pearson, publisher of the rival *Pearson's Magazine*, who offered Fletcher Robinson a job as a war correspondent for his new publishing endeavour, a morning newspaper called the *Daily Express*.[31] On his return from South Africa, Robinson was appointed editor of the *Express*, aged just 34.

After they got back from South Africa, Conan Doyle and Fletcher Robinson kept in touch, and arranged to go on a golfing holiday together, to the Royal Links Hotel in Cromer, on the Norfolk coast. It was from the Royal Links Hotel that Conan Doyle wrote to his mother, in March 1901: 'Fletcher Robinson came here with me and we are going to do a small book together "The Hound of the Baskervilles"—a real Creeper.'[32] The following month, Conan Doyle paid a visit to Fletcher Robinson's family home at Ipplepen, Devon, on the fringes of the unearthly wilderness of Dartmoor.

Our third returning South African is the man who precipitates the action of *The Hound of the Baskervilles*, Sir Charles Baskerville. Sir Charles has made a fortune in the South African goldfields, 'realized his gains and returned to England with them' (p. 13), and moved into his ancestral home of Baskerville Hall, which he plans to modernize and renovate: 'The total value of the estate was close on to a million'

[29] Max Pemberton, *Sixty Years Ago and After* (London: Hutchinson & Co., 1936), 124.
[30] See Brian W. Pugh and Paul R. Spiring, *Bertram Fletcher Robinson: A Footnote to The Hound of the Baskervilles* (London: MX Publishing, 2008), 3–4.
[31] Ibid., 68–70. [32] ACD, *A Life in Letters*, 477.

(p. 39).[33] As Andrew Glazzard points out, Sir Charles has made his money in 'speculation'—investment in goldmines rather than ownership of them. Conan Doyle himself had investments in Australian and South African goldmines from 1892, and bought shares in the Robinson Central Deep Mine in Johannesburg in 1902.[34] He had a personal interest in South African gold. South Africa, with its unparalleled mineral resources—its fabulous goldfields and legendary diamond mines—was strategically and economically vital to the British Empire, and had been one of the imaginative centres of British imperial fiction since the spectacular success of H. Rider Haggard's *King Solomon's Mines* in 1885. A letter from the explorer Verney Lovett Cameron, read to the Royal Geographical Society and published in *The Times* in 1876, was messianic about the whole continent's economic opportunities:

The interior [of Africa] is mostly a magnificent and healthy country of unspeakable richness. I have a small specimen of good coal; other minerals such as gold, copper, iron and silver are abundant, and I am confident that with a wise and liberal (not lavish) expenditure of capital, one of the greatest systems of inland navigation in the world might be utilized, and from 30 months to 36 months begin to repay any enterprising capitalist that might take the matter in hand.[35]

Conan Doyle's literary imagination travelled to South Africa several times over many years. In 1879, he published his first story, 'The Mystery of Sasassa Valley', a tale of South African diamond prospectors. The eponymous narrator of his first, unfinished, and unpublished novel, *The Narrative of John Smith* (1883), once worked as 'a diamond digger at the Cape'.[36] In 1903, the year after the book publication of *Baskervilles*, he published 'The Solitary Cyclist', another tale of returning South Africans and fabulous fortunes in gold and jewels, 'the finest diamonds in London'.[37]

---

[33] 'I believe that readers will not go far wrong if they think of a nineteenth-century pound as equivalent to £100 now. That holds broadly true for the century as a whole.' Jerry White, *London in the Nineteenth Century: A Human Awful Wonder of God* (London: Jonathan Cape, 2007), xv.

[34] Andrew Glazzard, *The Case of Sherlock Holmes: Secrets and Lies in Conan Doyle's Detective Fiction* (Edinburgh: Edinburgh University Press, 2018), 30–6.

[35] 'African Exploration', *The Times* (11 January 1876), 11.

[36] ACD, *The Narrative of John Smith*, ed. Jon Lellenberg, Daniel Stashower, and Rachel Foss (London: British Library, 2011), 27.

[37] ACD, 'The Solitary Cyclist', *Sherlock Holmes: The Complete Short Stories*, 642.

More generally, at least since Wilkie Collins's *The Moonstone* (1868), British imperial fiction had been fascinated by the far-flung empire as the source of endless loot. As the Indian intellectual Shashi Tharoor has written, 'India was governed for the benefit of Britain. Britain's rise for 200 years was financed by its depredations in India.'[38] The Moonstone itself, plundered from a Hindu temple, is closely modelled on the most legendary of all imperial gemstones, the fabulous, cursed Koh-I-Noor diamond, the Mountain of Light, a stone around which legends have swirled for centuries.[39] *The Moonstone* was an important influence on the young Conan Doyle, providing some of the inspiration for his early novel *The Mystery of Cloomber* (1888), in which a trio of Indian mystics pursue a British soldier to his remote home in Scotland to enact retribution for an atrocity he committed as a younger man. *The Moonstone* also lies somewhere behind *The Sign of the Four* (1890), the second Holmes novel, about the search for a priceless collection of jewels, including ' "the Great Mogul" . . . said to be the second largest stone in existence', stolen from Agra Fort during the First War of Indian Independence of 1857.[40] In the same novel, Dr. Watson reveals that he has himself spent time in the Australian goldfields, where he visited 'a hill near Ballarat, where the prospectors had been at work.'[41]

Baskervilles is, in fact, full of returning colonials. Sir Henry Baskerville, Sir Charles's heir, has been 'farming in Canada' (p. 20), and still speaks with a North American drawl. Stapleton is the son of the wicked Rodger Baskerville, who 'fled to Central America, and died there in 1876 of yellow fever' (p. 20)—but not before fathering a son with his Latin American wife. This is Rodger Baskerville Jr, who comes to England to get his hands on the Baskerville fortune, and changes his name to Vandeleur, and then to Stapleton. He brings with him his own exotic jewel, his wife 'Beryl Garcia, one of the beauties of Costa Rica' (p. 135). Dr. Watson himself had returned to London

---

[38] Shashi Tharoor, *Inglorious Empire: What the British Did to India* (London: Penguin, 2016), 3. Tharoor notes that in 1700, India's share of the world economy was 27%; by 1946, when the British left, it was just 3%.

[39] For a history of this diamond and its legends, see William Dalrymple and Anita Anand, *Koh-I-Noor: The History of the World's Most Infamous Diamond* (London: Bloomsbury, 2017).

[40] ACD, *The Sign of [the] Four*, in *The Complete Sherlock Holmes Long Stories* (London: John Murray, 1929), 258.

[41] Ibid., 178.

only a few years earlier, having been invalided out of the British army after being wounded during the Afghan Wars.

So, during their stay in the Royal Links Hotel in Cromer, Conan Doyle and Fletcher Robinson cooked up an idea for a novel called *The Hound of the Baskervilles*. But this was *not* the novel you have in your hands, or not exactly. The precise nature and extent of Fletcher Robinson's contribution to *Baskervilles* has been a much-disputed and at times controversial subject down the years.[42] What seems to have happened is that the pair began talking about Norfolk folklore, and most particularly about the local legend of 'Black Shuck', a local demon hound ('Shuck' is from the Anglo-Saxon 'scucca', meaning 'devil' or 'Satan'), which led in turn to a discussion of the many analogous Black Dog legends from around Robinson's native Dartmoor. And so the pair began to draw up the plot for a supernatural tale, a Gothic novel set on Dartmoor, about the legend of a demonic hound. This is what animates the letter which Conan Doyle sent to Greenhough Smith on the subject of his new novel:

I have the idea of a real creeper for *The Strand*. It is full of surprises, breaking naturally into good lengths for serial purposes. There is one stipulation. I must do it with my friend Fletcher-Robinson [*sic*], and his name must appear with mine. I can answer for the yarn being all my own in my own style without dilution, since your readers like that. But he gave me the central idea and the local colour, and so I feel his name must appear.[43]

What *doesn't* appear in this early description of *Baskervilles* is any account of Sherlock Holmes. But the idea to write a new Holmes story, too good to resist, came to Doyle as he was working on the early drafting of *Baskervilles*: it was certainly clear in his mind by the time he visited Ipplepen the following month. And so, what we have here

---

[42] W. W. Robson actually begins his introduction to the OUP edition of *Baskervilles* with a discussion of the novel's authorship: for him, this is 'The first matter for the critic to investigate' (Robson, 'Introduction' to ACD, *The Hound of the Baskervilles*, ed. W. W. Robson (Oxford: Oxford University Press, 1993), vii). Christopher Frayling, another of the novel's editors, has returned to this subject several times: see Frayling, *Nightmare: The Birth of Horror* (London: BBC Books, 1996), 168–96; 'Introduction' to ACD, *The Hound of the Baskervilles*, ed. Christopher Frayling (London: Penguin, 2001), xiv–xxiv; 'Nothing But a Hound Dog', in *Inside the Bloody Chamber: On Angela Carter, the Gothic, and Other Weird Tales* (London: Oberon Books, 2015), 193–211.

[43] Greenhough Smith, 391.

is a Sherlock Holmes novel overlaid onto the original structure of a Gothic novel. This explains a number of the novel's features. It accounts for its highly creative sense of tension between the material and the supernatural worlds, a tension which gives the novel a good deal of its power and appeal, as the readers, like the characters themselves, are faced with a generic and categorical mystery: what *kind* of novel are we reading? It also accounts for Sherlock Holmes's own absence from large parts of the novel, from the beginning of Chapter 6 to the beginning of Chapter 12, as Watson's narrative describes the uncanny landscape of Dartmoor, a space of epistemological uncertainty, and possibly of magic.

The published novel, then, is not the proposed novel; and by the time *Baskervilles* began its serialization, Conan Doyle had changed his position on shared authorship. The first instalment, in *The Strand Magazine* of August 1901, was entitled:

> The Hound of the Baskervilles.*
> ANOTHER ADVENTURE OF
> SHERLOCK HOLMES.
>   By CONAN DOYLE.

The asterisk led readers to a footnote: 'This story owes its inception to my friend, Mr. Fletcher Robinson, who has helped me both in the general plot and in the local details.—A.C.D.'[44] By the time of the first book edition in 1902, the dedication had changed again:

> MY DEAR ROBINSON,
>   It was to your account of a West-Country legend that this tale owes its inception. For this and for your help in the details all thanks.
>   Yours most truly,
>   A. CONAN DOYLE.[45]

For the American edition a few weeks later, the phrase 'this tale owes its inception' had been considerably weakened to 'first suggested the idea of this little tale to my mind'.[46] For the John Murray collected

---

[44] *Strand Magazine*, 22:128 (August 1901), 123.

[45] ACD, *The Hound of the Baskervilles: Another Adventure of Sherlock Holmes* (London: George Newnes, 1902), Dedication page.

[46] ACD, *The Hound of the Baskervilles* (New York: McClure, Phillips, & Co., 1902), Dedication page.

edition of 1929, Conan Doyle felt obliged to gloss further: 'I should add that the plot and every word of the actual narrative was my own.'[47] In his account of the authorship of *Baskervilles*, Greenhough Smith downplayed Fletcher Robinson's role yet further: 'As readers of the story are aware, Fletcher-Robinson's name was fully acknowledged. His share in the transaction was to draw the attention of Conan Doyle to the tradition of the fiery hound in a Welsh guide-book.'[48]

Some of Fletcher Robinson's friends certainly believed he had been cheated. The prolific novelist Archibald Marshall, a Cambridge chum, was adamant that Robinson 'wrote most of its first instalment for the *Strand Magazine*'.[49] (Presumably, Marshall means the legend of the curse of the Baskervilles here, not the actual Holmes material.) Marshall believed that Doyle had agreed to pay Robinson 25% of the earnings from *Baskervilles*. Andrew Lycett, Conan Doyle's most authoritative biographer, believes that the original agreement was even more generous, with Fletcher Robinson promised a third of the earnings. In the event, he got much less: Conan Doyle wrote him a cheque for £500 in the latter part of 1901, 'but subsequent payments were more sporadic'.[50]

(Many years after the fact, in an article published in 1939, Max Pemberton maintained that *he* had in fact given Fletcher Robinson the idea for the story: 'Fletcher Robinson . . . was dining in my house in Hampstead one night when the talk turned upon phantom dogs. . . . Three nights afterwards, Fletcher Robinson was dining with Sir Arthur. The talk in my house was still fresh in my mind, and he told Doyle what I had said.'[51])

In the event, Fletcher Robinson did get to write his own, much less successful story of a phantom hound. 'The Terror in the Snow' is one of *The Chronicles of Addington Peace*, a volume of detective stories he published in 1905. Set in Cloudham, Norfolk (that is, Cromer), the story begins, like *Baskervilles*, with an ancestral legend: in the eighteenth century, the nobleman Phillip de Laune brings home an albino wolf from St Petersburg, as a pet. The wolf kills de Laune's young son, tearing his throat out, and so de Laune kills the beast with his

[47] ACD, *Complete Sherlock Holmes Long Stories*, vi.
[48] Greenhough Smith, 391.
[49] Archibald Marshall, *Out and About: Random Reminiscences* (London: John Murray, 1933), 5.
[50] Lycett, 279.   [51] Weller, 45.

own hands. Cursed, the de Laune family falls into ruin, and Cloudham is haunted by the spirit of the wolf: 'The beast walks, man. There's not a labourer in Norfolk who would go into the lower garden on any night of the year, much less Christmas Eve.'[52]

Bertram Fletcher Robinson died in 1907, aged just 36, of typhoid caused by drinking contaminated water in a Parisian hotel. Occult rumours hung around his death for decades afterwards, beginning with the persistent story that he was killed by an Egyptian mummy's curse: in 1904, he had published a front-page story in the *Express* entitled 'A Priestess of Death: The Weird Story of an Egyptian Coffin'.[53] Conan Doyle came to believe this story: years later, after the death of Lord Caernarvon at the excavation of the Tomb of Tutankhamun in 1923, the *Daily Express* reported him as saying: 'The death of Mr. Fletcher Robinson . . . was caused by Egyptian "elementals" guarding a female mummy, because Mr. Robinson had begun an investigation of the stories of the mummy's malevolence. . . . I warned Mr. Robinson against concerning himself with the mummy at the British Museum. He persisted, and his death occurred.'[54]

Arthur Conan Doyle was a lifelong believer in the supernatural, but Sherlock Holmes was not. In 'The Sussex Vampire', Holmes famously dismisses the possibility of the supernatural: 'Rubbish, Watson, rubbish! . . . This Agency stands flat-footed upon the ground, and there it must remain. The world is big enough for us. No ghosts need apply.'[55] But in the uncertain terrain of the Great Grimpen Mire, as we shall see, it was impossible to stand 'flat-footed upon the ground' without sinking in and being swallowed up. And so *The Hound of the Baskervilles* maintains a delicately balanced undecidability throughout, in a manner that seems to affect even Holmes's fundamentalist materialism. Is it a rational detective story set in the positivistic, scientific, industrial world of Victorian England, or is it a supernatural Gothic tale set in a haunted, ambiguous landscape in which past and present collide? As the history of its composition and

[52] B. Fletcher Robinson, 'The Terror in the Snow', in *The Chronicles of Addington Peace* (London and New York: Harper & Brothers, 1905), 58.

[53] Roger Luckhurst, *The Mummy's Curse: The True History of a Dark Fantasy* (Oxford: Oxford University Press, 2012), 27–8.

[54] Ibid., 31.

[55] ACD, 'The Sussex Vampire', in *Sherlock Holmes: The Complete Short Stories* (London: John Murray, 1928), 1179.

the practice of reading it demonstrate, the novel is simultaneously both things.

The Hound of the Baskervilles stands on the threshold between two worlds, with a foot in each: a phantom hound which leaves material footprints. On hearing of the legend of the 'Baskerville demon', Holmes remarks: 'In a modest way I have combated evil, but to take on the Father of Evil himself would, perhaps, be too ambitious a task' (p. 20). The parenthetical 'perhaps' here signals the novel's categorical slipperiness: Holmes is *probably* not up to taking on Satan himself, in whom, it would seem, he *probably* does not believe (but, 'when you have eliminated the impossible, whatever remains, *however improbable*, must be the truth').[56] Holmes advises Sir Henry to 'avoid the moor in those hours of darkness when the powers of evil are exalted' (p. 46); Sir Henry in turn vows, 'We'll see it through if all the fiends of the pit were loose upon the moor' (p. 82).

In *The Hound of the Baskervilles*, Sherlock Holmes is himself an ambiguous presence, simultaneously alive and dead. Conan Doyle did not precisely bring Holmes back from the dead for *Baskervilles*. Rather, the novel presents itself as a posthumous tale, a recounting of an earlier adventure, which takes place before the fateful encounter on the Reichenbach Falls (there is some dispute as to *when* the events of the novel are supposed to have taken place, but 1888 or 1889 seem most likely).[57] But, in the autumn of 1903, some eighteen months after the publication of the book version of *Baskervilles*, Doyle published a new Holmes story, 'The Empty Room', in which Holmes is unambiguously brought back to life—but in a manner which has decidedly mystical overtones. Having miraculously survived the Reichenbach Falls, Holmes tells Watson that for the past three years he has walked the earth on a spiritual (or even Spiritualist) odyssey, travelling for two of those years in Tibet, where he spends time with the Dalai Lama in Lhasa, and going on a pilgrimage to Mecca.

In travelling to Dartmoor in *Baskervilles*, Holmes goes on another spiritual journey of sorts. Early in the novel, he and Watson have the following discussion:

[56] ACD, *The Sign of the Four*, 185.

[57] See 'Appendix 5: The Dating of *The Hound of the Baskervilles*', in ACD, *The New Annotated Sherlock Holmes*, Vol. III: *The Novels*, ed. Leslie S. Klinger (New York: W. W. Norton, 2006), 626–7.

'Where do you think I have been?' [asks Holmes]. . . . I have been to Devonshire.'

'In spirit?'

'Exactly. My body has remained in this arm-chair and has, I regret to observe, consumed in my absence two large pots of coffee and an incredible amount of tobacco. After you left I sent down to Stanford's for the Ordnance map of this portion of the moor, and my spirit has hovered about it all day.' (p. 23)[58]

Holmes is evoking the language of astral projection here, a subject in which Doyle had been interested from the very beginning of his writing career. He appended an essay on 'The Occult Philosophy' to *The Mystery of Cloomber*, in which he discusses 'The eastern adepts [who] exist at present principally in the north of India and in Thibet': 'An adept can put off his soul as he would put off his great-coat, and can travel in his soul with the rapidity of thought to the other end of the world. This endows him with practical omniscience as far as mundane affairs are concerned.'[59] There was, in fact, always something bordering on the supernatural about Holmes's 'practical omniscience': as far back as *A Study in Scarlet* (1887), in his first-ever account of Holmes's methods, Watson observes that 'the uninitiated . . . might well consider him as a necromancer'.[60] Although materially absent from the whole central portion of the novel, Holmes's spirit does indeed 'hover' over Dartmoor, as for Watson he takes on the guise of a mysterious, supernatural *genius loci*, the Man on the Tor, 'the unseen watcher, the man of darkness': 'He stood with his legs a little separated, his arms folded, his head bowed, as if he were brooding over that enormous wilderness of peat and granite that lay behind him. He might have been the very spirit of that terrible place' (p. 84).

In April 1901, Conan Doyle wrote to his mother from Rowe's Duchy Hotel in Princetown on Dartmoor. By this time, we can see, he was definitely writing a Sherlock Holmes novel:

---

[58] For a superb reading of this passage, see Janice M. Allan, 'Gothic Returns: *The Hound of the Baskervilles*', in Janice M. Allan and Christopher Pittard, eds, *The Cambridge Companion to Sherlock Holmes* (Cambridge: Cambridge University Press, 2019), 169–71.

[59] ACD, *The Mystery of Cloomber* (1888; London: Ward & Downey, 1896), 146, 148.

[60] ACD, 'A Study in Scarlet', in *The Complete Sherlock Holmes Long Stories*, 20.

Here I am in the highest town in England. Robinson and I are exploring the moor over our Sherlock Holmes book. I think it will work out splendidly— indeed I have already done nearly half of it. Holmes is at his very best, and it is a very dramatic idea—which I owe to Robinson.

We did 14 miles over the moor today and we are now pleasantly weary. It is a great place, very sad & wild, dotted with the dwellings of prehistoric man, strange monoliths and huts and graves. In the old days there was evidently a population of very many thousands here & now you may walk all day and never see one human being.[61]

This was not, it should be said, Conan Doyle's first visit to Dartmoor. In the summer of 1882, he spent a couple of rain-sodden days taking photographs of the moor in the company of Dr. George Budd, the eccentric and (according to Doyle) corrupt doctor with whom he briefly went into business in Plymouth (a period of his life memorialized in Doyle's autobiographical *The Stark Munro Letters* of 1895). 'Rugged "tors" and tangled masses of half-withered vegetation shut us in', he wrote in 1882, 'and the narrow road wound through a wilderness . . . where men had wandered in circles until they had dropped dead of hunger and fatigue.'[62] This visit provided the inspiration for one of Doyle's most strikingly Gothic early stories, 'The Winning Shot' (1883), in which a group of day-trippers on Dartmoor find themselves in 'a charnel-house place' at the foot of a tor, where the water sounds 'like the gurgling on the throat of a dying man':

On top of this mound, about sixty feet above our heads, a tall dark figure was standing, peering down, apparently into the rugged hollow in which we were.

The moon was just topping the ridge behind, and the gaunt, angular outlines of the stranger stood out hard and clear against its silvery radiance.

There was something ghastly in the sudden and silent appearance of this solitary wanderer, especially when coupled with the weird nature of the scene.

This, then, is the first appearance in Conan Doyle's fiction of the Man on the Tor. But here, he is not the benign and protective figure

---

[61] ACD, *A Life in Letters*, 479–80.

[62] ACD, 'Dry Plates on a Wet Moor', in *The Unknown Conan Doyle: Essays on Photography*, ed. John Michael Gibson and Richard Lancelyn Green (London: Secker & Warburg, 1982), 34.

of Sherlock Holmes, but an unambiguously supernatural presence, the evil, vampiric occultist Octavius Gaster: 'There was something in his angular proportions and the bloodless face which, taken in conjunction with the black cloak which fluttered from his shoulders, irresistibly reminded me of a bloodsucking species of bat.'[63]

Before *Baskervilles*, Conan Doyle's fiction had returned to Dartmoor for a Brigadier Gerard story, 'How the King Held the Brigadier' (1895), in which Gerard attempts an escape from Dartmoor prison, and even for another Holmes story, 'Silver Blaze' (1892). Here, the horse trainer John Straker appears to have been beaten to death by a 'Penang lawyer'—the same walking stick used by Dr. Mortimer, discussed in the opening paragraph of *Baskervilles*. Like *Baskervilles*, 'Silver Blaze' all hangs on 'the curious incident of the dog in the night-time'.[64]

Conan Doyle's Dartmoor is a phantasmagoric place. Even the stolid, foursquare Watson understands this. His first impression of the moor is that it is 'like some fantastic landscape in a dream' (p. 46). Like an English Lost World, the moor contains its own unique ecosystem: fabulous moths, rare orchids, enormous, phosphorescent hounds. It is Stapleton, the Anglo-Costa Rican naturalist and murderer, who feels most at home on the moor (it is his family home), who best understands its meaning: 'It is a wonderful place, the moor. . . . You never tire of the moor. You cannot think of the wonderful secrets which it contains. It is so vast, and so barren, and so mysterious. . . . [A]ll things are possible upon the moor' (p. 59).

During their long day's hiking on the moor, Conan Doyle and Fletcher Robinson visited Fox Tor Mire, a peat bog over a granite floor, a few miles from their base in Princetown. 'I took Doyle to see the mighty bog, a thousand acres of quaking slime', Robinson wrote.[65] The novel's Gothic imagination transformed this already remarkable spot into one of the most extraordinary pieces of symbolic landscape in English literature, the Great Grimpen Mire.[66]

---

[63] ACD, 'The Winning Shot', in *Gothic Tales*, ed. Darryl Jones (Oxford: Oxford University Press, 2016), 36–7.

[64] ACD, 'Silver Blaze', in *Sherlock Holmes: The Complete Short Stories*, 326.

[65] Weller, 69.

[66] For a brilliant account of the Great Grimpen Mire and its analogues, see Catherine Wynne's chapter 'Colonial Topographies: Bogs, Moors and Shifting Grounds', in *The Colonial Conan Doyle: British Imperialism, Irish Nationalism, and the Gothic* (Westport, CT: Greenwood, 2002), 65–99.

The Great Grimpen Mire is the very emblem of the novel's categorical ambiguity and uncertainty, the place where you cannot find
your feet, into which characters may sink, hopelessly lost—'a false
step yonder means death to man or beast', Stapleton warns (p. 57)—
and out of which mysterious things may emerge. From the moment
he arrives in Dartmoor, Watson recognizes, 'I have been conscious of
shadows all round me. Life has become like that Great Grimpen
Mire, with little green patches everywhere into which one may sink
and with no guide to point the track' (p. 63). The mystery of the
Hound of the Baskervilles, he writes, is 'this bog in which we are
floundering' (p. 76). The mire may, indeed, be alive, a conscious actor
in the plot. It seems to let out 'a long low moan, indescribably sad'.
'It's the weirdest strangest thing that ever I heard in my life', Watson
says (p. 59). At the end of the novel, when he and Holmes venture into
the 'dark, quivering mire', he feels 'as if some malignant hand was
tugging us down into those obscene depths, so grim and purposeful
was the clutch in which it held us' (p. 132).

Conan Doyle's fiction returns frequently to the symbolic possibilities of bogs, quicksands, and other varieties of uncertain, shifting
terrain. For one thing, as several critics have suggested, in their very
instability, bogs and their analogues can be made to signify, in
Catherine Wynne's phrase, 'the control or ownership of land'.[67]
Discussing another late-Victorian bog novel, Bram Stoker's *The
Snake's Pass* (1890), Nicholas Daly writes: 'Not only does the
bog physically resist the surveyor's project, it also produces from
its depths disturbing reminders of the history of the colonial project.'[68] The mire, then, is a *disputed* landscape, over which a number
of returning colonials—a South African, a Canadian, a Costa
Rican—make plausible claims. As the son of Rodger Baskerville, in
a direct line from the ancestral Hugo, Stapleton may well have the
clearest moral (and perhaps legal) claim to ownership—certainly, he
is the one, as we have seen, who identifies most strongly by far with
the landscape, even to the extent of being absorbed into it at the end
of the novel. Sir Charles (the hereditary title seems to be his, not his
family's—neither Hugo nor Rodger are titled—and so may well be

[67] Wynne, 65.

[68] Nicholas Daly, *Modernism: Romance and the Fin de Siècle: Popular Fiction and
British Culture, 1880–1914* (Cambridge: Cambridge University Press, 1999), 54.

a product of his vast fortune rather than his lineage) has an unspecified claim on the Baskerville estate, and dies childless. Sir Henry is his nephew.

Dartmoor's very wildness and weirdness—rare moths and orchids, Costa Ricans, unearthly creatures—aligns it with the variety of exotic or colonial landscapes which recur across Conan Doyle's fiction. It resembles Flytrap Gulch, full of carnivorous plants, in one of his first stories, 'The American's Tale' (1880): 'a marshy, gloomy place . . . soft and deep, and a body thrown in would be gone by morning'.[69] It is like the West African landscape that Doyle visited while working as a ship's doctor on board the SS *Mayumba*, fresh out of medical school in 1881: 'Dark and terrible mangrove swamps . . . where nothing that is not horrible could exist'.[70] This is the landscape that he would recall in 1897 when writing 'The Fiend of the Cooperage', a colonial horror story about a monstrous snake, set amongst marshes containing 'singular orchids and curious-looking plants'.[71] It is also the landscape of the South African veldt, 'a strange, wild place' full of 'relics of some extraordinary geological episode', or of the Sahara of *The Tragedy of the Korosko* (1898), in which a man and his camel can be 'sucked in and swallowed'.[72] It is like Maple White Land, the South American plateau of *The Lost World*, which also has its own unique flora and (especially) fauna, and which resembles 'a dream of fairyland'. At its centre, the explorers discover a swamp of pterodactyls: 'pools of green-scummed, stagnant water, fringed with bulrushes. It was a weird place in itself, but its occupants made it seem like a scene from the Seven Circles of Dante.'[73] And also it is like the ancestral Ireland of the Doyle family, a contested, boggy land. Conan Doyle's only Irish-set story, 'The Heiress of Glenmahowley' (1884), is set at 'the centre of an enormous area of peat cuttings and bog land', into which Fenians throw the body of an oppressive landlord, 'Mr. Lyons of Glenmorris . . . afther [*sic*] they shot him.'[74]

---

[69] ACD, 'The American's Tale', in *Gothic Tales*, 6.

[70] ACD, *Memories and Adventures*, 55.

[71] ACD, 'The Fiend of the Cooperage', in *Gothic Tales*, 293.

[72] ACD, *Memories and Adventures*, 177; ACD, The Crowborough Edition, Volume III: *The Tragedy of the Korosko / The Exploits of Brigadier Gerard* (Garden City, NY: Doubleday, Doran & Co. 1930), 90.

[73] ACD, *The Lost World* (London: Hodder and Stoughton, 1912), 114, 175.

[74] ACD, 'The Heiress of Glanmahowley', in *The Unknown Conan Doyle: Uncollected Stories*, ed. John Michael Gibson and Richard Lancelyn Green (London: Secker & Warburg, 1982), 144, 146.

The Mystery of Cloomber reaches its dramatic climax at 'the great bog of Cree', a landscape of 'dangerous swamps and treacherous pitfalls of liquid mud'. Colonial vengeance catches up with General Heatherstone in the form of the pursuing trio of Indian mystics, and it is into this 'bottomless pit' that he sinks without trace.[75] Published a couple of months later, in February 1889, the historical novel *Micah Clarke* is set in a West Country of moorlands and bogs, across which the protagonists are pursued by 'great hounds', that 'might have been grim silent spirits of the night, the phantom dogs of Herne the Hunter'.[76] One villainous character meets a horrible end in this 'boggy and treacherous' terrain: 'he sank of a sudden with a gurgling sound, and the green marsh scum met above his head, No ripple was there and no splash to mark the spot. It was sudden and silent, as though some strange monster of the marshes had seized him and dragged him down into the depths.'[77] In *The Sign of the Four*, published the following year, Jonathan Small is imprisoned on the Andaman Islands, spending 'Twenty long years in that fever-ridden swamp' before escaping to London.[78] He is caught by Holmes when he gets his wooden leg caught in the mud of the Thames (he lost his leg to a crocodile while swimming in the Ganges)—but not before jettisoning his priceless cargo of jewels into the river. Into the Thames also goes his companion, Tonga the Andaman Islander: 'Somewhere in the dark ooze at the bottom of the Thames lie the bones of that strange visitor to our shores.' Small will be sentenced to spend the rest of his life 'digging drains at Dartmoor'.[79]

The Great Grimpen Mire has a literary provenance well outside Conan Doyle's own writing. We have already discussed the importance of *The Moonstone* for Doyle's work, and part of that novel's mystery lies beneath the Shivering Sands, a quicksand which 'looks as if it had hundreds of suffocating people under it—all struggling to get to the surface, and all sinking lower in the dreadful deeps!': 'whatever goes into the Shivering Sand is sucked down and seen no more. . . .

---

[75] ACD, *The Mystery of Cloomber*, 137, 138.

[76] ACD, *Micah Clarke*, in *The Conan Doyle Historical Romances*, vol. 1 (London: John Murray, 1931), 885.

[77] Ibid., 1164, 1175.   [78] ACD, *The Sign of the Four*, 245.

[79] ACD, *The Sign of the Four*, 236, 238.

What the Sand gets, the Sand keeps forever.'[80] Conan Doyle was also a great admirer of Robert Louis Stevenson's 'The Pavilion on the Links', which he considered 'one of the great stories of the world'.[81] Another tale of vengeance carried out in remote corners of Britain (like *Cloomber*, it's set on the Scottish coast; like Collins's *The Woman in White* or Conan Doyle's own 'The Red Circle', the remorseless pursuers are members of an Italian nationalist secret society), the eponymous pavilion is built next to Graden Floe, an 'infamous' quicksand which 'would swallow a man in four minutes and a half'.[82]

But the work which most directly parallels *Baskervilles* is *A Book of Dartmoor*, published in 1900 by the Devon clergyman, man of letters, and Victorian all-rounder Sabine Baring-Gould. Baring-Gould was obsessed by Dartmoor, and in the words of his biographer, 'throughout his writing—whether on history, folklore, archaeology or in fiction—depicts it as charged with wonder.'[83] It's entirely possible that Conan Doyle actually read *A Book of Dartmoor* while he was there with Fletcher Robinson.[84] Certainly, the book prefigures many of *Baskervilles*' preoccupations and images: the tors, the Neolithic settlements and pre-historic inhabitants, the orchids and rare plants, the supernatural tales and folklore—and most especially the bogs. Baring-Gould begins the book with a long and detailed chapter on the bogs of Dartmoor: this is the first thing you need to know about this remarkable place. Of the 'quaking-bogs', he writes that 'It is a difficult matter to extricate horses when they flounder in . . .; every plunge sends the poor beasts in deeper'.[85] The worst of them is Fox Tor Mire, which 'once bore a very bad name', and is 'composed of . . . a horrible yellow slime . . . . and to cross it one must leap from tuft to tuft'.[86] Sabine Baring-Gould himself recalls how he once sank into a Dartmoor bog 'over my waist, and felt myself being sucked down as though an octopus had got hold of me'.[87] Dartmoor's bogs, he writes, were reputed to be populated by 'large, glaring-eyed monsters'.[88]

[80] Wilkie Collins, *The Moonstone*, ed. Sandra Kemp (London: Penguin, 1998), 39, 139, 165–6.

[81] ACD, *Memories and Adventures*, 289.

[82] Robert Louis Stevenson, 'The Pavilion on the Links', in *The Complete Stories of Robert Louis Stevenson*, ed. Barry Menikoff (New York: Modern Library, 2002), 139.

[83] J. E. Thomas, *Sabine Baring-Gold: The Life and Work of a Complete Victorian* (Stroud: Fonthill, 2015), 128.

[84] Frayling, 'Nothing But a Hound Dog', 207.

[85] Sabine Baring-Gould, *A Book of Dartmoor* (London: Methuen, 1900), 3.

[86] Ibid., 6, 8.   [87] Ibid., 10.   [88] Ibid., 5.

In 1897, Baring-Gould had written his own novel of Dartmoor, *Guavas the Tinner*. The novel is set against the background of a very Gothic moor, 'full of horror . . . ghostlike'. Its protagonist, Eldad Guavas, keeps a wolf as a companion, 'a foul fiend . . . his hair bristling, his eyes gleaming in the firelight, and his eyes glowing like carbuncles'.[89] The action comes to its dramatic conclusion in Fox Tor Mire, as the wolf attacks the villainous Dickon Rawle, who sinks to his death: 'Out of the mire emerged a hand, clutching wildly in the air . . . and then—sinking below the surface.'[90]

When he first hears of the legend of the Hound of the Baskervilles, Holmes dismisses it as only of interest 'To a collector of fairy-tales' (p. 12). But as Doyle knew, even if Holmes didn't, the collecting of fairytales, and the study of folklore more generally, was a business the Victorians took very seriously. The Folklore Society, formed in 1878, codified a renewed interest in folklore studies, often with a distinctly nationalist (or sometimes a regionalist) approach, from scholars, poets, and anthologists such as Andrew Lang, Fiona Macleod, Sir William and Lady Jane Wilde, Joseph Jacobs, and W. B. Yeats.[91] For the Victorians, there was nothing particularly unusual or outré about being 'a collector of fairy-tales'—and, in fact, Doyle's own father, Charles Altamont Doyle, was a commercial artist who specialized in pictures of fairies.

British folklore is rich in legends of black dogs and phantom hounds.[92] In folklore and legend, dogs are often understood as liminal beings, mediators between two worlds.[93] They mediate between the animal world and the human world, as exemplified by the folk legend that, after the Creation, a gulf opened up between Adam and the beasts, and the dog leaped over the gulf to join Adam. Dogs have their feet in both worlds. They also mediate between the worlds of the living and the dead, which is why they are often associated with boundaries.

[89]   Sabine Baring Gould, *Guavas the Tinner* (London: Methuen, 1897), 1, 138, 157.
[90]   Ibid., 273.
[91]   This is a much-condensed version of a longer argument I have made elsewhere: Darryl Jones, *Sleeping with the Lights On: The Unsettling Story of Horror* (Oxford: Oxford University Press, 2018), Chapter 2.
[92]   See Katharine M. Briggs, 'Black Dogs', in *A Dictionary of British Folk-Tales in the English Language, Part B: Folk Legends*, Volume 1 (London: Routledge and Kegan Paul, 1971), 3–19.
[93]   For this paragraph, I draw heavily on Patricia Dale-Green, *Dog* (London: Rupert Hart-Davis, 1966).

The dog Cerberus guards the entrance to the Underworld. Dogs are believed to howl at the death of their owners because they, unlike us, can actually see the Angel of Death, and more generally can see the spirit world. Thus, the appearance of a ghost dog could only be interpreted as an omen of death. Hell has its own hounds, of course, and Black Dogs are often thought to be the Devil in canine form. Phantom hounds are often described as flaming, or having fiery eyes (eyes that shine, burning red).[94] As the folklorist Theo Brown notes, Black Dogs are sometimes chthonic, 'coming out of, living in, or associated with the ground', and they have a particular affiliation with pits or holes, and occasionally with mines. Sometimes, they are seen sinking into the ground. They are significantly associated with prehistoric remains, with cromlechs and standing stones.[95]

Devon, and Dartmoor in particular, is home to several legends of Black Dogs and other phantom hounds. The folklorist Katharine Briggs recounts a Dartmoor Black Dog story with affiliations to some aspects of *Baskervilles*: a traveller sets out across the moor from the Royal Duchy Hotel in Princetown, and encounters 'an enormous dog, neither mastiff nor bloodhound, but what seemed to him to be a Newfoundland of immense size', which pursues him across the moor until he gets to a crossroads: 'Tradition says that a foul murder was many years ago committed at this spot, and the victim's dog is doomed to traverse this road and kill every man he encounters, until the perpetrator of the deed has perished by his instrumentality.'[96] In 1638, a Black Dog appeared 'from the sky, with lightning' at Widecombe-on-the-Moor; later versions of the tale have the hound accompanied by the Devil on horseback.[97] In their account of the folklore of Devon, Jennifer Westwood and Jacqueline Simpson list a number of phantom hound tales.[98] At the church of Buckfastleigh on the eastern fringes of the moor—not far from Fletcher Robinson's home at Ipplepen—lies the tomb of Richard Cabell, a wicked squire who reputedly hunted maidens for sport, and was doomed to be pursued through the afterlife by a pack of spectral hounds (I've visited

[94] Briggs, 8.
[95] Theo Brown, 'The Black Dog', *Folklore*, 69:3 (September 1958), 182–4.
[96] Briggs, 13.   [97] Brown, 'The Black Dog', 181–2.
[98] Jennifer Westwood and Jacqueline Simpson, *The Lore of the Land: A Guide to England's Legends, from Spring-Heeled Jack to the Witches of Warboys* (London: Penguin, 2005), 178–204.

Cabell's tomb, and it definitely looks as though it was built to keep something *in*). At the Dewerstone on the Moor, there is a legend of a headless hound; the rock itself is said to be named after Dewer, the demon huntsman of Dartmoor, who commands a supernatural pack of 'Whisht Hounds'. Further north, near Martinhoe, the ghost of cruel landowner Sir Robert Chichester is doomed to walk the countryside in the shape of a Black Dog. The Black Dog Inn at Uplyme, on the Devon–Dorset border, is named after a local legend of a spectral hound.

There were indeed Baskervilles in Devon—including Harry Baskerville, the Robinson family coachman, who drove Conan Doyle around on his 1901 visit, and who understandably was to make much of his surname in future years (it is a resonant surname, and one on which he dined out for the rest of his life—though Conan Doyle had come up with the novel's title *before* he met Harry Baskerville). But the main branch of the Baskervilles are from the Welsh border, around Herefordshire, and have as their family crest 'a wolf's head erased, or pierced through the mouth in bend sinister point upwards'.[99] The crest is attached to an old family legend, according to which one of the ancestral Baskervilles, in a drunken state, ran his faithful wolfhound through with his sword when the dog started barking to warn him of the approach of an enemy. 'Henceforth', Theo Brown was told, 'the death of a head of the family was announced by the baying of a hound.'[100] Conan Doyle unquestionably had a lot of material on which he could draw when he came to write *The Hound of the Baskervilles*.

A whole interrelated complex of symbols, themes, and patterns recurs throughout Arthur Conan Doyle's fiction: colonial retribution, unstable landscapes, priceless jewels, fantastic beasts. Especially, it seems, the beasts. Conan Doyle's England is a recognizably modern place, a place you can navigate by means of Ordnance Survey maps and *Bradshaw's Railway Guides*. But it is also a land of jaguars, leopards, baboons, swamp adders, cave bears, pterodactyls, lions,

---

[99] *Fairbairn's Book of Crests of the Families of Great Britain and Ireland*, 2 vols, 4th edn (London and Edinburgh: T. C. & E. C. Jack, 1905), 38.
[100] Brown, *Devon Ghosts* (Norwich: Jarrold Colour Publications, 1982).

mongooses, and demon hounds.[101] Any reader who believes that the mystery of the novel is solved with the discovery of the tin of phosphorescent paint, the 'proof' that there is no demonic hound, has missed the point of *The Hound of the Baskervilles*. The known and the unknown, the material and the spirit worlds, the natural and the supernatural, positivistic certainty and superstitious doubt, are all layered into the same landscape—into which you, the reader, are liable to sink and get lost. This is England—but England is not the place you thought it was.

[101] See, respectively, 'The Brazilian Cat', 'The Speckled Band', 'The Terror of Blue John Gap', *The Lost World*, 'The Veiled Lodger', 'The Crooked Man'—and *The Hound of the Baskervilles*. In the Holmes story 'The Copper Beeches' (1892), the villainous Jephro Rucastle has an enormous mastiff, 'a giant dog, as large as a calf': *Sherlock Holmes: The Complete Short Stories*, 292.

NOTE ON THE TEXT

THE HOUND OF THE BASKERVILLES first appeared in serial form in *The Strand Magazine*, August 1901–April 1902. The first book edition was published by George Newnes on 25 March 1902. A Colonial edition, published by Longmans' Colonial Library, followed on 2 April, with the American edition published by McClure, Phillips, & Co. on 15 April. The manuscript of the novel was broken up and sold as 185 individual sheets as part of the publicity campaign for the novel. Only 37 of these sheets are now known to exist, scattered across a variety of libraries and private collections. The only manuscript of a complete chapter (Chapter 11, 'The Man on the Tor') is in the Henry W. and Albert A. Berg Collection, New York Public Library. For a detailed account of the surviving manuscripts and their locations, see http://www.bestofsherlock.com/baskervilles-manuscript.htm.

The text for this edition is based on the 1993 Oxford University Press edition, edited by W. W. Robson, which in turn was based on the 1902 George Newnes first edition. Where there are significant differences between editions and manuscripts, I have discussed them in the Explanatory Notes.

SELECT BIBLIOGRAPHY

Biographical works

John Dickson Carr, *The Life of Sir Arthur Conan Doyle* (London: John Murray, 1949).

Arthur Conan Doyle, *A Life in Letters*, ed. Jon Lellenberg, Daniel Stashower, and Charles Foley (London: Harper, 2008).

Arthur Conan Doyle, *Memories and Adventures* (London: Hodder and Stoughton, 1924).

Owen Dudley Edwards, *The Quest for Sherlock Holmes: A Biographical Study of Arthur Conan Doyle* (Edinburgh: Mainstream, 1983).

Andrew Lycett, *Conan Doyle: The Man Who Created Sherlock Holmes* (London: Weidenfeld and Nicolson, 2007).

The literary background

Mike Ashley, *Adventures in the Strand: Arthur Conan Doyle and the Strand Magazine* (London: British Library, 2016).

Peter Keating, *The Haunted Study: A Social History of the English Novel 1875– 1914* (London, 1989).

Reginald Pound, *The Strand Mgazine 1891–1950* (London: Heinemann, 1966).

Philip Waller, *Writers, Readers and Reputations: Literary Life in Britain 1870– 1918* (Oxford, 2006).

Critical studies

Janice M. Allan and Christopher Pirratd, eds, *The Cambridge Companion to Sherlock Holmes* (Cambridge, UK: Cambridge University Press, 2019).

Mattias Boström, *The Life and Death of Sherlock Holmes* (London: Head of Zeus, 2017).

Clare Clarke, *British Detective Fiction 1891–1901: The Successors to Sherlock Holmes* (London: Palgrave Macmillan, 2020).

Clare Clarke, *Late-Victorian Crime Fiction in the Shadows of Sherlock* (London: Palgrave Macmillan, 2014).

Jonathan Cranfield, *Twentieth-Century Victorian: Arthur Conan Doyle and the Strand Magazine, 1891–1930* (Edinburgh: Edinburgh University Press, 2016).

Michael Dirda, *On Conan Doyle* (Princeton and Oxford: Princeton University Press, 2012).

Christopher Frayling, 'Nothing But a Hound Dog', in *Inside the Bloody Chamber: on Angela Carter, the Gothic, and Other Weird Tales* (London: Oberon, 2015).

Andrew Glazzard, *The Case of Sherlock Holmes: Secrets and Lies in Conan Doyle's Detective Fiction* (Edinburgh: Edinburgh University Press, 2018).

Douglas Kerr, *Conan Doyle: Writing, Profession, and Practice* (Oxford: Oxford University Press, 2013).

Brian McCuskey, *How Sherlock Pulled the Trick: Spiritualism and the Pseudoscientific Method* (University Park, PA: Pennsylvania University Press, 2021).

Caroline Reitz, *Detecting the Nation: Fictions of Detection and the Imperial Venture* (Columbus: Ohio State University Press, 2004).

Michael Sims, *Arthur & Sherlock: Conan Doyle and the Creation of Holmes* (London: Bloomsbury, 2017).

Catherine Wynne, *The Colonial Conan Doyle: British Imperialism, Irish Nationalism, and the Gothic* (Westport, CT, and London: Greenwood Press, 2002).

Folklore

Sabine Baring-Gould, *A Book of Dartmoor* (London: Methuen, 1900).

Katharine M. Briggs, *A Dictionary of British Folk-Tales*, 4 vols (London: Routledge and Kegan Paul, 1970).

Theo Brown, 'The Black Dog', *Folklore*, 69:3 (September 1958), 182–4.

Theo Brown, *Devon Ghosts* (Norwich: Jarrold Colour Publications, 1982).

Patricia Dale-Green, *Dog* (London: Rupert Hart-Davis, 1966).

Jennifer Westwood and Jacqueline Simpson, *The Lore of the Land: A Guide to England's Legends, from Spring-Heeled Jack to the Witches of Warboys* (London: Penguin, 2005).

Further Reading in Oxford World's Classics

Conan Doyle, Arthur, *A Study in Scarlet*, ed. Nicholas Daly.

Conan Doyle, Arthur, *The Memoirs of Sherlock Holmes*, ed. Jarlath Killeen.

Conan Doyle, Arthur, *The Return of Sherlock Holmes*, ed. Christopher Pittard.

Conan Doyle, Arthur, *Gothic Tales*, ed. Darryl Jones.

Conan Doyle, Arthur, *The Lost World*, ed. Ian Duncan.

A CHRONOLOGY OF ARTHUR CONAN DOYLE

Life	*Historical and Cultural Background*
1859 (22 May) Born at 11 Picardy Place, Edinburgh, to Mary Doyle (née Foley) and Charles Altamont Doyle, civil servant and artist.	Harper's Ferry Raid. Darwin, *On the Origin of Species* Mill, *On Liberty* Eliot, *Adam Bede* Collins, *Basil*
1868–75 Educated at the Jesuit school Hodder, and its senior college, Stonyhurst, in Lancashire. (Dec. 1874) Visits his Doyle relations in London.	Suez Canal opens. Married Woman's Property Act. Franco–Prussian War. Collins, *The Moonstone* Arnold, *Culture and Anarchy* Mayne Reid, *The Yellow Chief: A Romance of the Rocky Mountains* Pater, *Studies in the History of the Renaissance* Hardy, *Far from the Madding Crowd*
1875–6 (Sept.–June) Studies at Stella Matutina, a Jesuit school in Austria; comes home via Paris, where he stays with his great-uncle, Michael Conan. (Oct.) Begins his studies as a medical student at Edinburgh University.	Telephone patented by Alexander Graham Bell. The Great Sioux War of 1876. Eliot, *Daniel Deronda* Twain, *The Adventures of Tom Sawyer* Joaquin Miller, *First Fam'lies of the Sierras*
1877	Execution of John D. Lee for his role in the Mountain Meadows Massacre in Utah.
1878 Works as outpatient clerk to surgeon Joseph Bell. The Doyle family are now living at 23 George Square in the house of family friend Dr Bryan Waller.	Second Afghan War begins. Hardy, *The Return of the Native* Green, *The Leavenworth Case* James, *Daisy Miller*
1879 Publishes his first story, 'The Mystery of Sasassa Valley' in *Chambers's Journal* (6 Sept.). Works as assistant to Dr Reginald Hoare in Birmingham during the summer months.	Anglo–Zulu War. Ibsen, *A Doll's House*
1880 Spends six months as surgeon of the SS *Hope*, a whaling vessel. (Dec.) Publishes 'The American's Tale' in *London Society*.	First Anglo–Boer War begins. Zola, *Nana* James, *Washington Square* Spyri, *Heidi*

Life	*Historical and Cultural Background*
1881–2 (July–Aug.) Visits his wealthy Foley relatives in Lismore, Co. Waterford, where he becomes romantically involved with Elmo Weldon. Graduates from Edinburgh University. (Oct.–Jan.) Serves as surgeon on the West African steamer, SS *Mayumba*. Publishes six more stories in *London Society*, and one in *All the Year Round*. After a brief partnership with George Budd in Plymouth, he sets up in his own practice at Bush Villas, Southsea, Portsmouth.	President Garfield assassinated. H. G. Wells begins work as a draper's assistant in Southsea. Ibsen, *Ghosts* Births of James Joyce and Virginia Woolf
1883 'The Captain of the Pole-Star' (*Temple Bar*, Jan.), and other stories in *AYR*, *Bow Bells*, *London Society*, and the *Boy's Own Paper*.	Krakatoa erupts. R. L. and Fanny Van De Grift Stevenson, *The Dynamiter* Conway, *Called Back* Schreiner, *The Story of an African Farm* Collins, *Heart and Science*
1884 Receives twenty-nine guineas for 'J. Habakuk Jephson's Statement' (*Cornhill Magazine*, Jan.), and publishes stories in *Temple Bar* and *Cassell's Saturday Journal*. (Dec.) Meets Grant Allen, George du Maurier, F. Anstey, and other authors at the *Cornhill*'s annual dinner.	The Berlin Conference begins. Fabian Society founded. Zola, *Germinal* Huysmans, *À Rebours* Howells, *The Rise of Silas Lapham*
1885 (26 May) Charles Doyle is admitted to Montrose Royal Mental Hospital (Sunnyside). (July) 'The Great Keinplatz Experiment' (*Belgravia*). (1 Aug.) Receives his MD degree for his thesis on 'Vasomotor Influences on Tabes Dorsalis'. (6 Aug.) Marries Louise Hawkins. Honeymoons in Ireland.	The Rock Springs massacre of Chinese immigrants in Wyoming. Moore, *A Mummer's Wife* Rider Haggard, *King Solomon's Mines*
1886 *A Study in Scarlet* is rejected by several publishers before Ward, Lock purchase it outright.	The Benz Motorwagen is patented. Hume, *The Mystery of a Hansom Cab* James, *The Princess Casamassima* Stevenson, *Strange Case of Dr Jekyll and Mr Hyde*

Life	*Historical and Cultural Background*
1887 (Nov.) *A Study* appears in Beeton's Christmas Annual.	Queen Victoria's Golden Jubilee. Independent Labour Party founded. Rider Haggard, *She* Dujardin, *Les lauriers sont coupés*
1888 *A Study* published in volume form. (Aug.) *The Mystery of Cloomber* begins serialization in the *Pall Mall Budget*.	The Whitechapel murders begin. Mrs Humphry Ward, *Robert Elsmere* Kipling, *Plain Tales from the Hills*
1889 (Jan.) Birth of Mary Louise Doyle. (Feb.) *Micah Clarke*. (Aug.) Dinner at which Marshall Stoddard of *Lippincott's Magazine* commissions ACD to write *The Sign of the Four*, and Oscar Wilde *The Picture of Dorian Gray*.	Exposition Universelle in Paris. Dockers strike in London. Deaths of Wilkie Collins, Robert Browning, Gerard Manley Hopkins.
1890 Essay on R. L. Stevenson in the *National Review*. (Feb.) *The Sign of the Four* in *Lippincott's*. (Mar.) *The Captain of the Polestar and Other Tales*. (April) *The Firm of Girdlestone*. (Sept.) Hires A. P. Watt as his literary agent.	The Wounded Knee massacre in South Dakota. Wilde's *Dorian Gray* in *Lippincott's Magazine*.
1891 After a short period of study in Vienna ACD establishes himself at Wimpole Street, London, as an eye specialist. But as his income from writing increases he decides to write full time. Lives at 12 Tennison Road, South Norwood. (July) First Sherlock Holmes story, 'A Scandal in Bohemia', appears in the *Strand* magazine, and five more follow. (26 Oct.) *The White Company*.	German government takes control of the territory of the German East Africa Company. Hardy, *Tess of the d'Urbervilles* Gissing, *New Grub Street*
1892 'The Adventures of Sherlock Holmes' stories continue in the *Strand*, and appear in volume form in October. (Mar.) *The Doings of Raffles Haw*. Birth of son, Arthur Alleyne Kingsley. (Sept.) 'Lot No. 249' in *Harper's Magazine*. (Nov.) Diagnosed with tuberculosis, Louisa travels to Davos, Switzerland.	Ellis Island opens as an immigration centre. George and Weedon Grossmith, *Diary of a Nobody* Perkins Gilman, 'The Yellow Wallpaper' The Book of the Rhymers' Club

Life	*Historical and Cultural Background*
1893 Further 'Adventures' in the *Strand*, including (Dec.) 'The Final Problem'. (May) *The Refugees*. Collaborates with J. M. Barrie on a musical comedy. (27 Sept) ACD's sister Connie marries 'Raffles' author E. W. Hornung. (10 Oct.) Death of ACD's father. (Dec.) Visits Louisa in Davos. *The Memoirs of Sherlock Holmes*.	Coup against Queen Liliʻuokalani in Hawaii. Egerton, *Keynotes* Grand, *The Heavenly Twins*
1894 (21 Sept.) Henry Irving stages ACD's Waterloo. (Oct.) Lecture tour of the USA; spends Thanksgiving with Rudyard Kipling and his wife. *Round the Red Lamp*. (Dec.) *The Parasite*.	Death of Tsar Alexander III. Hope, *The Prisoner of Zenda* Weyman, *Under the Red Robe* Hepworth Dixon, *The Story of a Modern Woman*
1895 ACD and Louise visit Egypt. The semi-autobiographical *Stark Munro Letters*.	The Lumière brothers hold the first commercial screening of their Cinématographe Wells, *The Time Machine* Wilde, *The Importance of Being Earnest*
1896 As a stringer for the *Westminster Gazette* he accompanies a British expedition against Mahdist forces in Sudan. (Feb.) *The Exploits of Brigadier Gerard*. (Nov.) *Rodney Stone*. Contributes a two-page Holmes story, 'The Field Bazaar', to *The Student*.	The *Daily Mail* begins publication; within 6 years it has a circulation of over a million. Puccini, *La Bohème* A. E. Housman, *A Shropshire Lad* Morrison, *A Child of the Jago*
1897 (Mar.?) Meets Jean Leckie, his future second wife. Three 'Captain Sharkey' stories in *Pearson's Magazine*. (May–Dec.) *The Tragedy of the Korosko* in the *Strand*. (June) Speaks on the Irish contribution to English literature at a dinner of the Irish Literary Society. (Oct.) Family move into their new house, Undershaw, at Hindhead, Surrey.	Queen Victoria's Diamond Jubilee. Leopold II crowned King of the Belgians. Stoker, *Dracula* Marsh, *The Beetle*
1898 (Apr.) Visits Rome, where he dines with Hornung, George Gissing, and H. G. Wells. (June) *Songs of Action*. (Aug.) 'The Story of the Lost Special' in the *Strand*.	Spanish-American War. Wing Pinero, *Trelawney of the Wells* James, *The Turn of the Screw*

Life	*Historical and Cultural Background*
1899 (Mar.) *A Duet, with an Occasional Chorus.* (10 Apr.) His play *Halves* opens in Aberdeen. (May) 'The Story of the Brown Hand', *Strand.* (Oct. 23) William Gillette's version of ACD's Sherlock Holmes play opens in Buffalo, New York, and becomes a perennial international success.	'Aspirin' is patented. Irish Literary Theatre opens. Veblen, *The Theory of the Leisure Class* Chopin, *The Awakening* Norris, *McTeague* Conrad's *Heart of Darkness* is serialized.
1900 (Mar.–July) In South Africa with the charitable Langman Hospital during the Anglo–Boer war. Meets journalist Bertram Fletcher Robinson on the return voyage. *The Green Flag and Other Stories of War and Sport.* (May) *Sherlock Holmes Baffled*, a short Mutoscope film. (Oct.) Unsuccessful Liberal Unionist candidate for Edinburgh Central. *The Great Boer War.* (Dec.) Influenced by the Boers' effectiveness in South Africa, he starts the Undershaw Rifle Club.	Hawaii becomes a US territory. Boxer Uprising begins in China. Puccini, *Tosca* Conrad, *Lord Jim*
1901 (Mar.) Visits Dartmoor with Fletcher Robinson to research *The Hound of the Baskervilles.* (Aug.) *The Hound* begins in the *Strand*.	Death of Queen Victoria. Cook Islands annexed by New Zealand. President McKinley assassinated in Buffalo, New York. Shiel, *The Purple Cloud* Washington, *Up from Slavery*
1902 (Jan.) *The War in South Africa.* (Apr.) Visits Naples, meets writer Norman Douglas. (Aug.) Knighted by King Edward VII for his South African work. Becomes Deputy Lieutenant of Surrey. (Dec.) Appointed President of the Boys Empire League.	Texas Oil Company (Texaco) founded. First celebration of Empire Day in the UK. First private performance of Shaw's *Mrs Warren's Profession.* Nesbit, *Five Children and It* Mason, *The Four Feathers*
1903 (Sept.–Oct.) 'The Adventure of the Empty House' and other Sherlock Holmes stories in *Collier's* magazine (US) and the *Strand* (UK). Author's Edition of ACD's major works.	The Wright brothers make their first flight. The Women's Social and Political Union founded. Porter, *Life of an American Fireman* (film) Childers, *Riddle of the Sands* Du Bois, *The Souls of Black Folk*

Life	*Historical and Cultural Background*
1904	Works on *Sir Nigel*. Further Holmes stories appear in *Collier's* and the *Strand*.	Russo–Japanese War. Herero and Nama rebellion against German rule in South West Africa, and beginning of subsequent genocide. Puccini, *Madame Butterfly* Wallace, *The Four Just Men*
1905	(Mar.) *The Return of Sherlock Holmes*. (7 Apr.) Honorary doctorate from Edinburgh University. (Dec.) *Sir Nigel* begins in the Strand.	The Aliens Act (UK). Revolution in Russia. Albert Einstein publishes four significant papers on physics. Nesbit, *The Railway Children* serialized. Wharton, *The House of Mirth* Orczy, *The Scarlet Pimpernel* Hepworth Picture Plays, *Rescued By Rover*
1906	(Jan.) Unsuccessful bid as Unionist candidate for Hawick. (May) *Brigadier Gerard* at the Lyric Theatre. Discovers his late theatrical agent has embezzled £9000. (4 July) Death of Louise.	San Francisco Earthquake. Gandhi begins a campaign of civil disobedience against the Transvaal Government. Barrie, *Peter Pan in Kensington Gardens*
1907	Lobbies for the release of George Edalji. (18 Sept.) Marries Jean Leckie, and honeymoons in Italy, Greece, and Turkey. (Nov.) *Through the Magic Door.*	Suffragettes storm the British Parliament. Conrad, *The Secret Agent* Synge, *The Playboy of the Western World*
1908	*Round the Fire Stories*. Further Holmes stories in the *Strand*. ACD and Jean move into their new house, Windlesham, in Crowborough, Sussex.	Golden Jubilee of the Emperor Franz-Joseph. Baden-Powell, *Scouting for Boys* Forster, *A Room with a View*
1909	Describes Belgian colonial atrocities in *The Crime of the Congo*.	Japan occupies Korea. Blériot flies across the English Channel. Wells, *Tono Bungay* Marinetti, *Futurist Manifesto* Stein, *Three Lives*
1910	Meets President Roosevelt. *The Speckled Band* begins a run of 346 performances at the Adelphi Theatre.	Mexican Revolution begins. Post-Impressionist exhibition in London. Forster, *Howards End* Buchan, *Prester John*
1911	*The Last Galley*. ACD embraces Home Rule for Ireland, influenced by Sir Roger Casement. (25 May) Takes a flight in a biplane from	Italy annexes Libya. Chinese Republic proclaimed. Hodgson Burnett, *The Secret Garden* Wharton, *Ethan Frome*

Life	*Historical and Cultural Background*
Hendon aerodrome. (July) Participates in the Prince Henry Tour automobile rally.	

1912 *The Lost World.* The Case of Oscar Slater. Public clash with George Bernard Shaw about the RMS *Titanic* disaster.

Sinking of the RMS *Titanic.*
First Balkan War commences.
Tagore, *The Post Office*
Rice Burroughs, *Tarzan of the Apes*

1913 Two-reel film adaptation of *The Sign of the Four. The Poison Belt.* Campaigns for a Channel Tunnel.

Second Balkan War.
Suffragette Emily Davison killed at the Epsom Derby.
Shaw, *Pygmalion*
Proust, *Swann's Way*

1914 (May–July) Tours the USA and Canada in a private railway carriage. (Mar.) *Der Hund von Baskerville* released, the first of seven German Holmes films. British and American screen versions of *A Study in Scarlet.* (Sept.) *The Valley of Fear* begins serialization in the *Strand.* Forms local civil defence force, and joins other authors in Wellington House war propaganda work.

Assassination of Archduke Franz Ferdinand in Sarajevo triggers the First World War.
Joyce, *Dubliners*
Sōseki, *Kokoro*
Pastrone, *Cabiria* (film)
Tressell (Noonan), *The Ragged-Trousered Philanthropists*

1915 *The Firm of Girdlestone* (film version).

German U-Boat sinks the RMS *Lusitania.*
Buchan, *The Thirty-Nine Steps*
Richardson, *Pointed Roofs*

1916 Visits the Western Front. *The British Campaign in France and Flanders 1914* serialized in the *Strand. A Visit to Three Fronts.* Unsuccessfully campaigns for clemency for Sir Roger Casement, who is executed for treason.

The Easter Rising in Dublin.
Trial and execution of Sir Roger Casement.
Wells, *Mr Britling Sees It Through*
Joyce, *A Portrait of the Artist as a Young Man*
Buchan, *Greenmantle*

1917 (Sept.) 'His Last Bow' in the *Strand*, followed (Oct.) by *His Last Bow: Some Reminiscences of Sherlock Holmes.*

The Russian Revolution.
The United States enters the war.
Rice Burroughs, *A Princess of Mars*
Eliot, *Prufrock, and Other Observations*

1918 (Apr.) *The New Revelation*, in which ACD declares himself a Spiritualist. (Oct.) ACD's son Kingsley, who had been seriously

The war ends.
Beginning of the 'Spanish flu' pandemic.
Cather, *My Ántonia*

Life

Historical and Cultural Background

wounded during the Battle of the Somme, completes his military service, but dies during the influenza pandemic.

Lewis, *Tarr*
Thomas, *Last Poems*

1919 (Feb.) ACD's brother, Brigadier-General Innes Doyle, also succumbs to the flu pandemic. (Nov.) *The Vital Message,* another spiritualist book.

Spartacist protests in Berlin.
Civil War in Russia.
Amritsar Massacre in India.
Wodehouse, *My Man Jeeves*
Woolf, *Night and Day*

1920 The anti-spiritualist magician Harry Houdini visits Windlesham, and he and ACD become friends. Spiritualist lecture tour in Australia and New Zealand. (30 Dec.) ACD's mother dies.

Prohibition begins in the United States.
The German Workers' Party adopts Hitler's National Socialism.
Fitzgerald, *This Side of Paradise*
Christie, *The Mysterious Affair at Styles*
Lawrence, *Women in Love*

1921 E. W. Hornung dies. ACD visits Australia. Following a deal between ACD and Stoll Pictures, *The Yellow Face* becomes the first of forty-seven Holmes films (1921–3), all starring Eille Norwood as Holmes.

Irish War of Independence ends.
Marie Stopes opens a birth-control clinic in London.
Sabatini, *Scaramouche*
Čapek, *R.U.R.*

1922 (Feb.–Mar.) 'The Problem of Thor Bridge' (*Strand*). (Apr.) Begins another tour of the USA. John Murray publishes a six-volume edition of the non-Holmes stories, and a volume of ACD's poetry. *The Coming of the Fairies.*

The Teapot Dome corruption scandal in the United States.
Irish Civil War.
Joyce, *Ulysses*
Woolf, *Jacob's Room*
Eliot, *The Waste Land*

1923 (Mar.) 'The Creeping Man' (*Strand*).

Rosewood Massacre of African Americans in Florida.
The British Mandate for Palestine comes into effect.
Sayers, *Whose Body*
Huxley, *Antic Hay*

1924 (Jan.) 'The Sussex Vampire' (*Strand*). Writes a Holmes pastiche for the library of Queen Mary's Dolls' House. *Memories and Adventures.*

Ramsay MacDonald becomes Britain's first Labour Prime Minister.
Asian Exclusion Act becomes law in the United States.
Mann, *The Magic Mountain*
Forster, *A Passage to India*

Life	*Historical and Cultural Background*
1925 Opens the Psychic Bookshop at 2 Victoria Street in London. (July) *The Land of Mist* commences in the *Strand*.	Mussolini tightens his grip on Italian politics. In 'Pink's War' the RAF is deployed against Mahsud forces in South Waziristan. Woolf, *Mrs Dalloway* Fitzgerald, *The Great Gatsby*
1926 *Strand* publishes three new stories. *The History of Spiritualism*. Offers his assistance to the police in their search for Agatha Christie.	General Strike in the UK. Rif War in Morocco ends. Townsend Warner, *Lolly Willowes* Hughes, *The Weary Blues*
1927 (Apr.) 'The Adventure of Shoscombe old Place' (*Strand*), the last Holmes story. (June) *The Case-Book of Sherlock Holmes*. (Oct.) *The Maracot Deep* begins in the *Strand*.	Pan-Am is founded;. The People's Liberation Army is formed in China. Forster, *Aspects of the Novel* Heidegger, *Being and Time*
1928 (Oct.) Begins a spiritualist lecture tour in Africa. *The Complete Sherlock Holmes Short Stories*.	The first Zeppelin passenger flights from Germany to the United States. Logie Baird broadcasts a transatlantic television signal. Hall, *The Well of Loneliness* Larsen, *Quicksand*
1929 Gives an interview to Movietone News. (July) *The Maracot Deep and Other Stories*. (Oct.) Despite his declining health he begins a lecture tour of the Netherlands and Scandinavia.	The Wall Street Crash. Signing of the Geneva Convention. Faulkner, *The Sound and the Fury* Bowen, *The Last September*
1930 (7 July) Dies at Windlesham.	Gandhi's Salt March. Hollywood adopts the Hays Code. Hammett, *The Maltese Falcon* Waugh, *Vile Bodies*

This story owes its inception to my friend, Mr. Fletcher Robinson, who has helped me both in the general plot and in the local details.

A.C.D.*

MY DEAR ROBINSON,

   It was to your account of a West-Country legend that this tale owes its inception. For this and for your help in the details all thanks.

Yours most truly,
A. CONAN DOYLE

Hindhead
       Haslemere*

MY DEAR ROBINSON

   It was your account of a west country legend which first suggested the idea of this little tale to my mind.
   For this, and for the help in which you have me in its evolution, all thanks.

Yours most truly,
A. CONAN DOYLE*

THE HOUND OF THE BASKERVILLES

CHAPTER 1

MR SHERLOCK HOLMES

MR SHERLOCK HOLMES, who was usually very late in the mornings, save upon those not infrequent occasions when he stayed up all night,* was seated at the breakfast table. I stood upon the hearth-rug and picked up the stick which our visitor had left behind him the night before. It was a fine, thick piece of wood, bulbous-headed, of the sort which is known as a 'Penang lawyer'.* Just under the head was a broad silver band, nearly an inch across. 'To James Mortimer, MRCS,* from his friends of the CCH', was engraved upon it, with the date '1884'. It was just such a stick as the old-fashioned family practitioner used to carry—dignified, solid, and reassuring.

'Well, Watson, what do you make of it?'

Holmes was sitting with his back to me, and I had given him no sign of my occupation.

'How did you know what I was doing? I believe you have eyes in the back of your head.'

'I have, at least, a well-polished, silver-plated coffee-pot in front of me,' said he. 'But, tell me, Watson, what do you make of our visitor's stick? Since we have been so unfortunate as to miss him and have no notion of his errand, this accidental souvenir becomes of importance. Let me hear you reconstruct the man by an examination of it.'

'I think,' said I, following so far as I could the methods of my companion, 'that Dr Mortimer is a successful elderly medical man, well-esteemed, since those who know him give him this mark of their appreciation.'

'Good!' said Holmes. 'Excellent!'

'I think also that the probability is in favour of his being a country practitioner who does a great deal of his visiting on foot.'

'Why so?'

'Because this stick, though originally a very handsome one, has been so knocked about that I can hardly imagine a town practitioner carrying it. The thick iron ferrule* is worn down, so it is evident that he has done a great amount of walking with it.'

'Perfectly sound!' said Holmes.

'And then again, there is the "friends of the CCH". I should guess that to be the Something Hunt, the local hunt to whose members he has possibly given some surgical assistance, and which has made him a small presentation in return.'

'Really, Watson, you excel yourself,' said Holmes, pushing back his chair and lighting a cigarette. 'I am bound to say that in all the accounts which you have been so good as to give of my own small achievements you have habitually underrated your own abilities. It may be that you are not yourself luminous, but you are a conductor of light. Some people without possessing genius have a remarkable power of stimulating it. I confess, my dear fellow, that I am very much in your debt.'

He had never said as much before, and I must admit that his words gave me keen pleasure, for I had often been piqued by his indifference to my admiration and to the attempts which I had made to give publicity to his methods. I was proud, too, to think that I had so far mastered his system as to apply it in a way which earned his approval. He now took the stick from my hands and examined it for a few minutes with his naked eyes. Then, with an expression of interest, he laid down his cigarette, and, carrying the cane to the window, he looked over it again with a convex lens.

'Interesting, though elementary,'* said he, as he returned to his favourite corner of the settee. 'There are certainly one or two indications upon the stick. It gives us the basis for several deductions.'

'Has anything escaped me?' I asked, with some self-importance. 'I trust that there is nothing of consequence which I have overlooked?'

'I am afraid, my dear Watson, that most of your conclusions were erroneous. When I said that you stimulated me I meant, to be frank, that in noting your fallacies I was occasionally guided towards the truth. Not that you are entirely wrong in this instance. The man is certainly a country practitioner. And he walks a good deal.'

'Then I was right.'

'To that extent.'

'But that was all.'

'No, no, my dear Watson, not all—by no means all. I would suggest, for example, that a presentation to a doctor is more likely to come from a hospital than from a hunt, and that when the initials "CC" are placed before that hospital the words "Charing Cross" very naturally suggest themselves.'

'You may be right.'

'The probability lies in that direction. And if we take this as a working hypothesis we have a fresh basis from which to start our construction of this unknown visitor.'

'Well, then, supposing that "CCH" does stand for "Charing Cross Hospital",* what further inferences may we draw?'

'Do none suggest themselves? You know my methods. Apply them!'

'I can only think of the obvious conclusion that the man has practised in town before going to the country.'

'I think that we might venture a little farther than this. Look at it in this light. On what occasion would it be most probable that such a presentation would be made? When would his friends unite to give him a pledge of their good will? Obviously at the moment when Dr Mortimer withdrew from the service of the hospital in order to start in practice for himself. We know there has been a presentation. We believe there has been a change from a town hospital to a country practice. Is it, then, stretching our inference too far to say that the presentation was on the occasion of the change?'

'It certainly seems probable.'

'Now, you will observe that he could not have been on the *staff* of the hospital,* since only a man well-established in a London practice could hold such a position, and such a one would not drift into the country. What was he, then? If he was in the hospital and yet not on the staff, he could only have been a house-surgeon or a house-physician*—little more than a senior student. And he left five years ago—the date is on the stick. So your grave, middle-aged family practitioner vanishes into thin air, my dear Watson, and there emerges a young fellow under thirty, amiable, unambitious, absent-minded, and the possessor of a favourite dog, which I should describe roughly as being larger than a terrier and smaller than a mastiff.'

I laughed incredulously as Sherlock Holmes leaned back in his settee and blew little wavering rings of smoke up to the ceiling.

'As to the latter part, I have no means of checking you,' said I, 'but at least it is not difficult to find out a few particulars about the man's age and professional career.'

From my small medical shelf I took down the Medical Directory* and turned up the name. There were several Mortimers, but only one who could be our visitor. I read his record aloud.

Mortimer, James, MRCS, 1882, Grimpen,* Dartmoor, Devon, House-surgeon, from 1882 to 1884, at Charing Cross Hospital. Winner of the Jackson Prize for Comparative Pathology,* with essay entitled 'Is Disease a Reversion?'* Corresponding member of the Swedish Pathological Society.* Author of 'Some Freaks of Atavism'* (*Lancet*,* 1882), 'Do We Progress?' (*Journal of Psychology*,* March, 1883). Medical Officer for the parishes of Grimpen, Thorsley, and High Barrow.*

'No mention of that local hunt, Watson,' said Holmes, with a mischievous smile, 'but a country doctor, as you very astutely observed. I think that I am fairly justified in my inferences. As to the adjectives, I said, if I remember right, amiable, unambitious, and absent-minded. It is my experience that it is only an amiable man in this world who receives testimonials, only an unambitious one who abandons a London career for the country, and only an absent-minded one who leaves his stick and not his visiting-card after waiting an hour in your room.'

'And the dog?'

'Has been in the habit of carrying this stick behind his master. Being a heavy stick the dog has held it tightly by the middle, and the marks of his teeth are very plainly visible. The dog's jaw, as shown in the space between these marks, is too broad in my opinion for a terrier and not broad enough for a mastiff. It may have been—yes, by Jove, it *is* a curly-haired spaniel.'

He had risen and paced the room as he spoke. Now he halted in the recess of the window. There was such a ring of conviction in his voice that I glanced up in surprise.

'My dear fellow, how can you possibly be so sure of that?'

'For the very simple reason that I see the dog himself on our very doorstep, and there is the ring of its owner. Don't move, I beg you, Watson. He is a professional brother of yours, and your presence may be of assistance to me. Now is the dramatic moment of fate, Watson, when you hear a step upon the stair which is walking into your life, and you know not whether for good or ill. What does Dr James Mortimer, the man of science, ask of Sherlock Holmes, the specialist in crime? Come in!'

The appearance of our visitor was a surprise to me since I had expected a typical country practitioner. He was a very tall, thin man, with a long nose like a beak, which shot out between two keen, grey eyes, set closely together and sparkling brightly from behind a pair of gold-rimmed glasses. He was clad in a professional but rather slovenly fashion, for his frock-coat was dingy and his trousers frayed. Though young, his long back was already bowed, and he walked with a forward thrust of his head and a general air of peering benevolence. As he entered his eyes fell upon the stick in Holmes's hand, and he ran towards it with an exclamation of joy.

'I am so very glad,' said he. 'I was not sure whether I had left it here or in the Shipping Office. I would not lose that stick for the world.'

'A presentation, I see,' said Holmes.

'Yes, sir.'

'From Charing Cross Hospital?'

'From one or two friends there on the occasion of my marriage.'

'Dear, dear, that's bad!' said Holmes, shaking his head.

Dr Mortimer blinked through his glasses in mild astonishment.

'Why was it bad?'

'Only that you have disarranged our little deductions. Your marriage, you say?'

'Yes, sir. I married, and so left the hospital, and with it all hopes of a consulting practice. It was necessary to make a home of my own.'

'Come, come, we are not so far wrong after all,' said Holmes. 'And now, Dr James Mortimer—'

'Mister, sir, Mister—a humble MRCS.'*

'And a man of precise mind, evidently.'

'A dabbler in science, Mr Holmes, a picker up of shells on the shores of the great unknown ocean.* I presume that it is Mr Sherlock Holmes whom I am addressing and not—'

'No, this is my friend Dr Watson.'

'Glad to meet you, sir. I have heard your name mentioned in connection with that of your friend. You interest me very much, Mr Holmes. I had hardly expected so dolichocephalic a skull or such well-marked supra-orbital development. Would you have any objection to my running my finger along your parietal fissure?* A cast of your skull, sir, until the original is available, would be an ornament to any anthropological museum.* It is not my intention to be fulsome, but I confess that I covet your skull.'

Sherlock Holmes waved our strange visitor into a chair.

'You are an enthusiast in your line of thought, I perceive, sir, as I am in mine,' said he. 'I observe from your forefinger that you make your own cigarettes. Have no hesitation in lighting one.'

The man drew out paper and tobacco and twirled the one up in the other with surprising dexterity. He had long, quivering fingers as agile and restless as the antennae of an insect.

Holmes was silent, but his little darting glances showed me the interest which he took in our curious companion.

'I presume, sir,' said he at last, 'that it was not merely for the purpose of examining my skull that you have done me the honour to call here last night and again to-day?'

'No, sir, no; though I am happy to have had the opportunity of doing that as well. I came to you, Mr Holmes, because I recognise that I am myself an unpractical man, and because I am suddenly confronted with a most serious and extraordinary problem. Recognising, as I do, that you are the second highest expert in Europe—'

'Indeed, sir! May I inquire who has the honour to be the first?' asked Holmes, with some asperity.

'To the man of precisely scientific mind the work of Monsieur Bertillon* must always appeal strongly.'

'Then had you not better consult him?'

'I said, sir, to the precisely scientific mind. But as a practical man of affairs it is acknowledged that you stand alone. I trust, sir, that I have not inadvertently—'

'Just a little,' said Holmes. 'I think, Dr Mortimer, you would do wisely if without more ado you would kindly tell me plainly what the exact nature of the problem is in which you demand my assistance.'

CHAPTER 2

THE CURSE OF THE BASKERVILLES

'I HAVE in my pocket a manuscript,' said Dr James Mortimer.

'I observed it as you entered the room,' said Holmes.

'It is an old manuscript.'

'Early eighteenth century, unless it is a forgery.'

'How can you say that, sir?'

'You have presented an inch or two of it to my examination all the time that you have been talking. It would be a poor expert who could not give the date of a document within a decade or so. You may possibly have read my little monograph upon the subject. I put that at 1730.'

'The exact date is 1742.' Dr Mortimer drew it from his breast-pocket. 'This family paper was committed to my care by Sir Charles Baskerville, whose sudden and tragic death some three months ago created so much excitement in Devonshire. I may say that I was his personal friend as well as his medical attendant. He was a strong-minded man, sir, shrewd, practical, and as unimaginative as I am myself. Yet he took this document very seriously, and his mind was prepared for just such an end as did eventually overtake him.'

Holmes stretched out his hand for the manuscript and flattened it upon his knee.

'You will observe, Watson, the alternative use of the long *s* and the short.* It is one of several indications which enabled me to fix the date.'

I looked over his shoulder at the yellow paper and the faded script. At the head was written: 'Baskerville Hall', and below, in large, scrawling figures: '1742'.

'It appears to be a statement of some sort.'

'Yes, it is a statement of a certain legend which runs in the Baskerville family.'

'But I understand that it is something more modern and practical upon which you wish to consult me?'

'Most modern. A most practical, pressing matter, which must be decided within twenty-four hours. But the manuscript is short and is intimately connected with the affair. With your permission I will read it to you.'

Holmes leaned back in his chair, placed his finger-tips together, and closed his eyes, with an air of resignation. Dr Mortimer turned the manuscript to the light, and read in a high, crackling voice the following curious, old-world narrative.

'Of the origin of the Hound of the Baskervilles there have been many statements, yet as I come in a direct line from Hugo Baskerville, and as I had the story from my father, who also had it from his, I have set it down with all belief that it occurred even as is here set forth. And I would have you believe, my sons, that the same Justice which punishes sin may also most graciously forgive it, and that no ban is so heavy but that by prayer and repentance it may be removed. Learn then from this story not to fear the fruits of the past, but rather to be circumspect in the future, that those foul passions whereby our family has suffered so grievously may not again be loosed to our undoing.

'Know then that in the time of the Great Rebellion (the history of which by the learned Lord Clarendon* I most earnestly commend to your attention) this Manor of Baskerville was held by Hugo of that name, nor can it be gainsaid that he was a most wild, profane, and godless man. This, in truth, his neighbours might have pardoned, seeing that saints have never flourished in those parts, but there was in him a certain wanton and cruel humour which made his name a by-word through the West.* It chanced that this Hugo came to love (if, indeed, so dark a passion may be known under so bright a name) the daughter of a yeoman who held lands near the Baskerville estate. But the young maiden, being discreet and of good repute, would ever avoid him, for she feared his evil name. So it came to pass that one Michaelmas* this Hugo, with five or six of his idle and wicked companions, stole down upon the farm and carried off the maiden, her father and brothers being from home, as he well knew. When they had brought her to the Hall the maiden was placed in an upper chamber, while Hugo and his friends sat down to a long carouse, as was their nightly custom. Now, the poor lass upstairs was like to have her wits turned at the singing and shouting and terrible oaths which came up to her from below, for they say that the words used by Hugo Baskerville, when he was in wine, were such as might blast the man who said them. At last in the stress of her fear she did that which might have daunted the bravest or most active man, for by the aid of the growth of ivy which covered (and still covers) the south wall, she came down from under the eaves, and so homeward across the moor, there being three leagues* betwixt the Hall and her father's farm.

'It chanced that some little time later Hugo left his guests to carry food and drink—with other worse things, per-chance—to his captive, and so found the cage empty and the bird escaped. Then, as it would seem, he became as one that hath a devil, for, rushing down the stairs into the dining-hall, he sprang upon the great table, flagons and trenchers* flying before him, and he cried aloud before all the company that he would that very night render his body and soul to the Powers of Evil if he might but overtake the wench. And while the revellers stood aghast at the fury of the man, one more wicked or, it may be, more drunken than the rest, cried out that they should put the hounds upon her. Whereat Hugo ran from the house, crying to his grooms that they should saddle his mare and unkennel the pack, and giving the hounds a kerchief of the maid's he swung them to the line,* and so off full cry in the moonlight over the moor.

'Now, for some space the revellers stood agape, unable to understand all that had been done in such haste. But anon their bemused wits awoke to the nature of the deed which was like to be done upon the moorlands. Everything was now in an uproar, some calling for their pistols, some for their horses, and some for another flask of wine. But at length some sense came back to their crazed minds, and the whole of them, thirteen in number, took horse and started in pursuit. The moon shone clear above them, and they rode swiftly abreast, taking that course which the maid must needs have taken if she were to reach her own home.

'They had gone a mile or two when they passed one of the night shepherds upon the moorlands, and they cried to him to know if he had seen the hunt. And the man, as the story goes, was so crazed with fear that he could scarce speak, but at last he said that he had indeed seen the unhappy maiden, with the hounds upon her track. "But I have seen more than that," said he, "for Hugo Baskerville passed me upon his black mare, and there ran mute behind him such a hound of hell as God forbid should ever be at my heels."

'So the drunken squires cursed the shepherd and rode onwards. But soon their skins turned cold, for there came a sound of galloping* across the moor, and the black mare, dabbled with white froth, went past with trailing bridle and empty saddle. Then the revellers rode close together, for a great fear was on them, but they still followed over the moor, though each, had he been alone, would have been right glad to have turned his horse's head. Riding slowly in this fashion, they came at last upon the hounds. These, though known for their valour and their breed, were whimpering in a cluster at the head of a deep dip or goyal,* as we call it, upon the moor, some slinking away and some, with starting hackles* and staring eyes, gazing down the narrow valley before them.

'The company had come to a halt, more sober men, as you may guess, than when they started. The most of them would by no means advance, but three of them, the boldest, or, it may be the most drunken, rode forward down the goyal. Now it opened into a broad space in which stood two of those great stones,* still to be seen there, which were set by certain forgotten peoples in the days of old. The moon was shining bright upon the clearing, and there in the centre lay the unhappy maid where she had fallen, dead of fear and of fatigue. But it was not the sight of her body, nor yet was it that of the body of Hugo Baskerville lying near her, which raised the hair upon the heads of these three dare-devil roisterers, but it was that, standing over Hugo, and plucking at his throat, there stood a foul thing, a great, black beast, shaped like a hound, yet larger than any hound that ever mortal eye has rested upon. And even as they looked the thing tore the throat out of Hugo Baskerville, on which, as it turned its blazing eyes and dripping jaws upon them, the three shrieked with fear and rode for dear life, still screaming, across the moor. One, it is said, died that very night of what he had seen, and the other twain were but broken men for the rest of their days.

'Such is the tale, my sons, of the coming of the hound which is said to have plagued the family so sorely ever since. If I have set it down it is because that which is clearly known hath less terror than that which is but hinted at and guessed. Nor can it be denied that many of the family have been unhappy in their deaths, which have been sudden, bloody, and mysterious. Yet may we shelter ourselves in the infinite goodness of Providence, which would not for ever punish the innocent beyond that third or fourth generation which is threatened in Holy Writ.* To that Providence, my sons, I hereby commend you, and I counsel you by way of caution to forbear from crossing the moor in those dark hours when the powers of evil are exalted.

'(This from Hugo Baskerville to his sons Rodger and John, with instructions that they say nothing thereof to their sister Elizabeth.)'

When Dr Mortimer had finished reading this singular narrative he pushed his spectacles up on his forehead and stared across at Mr Sherlock Holmes. The latter yawned and tossed the end of his cigarette into the fire.

'Well?' said he.

'Do you find it interesting?'

'To a collector of fairy-tales.'*

Dr Mortimer drew a folded newspaper out of his pocket.

'Now, Mr Holmes, we will give you something a little more recent. This is the *Devon County Chronicle** of June 14th* of this year. It is a short account of the facts elicited at the death of Sir Charles Baskerville which occurred a few days before that date.'

My friend leaned a little forward and his expression became intent. Our visitor readjusted his glasses and began:

'The recent sudden death of Sir Charles Baskerville, whose name has been mentioned as the probable Liberal candidate for Mid-Devon* at the next election, has cast a gloom over the county. Though Sir Charles had resided at Baskerville Hall for a comparatively short period his amiability of character and extreme generosity had won the affection and respect of all who had been brought into contact with him. In these days of *nouveaux riches** it is refreshing to find a case where the scion of an old county family which has fallen upon evil days is able to make his own fortune and to bring it back with him to restore the fallen grandeur of his line. Sir Charles, as is well known, made large sums of money in South African speculation.* More wise than those who go on until the wheel turns against them, he realized his gains and returned to England with them. It is only two years since he took up his residence at Baskerville Hall, and it is common talk how large were those schemes of reconstruction and improvement which have been interrupted by his death. Being himself childless, it was his openly expressed desire that the whole country-side should, within his own lifetime, profit by his good fortune, and many will have personal reasons for bewailing his untimely end. His generous donations to local and county charities have been frequently chronicled in these columns.

'The circumstances connected with the death of Sir Charles cannot be said to have been entirely cleared up by the inquest, but at least enough has been done to dispose of those rumours to which local superstition has given rise. There is no reason whatever to suspect foul play, or to imagine that death could be from any but natural causes. Sir Charles was a widower, and a man who may be said to have been in some ways of an eccentric habit of mind. In spite of his considerable wealth he was simple in his personal tastes, and his indoor servants at Baskerville Hall consisted of a married couple named Barrymore, the husband acting as butler and the wife as housekeeper. Their evidence, corroborated by that of several friends, tends to show that Sir Charles's health has for some time been impaired, and points especially to some affection of the heart, manifesting itself in changes of colour, breathlessness, and acute attacks of nervous depression. Dr James Mortimer, the friend and medical attendant of the deceased, has given evidence to the same effect.

'The facts of the case are simple. Sir Charles Baskerville was in the habit every night before going to bed of walking down the famous Yew Alley of Baskerville Hall. The evidence of the Barrymores shows that this had been his custom. On the 4th of June* Sir Charles had declared his intention of starting next day for London, and had ordered Barrymore to prepare his luggage. That night he went out as usual for his nocturnal walk, in the course of which he was in the habit of smoking a cigar. He never returned. At twelve o'clock Barrymore, finding the hall door still open, became alarmed and, lighting a lantern, went in search of his master. The day had been wet, and Sir Charles's footmarks were easily traced down the Alley. Half-way down this walk there is a gate which leads out on to the moor. There were indications that Sir Charles had stood for some little time here. He then proceeded down the Alley, and it was at the far end of it that his body was discovered. One fact which has not been explained is the statement of Barrymore that his master's foot-prints altered their character from the time he passed the moor-gate, and that he appeared from thence onwards to have been walking upon his toes. One Murphy, a gipsy horse-dealer, was on the moor at no great distance at the time, but he appears by his own confession to have been the worse for drink. He declares that he heard cries, but is unable to state from what direction they came. No signs of violence were to be discovered upon Sir Charles's person, and though the doctor's evidence pointed to an almost incredible facial distortion—so great that Dr Mortimer refused at first to believe that it was indeed his friend and patient who lay before him—it was explained that that is a symptom which is not unusual in cases of dyspnoea* and death from cardiac exhaustion. This explanation was borne out by the post-mortem examination, which showed long-standing organic disease, and the coroner's jury* returned a verdict in accordance with the medical evidence. It is well that this is so, for it is obviously of the utmost importance that Sir Charles's heir should settle at the Hall, and continue the good work which has been so sadly interrupted. Had the prosaic finding of the coroner not finally put an end to the romantic stories which have been whispered in connection with the affair, it might have been difficult to find a tenant for Baskerville Hall.* It is understood that the next-of-kin is Mr Henry Baskerville, if he be still alive, the son of Sir Charles Baskerville's younger brother. The young man, when last heard of, was in America, and inquiries are being instituted with a view to informing him of his good fortune.'

Dr Mortimer refolded his paper and replaced it in his pocket.

'Those are the public facts, Mr Holmes, in connection with the death of Sir Charles Baskerville.'

'I must thank you', said Sherlock Holmes, 'for calling my attention to a case which certainly presents some features of interest. I had observed some newspaper comment at the time, but I was exceedingly preoccupied by that little affair of the Vatican cameos, and in my anxiety to oblige the Pope* I lost touch with several interesting English cases. This article, you say, contains all the public facts?'

'It does.'

'Then let me have the private ones.' He leaned back, put his finger-tips together, and assumed his most impassive and judicial expression.

'In doing so,' said Dr Mortimer, who had begun to show signs of some strong emotion, 'I am telling that which I have not confided to anyone. My motive for withholding it from the coroner's inquiry is that a man of science shrinks from placing himself in the public position of seeming to endorse a popular superstition. I had the further motive that Baskerville Hall, as the paper says, would certainly remain untenanted if anything were done to increase its already rather grim reputation. For both these reasons I thought that I was justified in telling rather less than I knew, since no practical good could result from it, but with you there is no reason why I should not be perfectly frank.

'The moor is very sparsely inhabited, and those who live near each other are thrown very much together. For this reason I saw a good deal of Sir Charles Baskerville. With the exception of Mr Frankland, of Lafter Hall,* and Mr Stapleton, the naturalist, there are no other men of education within many miles. Sir Charles was a retiring man, but the chance of his illness brought us together, and a community of interests in science kept us so. He had brought back much scientific information from South Africa, and many a charming evening we have spent together discussing the comparative anatomy of the Bushman and the Hottentot.*

'Within the last few months it became increasingly plain to me that Sir Charles's nervous system was strained to breaking point. He had taken this legend which I have read you exceedingly to heart—so much so that, although he would walk in his own grounds, nothing would induce him to go out upon the moor at night. Incredible as it may appear to you, Mr Holmes, he was honestly convinced that a dreadful fate overhung his family, and certainly the records which he was able to give of his ancestors were not encouraging. The idea of some ghastly presence constantly haunted him, and on more than one occasion he has asked me whether I had on my medical journeys at night ever seen any strange creature or heard the baying of a hound. The latter question he put to me several times, and always with a voice which vibrated with excitement.

'I can well remember driving up to his house in the evening, some three weeks before the fatal event. He chanced to be at his hall door. I had descended from my gig* and was standing in front of him, when I saw his eyes fix themselves over my shoulder, and stare past me with an expression of the most dreadful horror. I whisked round and had just time to catch a glimpse of something which I took to be a large black calf passing at the head of the drive. So excited and alarmed was he that I was compelled to go down to the spot where the animal had been and look around for it. It was gone, however, and the incident appeared to make the worst impression upon his mind. I stayed with him all the evening, and it was on that occasion, to explain the emotion which he had shown, that he confided to my keeping that narrative which I read to you when first I came. I mention this small episode because it assumes some importance in view of the tragedy which followed, but I was convinced at the time that the matter was entirely trivial and that his excitement had no justification.

'It was at my advice that Sir Charles was about to go to London. His heart was, I knew, affected, and the constant anxiety in which he lived, however chimerical* the cause of it might be, was evidently having a serious effect upon his health. I thought that a few months among the distractions of town would send him back a new man. Mr Stapleton, a mutual friend who was much concerned at his state of health, was of the same opinion. At the last instant came this terrible catastrophe.

'On the night of Sir Charles's death Barrymore the butler, who made the discovery, sent Perkins the groom on horse-back to me, and as I was sitting up late I was able to reach Baskerville Hall within an hour of the event. I checked and corroborated all the facts which were mentioned at the inquest. I followed the footsteps down the Yew

Alley, I saw the spot at the moor-gate where he seemed to have waited. I remarked the change in the shape of the prints after that point, I noted that there were no other footsteps save those of Barrymore on the soft gravel, and finally I carefully examined the body, which had not been touched until my arrival. Sir Charles lay on his face, his arms out, his fingers dug into the ground, and his features convulsed with some strong emotion to such an extent that I could hardly have sworn to his identity. There was certainly no physical injury of any kind. But one false statement was made by Barrymore at the inquest. He said that there were no traces upon the ground round the body. He did not observe any. But I did—some little distance off, but fresh and clear.'

'Footprints?'

'Footprints.'

'A man's or a woman's?'

Dr Mortimer looked strangely at us for an instant, and his voice sank almost to a whisper as he answered:

'Mr Holmes, they were the footprints of a gigantic hound!'*

CHAPTER 3

THE PROBLEM

I CONFESS that at these words a shudder passed through me. There was a thrill in the doctor's voice which showed that he was himself deeply moved by that which he told us. Holmes leaned forward in his excitement, and his eyes had the hard, dry glitter which shot from them when he was keenly interested.

'You saw this?'

'As clearly as I see you.'

'And you said nothing?'

'What was the use?'

'How was it that no one else saw it?'

'The marks were some twenty yards from the body, and no one gave them a thought. I don't suppose I should have done so had I not known this legend.'

'There are many sheep-dogs on the moor?'

'No doubt, but this was no sheep-dog.'

'You say it was large?'

'Enormous.'

'But it had not approached the body?'

'No.'

'What sort of night was it?'

'Damp and raw.'

'But not actually raining?'

'No.'

'What is the alley like?'

'There are two lines of old yew hedge, twelve feet high and impenetrable. The walk in the centre is about eight feet across.'

'Is there anything between the hedges and the walk?'

'Yes, there is a strip of grass about six feet broad on either side.'

'I understand that the yew hedge is penetrated at one point by a gate?'

'Yes, the wicket-gate* which leads on to the moor.'

'Is there any other opening?'

'None.'

'So that to reach the Yew Alley one either has to come down it from the house or else to enter it by the moor-gate?'

'There is an exit through a summer-house at the far end.'

'Had Sir Charles reached this?'

'No; he lay about fifty yards from it.'

'Now, tell me, Dr Mortimer—and this is important—the marks which you saw were on the path and not on the grass?'

'No marks could show on the grass.'

'Were they on the same side of the path as the moor-gate?'

'Yes; they were on the edge of the path on the same side as the moor-gate.'

'You interest me exceedingly. Another point. Was the wicket-gate closed?'

'Closed and padlocked.'

'How high was it?'

'About four feet high.'

'Then anyone could have got over it?'

'Yes.'

'And what marks did you see by the wicket-gate?'

'None in particular.'

'Good Heaven! Did no one examine?'

'Yes, I examined myself.'

'And found nothing?'

'It was all very confused. Sir Charles had evidently stood there for five or ten minutes.'

'How do you know that?'

'Because the ash had twice dropped from his cigar.'

'Excellent! This is a colleague, Watson, after our own heart.* But the marks?'

'He had left his own marks all over that small patch of gravel. I could discern no others.'

Sherlock Holmes struck his hand against his knee with an impatient gesture.

'If I had only been there!' he cried. 'It is evidently a case of extraordinary interest, and one which presented immense opportunities to the scientific expert. That gravel page upon which I might have read so much has been long ere this smudged by the rain and defaced by the clogs of curious peasants. Oh, Dr Mortimer, Dr Mortimer, to think that you should not have called me in! You have indeed much to answer for.'

'I could not call you in, Mr Holmes, without disclosing these facts to the world, and I have already given my reasons for not wishing to do so. Besides, besides—'

'Why do you hesitate?'

'There is a realm in which the most acute and most experienced of detectives is helpless.'

'You mean that the thing is supernatural?'

'I did not positively say so.'

'No, but you evidently think it.'

'Since the tragedy, Mr Holmes, there have come to my ears several incidents which are hard to reconcile with the settled order of Nature.'

'For example?'

'I find that before the terrible event occurred several people had seen a creature upon the moor which corresponds with this Baskerville demon, and which could not possibly be any animal known to science. They all agreed that it was a huge creature, luminous, ghastly, and spectral. I have cross-examined these men, one of them a hard-headed countryman, one a farrier,* and one a moorland farmer, who all tell the same story of this dreadful apparition, exactly corresponding to the hell-hound of the legend. I assure you that there is a reign of terror in the district, and that it is a hardy man who will cross the moor at night.'

'And you, a trained man of science, believe it to be supernatural?'

'I do not know what to believe.'

Holmes shrugged his shoulders. 'I have hitherto confined my investigations to this world,' said he. 'In a modest way I have combated evil, but to take on the Father of Evil himself would, perhaps, be too ambitious a task. Yet you must admit that the footmark is material.'

'The original hound was material enough to tug a man's throat out, and yet he was diabolical as well.'

'I see that you have quite gone over to the supernaturalists. But now, Dr Mortimer, tell me this. If you hold these views, why have you come to consult me at all? You tell me in the same breath that it is useless to investigate Sir Charles's death, and that you desire me to do it.'

'I did not say that I desired you to do it.'

'Then, how can I assist you?'

'By advising me as to what I should do with Sir Henry Baskerville, who arrives at Waterloo Station'*—Dr Mortimer looked at his watch—'in exactly one hour and a quarter.'

'He being the heir?'

'Yes. On the death of Sir Charles we inquired for this young gentleman, and found that he had been farming in Canada. From the accounts which have reached us he is an excellent fellow in every way. I speak now not as a medical man but as a trustee and executor* of Sir Charles's will.'

'There is no other claimant, I presume?'

'None. The only other kinsman whom we have been able to trace was Rodger Baskerville, the youngest of three brothers of whom poor Sir Charles was the elder. The second brother, who died young, is the father of this lad Henry. The third, Rodger, was the black sheep of the family. He came of the old masterful Baskerville strain, and was the very image, they tell me, of the family picture of old Hugo. He made England too hot to hold him, fled to Central America, and died there in 1876 of yellow fever.* Henry is the last of the Baskervilles. In one hour and five minutes I meet him at Waterloo Station. I have had a wire* that he arrived at Southampton this morning. Now, Mr Holmes, what would you advise me to do with him?'

'Why should he not go to the home of his fathers?'

'It seems natural, does it not? And yet, consider that every Baskerville who goes there meets with an evil fate. I feel sure that if Sir Charles could have spoken with me before his death he would have warned me against bringing this the last of the old race, and the heir to great wealth, to that deadly place. And yet it cannot be denied that the prosperity of the whole poor, bleak country-side depends upon his presence.* All the good work which has been done by Sir Charles will crash to the ground if there is no tenant of the Hall. I fear lest I should be swayed too much by my own obvious interest in the matter, and that is why I bring the case before you and ask for your advice.'

Holmes considered for a little time. 'Put into plain words, the matter is this,' said he. 'In your opinion there is a diabolical agency which makes Dartmoor an unsafe abode for a Baskerville—that is your opinion?'

'At least I might go the length of saying that there is some evidence that this may be so.'

'Exactly. But surely if your supernatural theory be correct, it could work the young man evil in London as easily as in Devonshire. A devil with merely local powers like a parish vestry* would be too inconceivable a thing.'

'You put the matter more flippantly, Mr Holmes, than you would probably do if you were brought into personal contact with these things. Your advice, then, as I understand it, is that the young man will be as safe in Devonshire as in London. He comes in fifty minutes. What would you recommend?'

'I recommend, sir, that you take a cab, call off your spaniel, who is scratching at my front door, and proceed to Waterloo to meet Sir Henry Baskerville.'

'And then?'

'And then you will say nothing to him at all until I have made up my mind about the matter.'

'How long will it take you to make up your mind?'

'Twenty-four hours. At ten o'clock tomorrow, Dr Mortimer, I will be much obliged to you if you will call upon me here, and it will be of help to me in my plans for the future if you will bring Sir Henry Baskerville with you.'

'I will do so, Mr Holmes.'

He scribbled the appointment on his shirt-cuff and hurried off in his strange, peering, absent-minded fashion. Holmes stopped him at the head of the stair.

'Only one more question, Dr Mortimer. You say that before Sir Charles Baskerville's death several people saw this apparition upon the moor?'

'Three people did.'

'Did any see it after?'

'I have not heard of any.'

'Thank you. Good morning.'

Holmes returned to his seat with that quiet look of inward satisfaction which meant that he had a congenial task before him.

'Going out, Watson?'

'Unless I can help you.'

'No, my dear fellow, it is at the hour of action that I turn to you for aid. But this is splendid, really unique from some points of view. When you pass Bradley's, would you ask him to send up a pound of the strongest shag tobacco?* Thank you. It would be as well if you could make it convenient not to return before evening. Then I should be very glad to compare impressions as to this most interesting problem which has been submitted to us this morning.'

I knew that seclusion and solitude were very necessary for my friend in those hours of intense mental concentration during which he weighed every particle of evidence, constructed alternative theories, balanced one against the other, and made up his mind as to which points were essential and which immaterial. I therefore spent the day at my club, and did not return to Baker Street until evening. It was nearly nine o'clock when I found myself in the sitting-room once more.

My first impression as I opened the door was that a fire had broken out, for the room was so filled with smoke that the light of the lamp upon the table was blurred by it. As I entered, however, my fears were set at rest, for it was the acrid fumes of strong, coarse tobacco, which took me by the throat and set me coughing. Through the haze I had a vague vision of Holmes in his dressing-gown coiled up in an armchair with his black clay pipe between his lips. Several rolls of paper lay around him.

'Caught cold, Watson?' said he.

'No, it's this poisonous atmosphere.'

'I suppose it *is* pretty thick, now that you mention it.'

'Thick! It is intolerable.'

'Open the window, then! You have been at your club all day, I perceive.'

'My dear Holmes!'

'Am I right?'

'Certainly, but how—?'

He laughed at my bewildered expression.

'There is a delightful freshness about you, Watson, which makes it a pleasure to exercise any small powers which I possess at your expense. A gentleman goes forth on a showery and miry day. He returns immaculate in the evening with the gloss still on his hat and his boots. He has been a fixture therefore all day. He is not a man with intimate friends. Where, then, could he have been? Is it not obvious?'

'Well, it is rather obvious.'

'The world is full of obvious things which nobody by any chance ever observes. Where do you think that I have been?'

'A fixture also.'

'On the contrary, I have been to Devonshire.'

'In spirit?'*

'Exactly. My body has remained in this arm-chair, and has, I regret to observe, consumed in my absence two large pots of coffee and an incredible amount of tobacco. After you left I sent down to Stanford's for the Ordnance map* of this portion of the moor, and my spirit has hovered over it all day. I flatter myself that I could find my way about.'

'A large scale map,* I presume?'

'Very large.' He unrolled one section and held it over his knee. 'Here you have the particular district which concerns us. That is Baskerville Hall in the middle.'

'With a wood round it?'

'Exactly. I fancy the Yew Alley, though not marked under that name, must stretch along this line, with the moor, as you perceive, upon the right of it. This small clump of buildings here is the hamlet of Grimpen, where our friend Dr Mortimer has his headquarters. Within a radius of five miles there are, as you see, only a very few scattered dwellings. Here is Lafter Hall, which was mentioned in the narrative. There is a house indicated here which may be the residence of the naturalist—Stapleton, if I remember right, was his name. Here are two moorland farmhouses, High Tor and Foulmire.* Then fourteen miles away the great convict prison of Princetown.* Between and around these scattered points extends the desolate, lifeless moor. This, then, is the stage upon which tragedy has been played, and upon which we may help to play it again.'

'It must be a wild place.'

'Yes, the setting is a worthy one. If the devil did desire to have a hand in the affairs of men—'

'Then you are yourself inclining to the supernatural explanation.'

'The devil's agents may be of flesh and blood, may they not? There are two questions waiting for us at the outset. The one is whether any crime has been committed at all; the second is, what is the crime and how was it committed? Of course, if Dr Mortimer's surmise should be correct, and we are dealing with forces outside the ordinary laws of Nature, there is an end of our investigation. But we are bound to exhaust all other hypotheses before falling back upon this one. I think we'll shut that window again, if you don't mind. It is a singular thing, but I find that a concentrated atmosphere helps a concentration of thought. I have not pushed it to the length of getting into a box to think, but that is the logical outcome of my convictions. Have you turned the case over in your mind?'

'Yes, I have thought a good deal of it in the course of the day.'

'What do you make of it?'

'It is very bewildering.'

'It has certainly a character of its own. There are points of distinction about it. That change in the footprints, for example. What do you make of that?'

'Mortimer said that the man had walked on tiptoe down that portion of the alley.'

'He only repeated what some fool had said at the inquest. Why should a man walk on tiptoe down the alley?'

'What then?'

'He was running, Watson—running desperately, running for his life, running until he burst his heart and fell dead upon his face.'

'Running from what?'

'There lies our problem. There are indications that the man was crazed with fear before ever he began to run.'

'How can you say that?'

'I am presuming that the cause of his fears came to him across the moor. If that were so, and it seems most probable, only a man who had lost his wits would have run *from* the house instead of towards it. If the gipsy's evidence may be taken as true, he ran with cries for help in the direction where help was least likely to be. Then again, whom was he waiting for that night, and why was he waiting for him in the Yew Alley rather than in his own house?'

'You think that he was waiting for someone?'

'The man was elderly and infirm. We can understand his taking an evening stroll, but the ground was damp and the night inclement. Is it natural that he should stand for five or ten minutes, as Dr Mortimer, with more practical sense than I should have given him credit for, deduced from the cigar ash?'

'But he went out every evening.'

'I think it unlikely that he waited at the moor-gate every evening. On the contrary, the evidence is that he avoided the moor. That night he waited there. It was the night before he was to take his departure for London. The thing takes shape, Watson. It becomes coherent. Might I ask you to hand me my violin, and we will postpone all further thought upon this business until we have had the advantage of meeting Dr Mortimer and Sir Henry Baskerville in the morning.'

CHAPTER 4

SIR HENRY BASKERVILLE

OUR breakfast-table was cleared early, and Holmes waited in his dressing-gown for the promised interview. Our clients were punctual to their appointment, for the clock had just struck ten when Dr Mortimer was shown up, followed by the young Baronet.* The latter was a small, alert, dark-eyed man about thirty years of age, very sturdily built, with thick black eyebrows and a strong, pugnacious face. He wore a ruddy-tinted tweed suit,* and had the weather-beaten appearance of one who has spent most of his time in the open air, and yet there was something in his steady eye and the quiet assurance of his bearing which indicated the gentleman.

'This is Sir Henry Baskerville,' said Dr Mortimer.

'Why, yes,' said he, 'and the strange thing is, Mr Sherlock Holmes, that if my friend here had not proposed coming round to you this morning I should have come on my own. I understand that you think out little puzzles, and I've had one this morning which wants more thinking out than I am able to give it.'

'Pray take a seat, Sir Henry. Do I understand you to say that you have yourself had some remarkable experience since you arrived in London?'

'Nothing of much importance, Mr Holmes. Only a joke, as like as not. It was this letter, if you can call it a letter, which reached me this morning.'

He laid an envelope upon the table, and we all bent over it. It was of common quality, greyish in colour. The address, 'Sir Henry Baskerville, Northumberland Hotel',* was printed in rough characters; the post-mark 'Charing Cross', and the date of posting the preceding evening.

'Who knew that you were going to the Northumberland Hotel?' asked Holmes, glancing keenly across at our visitor.

'No one could have known. We only decided after I met Dr Mortimer.'

'But Dr Mortimer was, no doubt, already stopping there?'

'No, I had been staying with a friend,' said the doctor. 'There was no possible indication that we intended to go to this hotel.'

'Hum! Someone seems to be very deeply interested in your movements.' Out of the envelope he took a half-sheet of foolscap* paper folded into four. This he opened and spread flat upon the table. Across the middle of it a single sentence had been formed by the expedient of pasting printed words upon it. It ran: 'as you value your life or your reason keep away from the moor.' The word 'moor' only was printed in ink.

'Now,' said Sir Henry Baskerville, 'perhaps you will tell me, Mr Holmes, what in thunder is the meaning of that, and who it is that takes so much interest in my affairs?'

'What do you make of it, Dr Mortimer? You must allow that there is nothing supernatural about this, at any rate?'

'No, sir, but it might very well come from someone who was convinced that the business is supernatural.'

'What business?' asked Sir Henry, sharply. 'It seems to me that all you gentlemen know a great deal more than I do about my own affairs.'

'You shall share our knowledge before you leave this room, Sir Henry. I promise you that,' said Sherlock Holmes. 'We will confine

ourselves for the present, with your permission, to this very interesting document, which must have been put together and posted yesterday evening. Have you yesterday's *Times*,* Watson?'

'It is here in the corner.'

'Might I trouble you for it—the inside page, please, with the leading articles?' He glanced swiftly over it, running his eyes up and down
the columns. 'Capital article this on Free Trade.* Permit me to give
you an extract from it. "You may be cajoled into imagining that your
own special trade or your own industry will be encouraged by a protective tariff, but it stands to reason that such legislation must in the
long run keep away wealth from the country, diminish the value of
our imports, and lower the general conditions of life in this island."
What do you think of that, Watson?' cried Holmes, in high glee, rub-
bing his hands together with satisfaction. 'Don't you think that is an
admirable sentiment?'

Dr Mortimer looked at Holmes with an air of professional interest,
and Sir Henry Baskerville turned a pair of puzzled dark eyes upon me.

'I don't know much about the tariff and things of that kind,' said
he; 'but it seems to me we've got a bit off the trail so far as that note is
concerned.'

'On the contrary, I think we are particularly hot upon the trail, Sir
Henry. Watson here knows more about my methods than you do, but
I fear that even he has not quite grasped the significance of this
sentence.'

'No, I confess that I see no connection.'

'And yet, my dear Watson, there is so very close a connection that
the one is extracted out of the other. "You", "your", "your", "life",
"reason", "value", "keep away", "from the". Don't you see now
whence these words have been taken?'

'By thunder, you're right! Well, if that isn't smart!' cried Sir Henry.

'If any possible doubt remained it is settled by the fact that "keep
away" and "from the" are cut out in one piece.'

'Well, now—so it is!'

'Really, Mr Holmes, this exceeds anything which I could have
imagined,' said Dr Mortimer, gazing at my friend in amazement.
'I could understand anyone saying that the words were from a newspaper; but that you should name which, and add that it came from the
leading article, is really one of the most remarkable things which
I have ever known. How did you do it?'

'I presume, doctor, that you could tell the skull of a negro from that of an Esquimaux?'*

'Most certainly.'

'But how?'

'Because that is my special hobby. The differences are obvious. The supra-orbital crest, the facial angle, the maxillary curve,* the—'

'But this is my special hobby, and the differences are equally obvious. There is as much difference to my eyes between the leaded bourgeois type* of a *Times* article and the slovenly print of an evening halfpenny paper as there could be between your Negro and your Esquimaux. The detection of types* is one of the most elementary branches of knowledge to the special expert in crime, though I confess that once when I was very young I confused the *Leeds Mercury* with the *Western Morning News*.* But a *Times* leader is entirely distinctive, and these words could have been taken from nothing else. As it was done yesterday the strong probability was that we should find the words in yesterday's issue.'

'So far as I can follow you, then, Mr Holmes,' said Sir Henry Baskerville, 'someone cut out this message with a scissors—'

'Nail-scissors,' said Holmes. 'You can see that it was a very short-bladed scissors, since the cutter had to take two snips over "keep away".'

'That is so. Someone, then, cut out the message with a pair of short-bladed scissors, pasted it with paste—'

'Gum,' said Holmes.

'With gum on to the paper. But I want to know why the word "moor" should have been written?'

'Because he could not find it in print. The other words were all simple, and might be found in any issue, but "moor" would be less common.'

'Why, of course, that would explain it. Have you read anything else in this message, Mr Holmes?'

'There are one or two indications, and yet the utmost pains have been taken to remove all clues. The address, you observe, is printed in rough characters. But *The Times* is a paper which is seldom found in any hands but those of the highly educated. We may take it, therefore, that the letter was composed by an educated man who wished to pose as an uneducated one, and his effort to conceal his own writing suggests that that writing might be known, or come to be known, by you. Again, you will observe that the words are not gummed on in an accurate line, but that some are much higher than others. "Life", for example, is quite out of its proper place. That may point to carelessness or it may point to agitation and hurry upon the part of the cutter. On the whole I incline to the latter view, since the matter was evidently important, and it is unlikely that the composer of such a letter would be careless. If he were in a hurry it opens up the interesting question why he should be in a hurry, since any letter posted up to early morning would reach Sir Henry before he would leave his hotel. Did the composer fear an interruption—and from whom?'

'We are coming now rather into the region of guesswork,' said Dr Mortimer.

'Say, rather, into the region where we balance probabilities and choose the most likely. It is the scientific use of the imagination, but we have always some material basis on which to start our specula-tions. Now, you would call it a guess, no doubt, but I am almost cer-tain that this address has been written in an hotel.'

'How in the world can you say that?'

'If you examine it carefully you will see that both the pen and the ink have given the writer trouble. The pen has spluttered twice in a single word, and has run dry three times in a short address, showing that there was very little ink in the bottle. Now, a private pen or ink-bottle is seldom allowed to be in such a state, and the combination of the two must be quite rare. But you know the hotel ink and the hotel pen, where it is rare to get anything else. Yes, I have very little hesita-tion in saying that could we examine the waste-paper baskets of the hotels round Charing Cross until we found the remains of the muti-lated *Times* leader we could lay our hands straight upon the person who sent this singular message. Hullo! Hullo! What's this?'

He was carefully examining the foolscap, upon which the words were pasted, holding it only an inch or two from his eyes.

'Well?'

'Nothing,' said he, throwing it down. 'It is a blank half-sheet of paper, without even a water-mark* upon it. I think we have drawn as much as we can from this curious letter; and now, Sir Henry, has any-thing else of interest happened to you since you have been in London?'

'Why, no, Mr Holmes. I think not.'

'You have not observed anyone follow or watch you?'

'I seem to have walked right into the thick of a dime novel,'* said our visitor. 'Why in thunder should anyone follow or watch me?'

'We are coming to that. You have nothing else to report to us before we go into this matter?'

'Well, it depends upon what you think worth reporting.'

'I think anything out of the ordinary routine of life well worth reporting.'

Sir Henry smiled. 'I don't know much of British life yet, for I have spent nearly all my time in the States and in Canada. But I hope that to lose one of your boots is not part of the ordinary routine of life over here.'

'You have lost one of your boots?'

'My dear sir,' cried Dr Mortimer, 'it is only mislaid. You will find it when you return to the hotel. What is the use of troubling Mr Holmes with trifles of this kind?'

'Well, he asked me for anything outside the ordinary routine.'

'Exactly,' said Holmes, 'however foolish the incident may seem. You have lost one of your boots, you say?'

'Well, mislaid it, anyhow. I put them both outside my door last night, and there was only one in the morning. I could get no sense out of the chap who cleans them. The worst of it is that I only bought the pair last night in the Strand,* and I have never had them on.'

'If you have never worn them, why did you put them out to be cleaned?'

'They were tan boots, and had never been varnished. That was why I put them out.'

'Then I understand that on your arrival in London yesterday you went out at once and bought a pair of boots?'

'I did a good deal of shopping. Dr Mortimer here went round with me. You see, if I am to be squire down there I must dress the part,* and it may be that I have got a little careless in my ways out West. Among other things I bought these brown boots—gave six dollars for them—and had one stolen before ever I had them on my feet.'

'It seems a singularly useless thing to steal,' said Sherlock Holmes. 'I confess that I share Dr Mortimer's belief that it will not be long before the missing boot is found.'

'And now, gentlemen,' said the Baronet, with decision, 'it seems to me that I have spoken quite enough about the little that I know. It is time that you kept your promise, and gave me a full account of what we are all driving at.'

'Your request is a very reasonable one,' Holmes answered. 'Dr Mortimer, I think you could not do better than to tell your story as you told it to us.'

Thus encouraged, our scientific friend drew his papers from his pocket, and presented the whole case as he had done upon the morning before. Sir Henry Baskerville listened with the deepest attention and with an occasional exclamation of surprise.

'Well, I seem to have come into an inheritance with a vengeance,' said he, when the long narrative was finished. 'Of course, I've heard of the hound ever since I was in the nursery. It's the pet story of the family,* though I never thought of taking it seriously before. But as to my uncle's death—well, it all seems boiling up in my head, and I can't get it clear yet. You don't seem quite to have made up your mind whether it's a case for a policeman or a clergyman.'

'Precisely.'

'And now there's this affair of the letter to me at the hotel. I suppose that fits into its place.'

'It seems to show that someone knows more than we do about what goes on upon the moor,' said Dr Mortimer.

'And also,' said Holmes, 'that someone is not ill-disposed towards you, since they warn you of danger.'

'Or it may be that they wish for their own purposes to scare me away.'

'Well, of course, that is possible also. I am very much indebted to you, Dr Mortimer, for introducing me to a problem which presents several interesting alternatives. But the practical point which we now have to decide, Sir Henry, is whether it is or is not advisable for you to go to Baskerville Hall.'

'Why should I not go?'

'There seems to be danger.'

'Do you mean danger from this family fiend or do you mean danger from human beings?'

'Well, that is what we have to find out.'

'Whichever it is, my answer is fixed. There is no devil in hell, Mr Holmes, and there is no man upon earth who can prevent me from going to the home of my own people, and you may take that to be my final answer.' His dark brows knitted and his face flushed to a dusky red as he spoke. It was evident that the fiery temper of the Baskervilles was not extinct in this their last representative. 'Meanwhile,' said he,

'I have hardly had time to think over all that you have told me. It's a big thing for a man to have to understand and to decide at one sitting. I should like to have a quiet hour by myself to make up my mind. Now, look here, Mr Holmes, it's half-past eleven now, and I am going back right away to my hotel. Suppose you and your friend, Dr Watson, come round and lunch with us at two? I'll be able to tell you more clearly then how this thing strikes me.'

'Is that convenient to you, Watson?'

'Perfectly.'

'Then you may expect us. Shall I have a cab called?'

'I'd prefer to walk, for this affair has flurried me rather.'

'I'll join you in a walk, with pleasure,' said his companion.

'Then we meet again at two o'clock. Au revoir, and good morning!'

We heard the steps of our visitors descend the stair and the bang of the front door. In an instant Holmes had changed from the languid dreamer to the man of action.

'Your hat and boots, Watson, quick! Not a moment to lose!' He rushed into his room in his dressing-gown, and was back again in a few seconds in a frock-coat. We hurried together down the stairs and into the street. Dr Mortimer and Baskerville were still visible about two hundred yards ahead of us in the direction of Oxford Street.*

'Shall I run on and stop them?'

'Not for the world, my dear Watson. I am perfectly satisfied with your company, if you will tolerate mine. Our friends are wise, for it is certainly a very fine morning for a walk.'

He quickened his pace until we had decreased the distance which divided us by about half. Then, still keeping a hundred yards behind, we followed into Oxford Street and so down Regent Street.* Once our friends stopped and stared into a shop window, upon which Holmes did the same. An instant afterwards he gave a little cry of satisfaction, and, following the direction of his eager eyes, I saw that a hansom cab* with a man inside which had halted on the other side of the street was now walking slowly onwards again.

'There's our man, Watson! Come along! We'll have a good look at him, if we can do no more.'

At that instant I was aware of a bushy black beard and a pair of piercing eyes turned upon us through the side window of the cab. Instantly the trap-door at the top flew up, something was screamed to the driver, and the cab flew madly off down Regent Street. Holmes looked eagerly round for another, but no empty one was in sight. Then he dashed in wild pursuit amid the stream of the traffic, but the start was too great, and already the cab was out of sight.

'There now!' said Holmes, bitterly, as he emerged panting and white with vexation from the tide of vehicles. 'Was ever such bad luck and such bad management, too? Watson, Watson, if you are an honest man you will record this also and set it against my successes!'

'Who was the man?'

'I have not an idea.'

'A spy?'

'Well, it was evident from what we have heard that Baskerville has been very closely shadowed by someone since he has been in town. How else could it be known so quickly that it was the Northumberland Hotel which he had chosen? If they had followed him the first day I argued that they would follow him also the second. You may have observed that I twice strolled over to the window while Dr Mortimer was reading his legend.'

'Yes, I remember.'

'I was looking out for loiterers in the street, but I saw none. We are dealing with a clever man, Watson. This matter cuts very deep, and though I have not finally made up my mind whether it is a benevolent or a malevolent agency which is in touch with us, I am conscious always of power and design. When our friends left I at once followed them in the hopes of marking down their invisible attendant. So wily was he that he had not trusted himself upon foot, but he had availed himself of a cab, so that he could loiter behind or dash past them and so escape their notice. His method had the additional advantage that if they were to take a cab he was all ready to follow them. It has, however, one obvious disadvantage.'

'It puts him in the power of the cabman.'

'Exactly.'

'What a pity we did not get the number!'

'My dear Watson, clumsy as I have been, you surely do not seriously imagine that I neglected to get the number? 2704 is our man. But that is no use to us for the moment.'

'I fail to see how you could have done more.'

'On observing the cab I should have instantly turned and walked in the other direction. I should then at my leisure have hired a second cab and followed the first at a respectful distance, or, better still, have driven to the Northumberland Hotel and waited there. When our unknown had followed Baskerville home we should have had the opportunity of playing his own game upon himself, and seeing where he made for. As it is, by an indiscreet eagerness, which was taken advantage of with extraordinary quickness and energy by our opponent, we have betrayed ourselves and lost our man.'

We had been sauntering slowly down Regent Street during this conversation, and Dr Mortimer, with his companion, had long vanished in front of us.

'There is no object in our following them,' said Holmes. 'The shadow has departed and will not return. We must see what further cards we have in our hands, and play them with decision. Could you swear to that man's face within the cab?'

'I could swear only to the beard.'

'And so could I—from which I gather that in all probability it was a false one. A clever man upon so delicate an errand has no use for a beard save to conceal his features. Come in here, Watson!'

He turned into one of the district messenger offices,* where he was warmly greeted by the manager.

'Ah, Wilson, I see you have not forgotten the little case in which I had the good fortune to help you?'

'No, sir, indeed I have not. You saved my good name, and perhaps my life.'

'My dear fellow, you exaggerate. I have some recollection, Wilson, that you had among your boys a lad named Cartwright, who showed some ability during the investigation.'

'Yes, sir, he is still with us.'

'Could you ring him up? Thank you! And I should be glad to have change of this five-pound note.'

A lad of fourteen, with a bright, keen face, had obeyed the summons of the manager. He stood now gazing with great reverence at the famous detective.

'Let me have the Hotel Directory,'* said Holmes. 'Thank you! Now, Cartwright, there are the names of twenty-three hotels here, all in the immediate neighbourhood of Charing Cross. Do you see?'

'Yes, sir.'

'You will visit each of these in turn.'

'Yes, sir.'

'You will begin in each case by giving the outside porter one shilling. Here are twenty-three shillings.'

'Yes, sir.'

'You will tell him that you want to see the waste paper of yesterday. You will say that an important telegram has miscarried, and that you are looking for it. You understand?'

'Yes, sir.'

'But what you are really looking for is the centre page of *The Times* with some holes cut in it with scissors. Here is a copy of *The Times*. It is this page. You could easily recognize it, could you not?'

'Yes, sir.'

'In each case the outside porter will send for the hall porter, to whom also you will give a shilling. Here are twenty-three shillings. You will then learn in possibly twenty cases out of the twenty-three that the waste of the day before has been burned or removed. In the three other cases you will be shown a heap of paper, and will look for this page of *The Times* among it. The odds are enormously against your finding it. There are ten shillings over in case of emergencies. Let me have a report by wire at Baker Street before evening. And now, Watson, it only remains for us to find out by wire the identity of the cabman, No. 2704, and then we will drop into one of the Bond Street picture-galleries* and fill in the time until we are due at the hotel.'*

CHAPTER 5

THREE BROKEN THREADS

SHERLOCK HOLMES had, in a very remarkable degree, the power of detaching his mind at will. For two hours the strange business in which we had been involved appeared to be forgotten, and he was entirely absorbed in the pictures of the modern Belgian masters.* He would talk of nothing but art, of which he had the crudest ideas,* from our leaving the gallery until we found ourselves at the Northumberland Hotel.

'Sir Henry Baskerville is upstairs expecting you,' said the clerk. 'He asked me to show you up at once when you came.'

'Have you any objection to my looking at your register?' said Holmes.

'Not in the least.'

The book showed that two names had been added after that of Baskerville. One was Theophilus Johnson and family, of Newcastle; the other Mrs Oldmore and maid, of High Lodge, Alton.*

'Surely that must be the same Johnson whom I used to know,' said Holmes to the porter. 'A lawyer, is he not, grey-headed, and walks with a limp?'

'No, sir, this is Mr Johnson the coal-owner, a very active gentleman, not older than yourself.'

'Surely you are mistaken about his trade?'

'No, sir; he has used this hotel for many years, and he is very well known to us.'

'Ah, that settles it. Mrs Oldmore, too; I seem to remember the name. Excuse my curiosity, but often in calling upon one friend one finds another.'

'She is an invalid lady, sir. Her husband was once Mayor of Gloucester.* She always comes to us when she is in town.'

'Thank you; I am afraid I cannot claim her acquaintance. We have established a most important fact by these questions, Watson,' he continued, in a low voice, as we went upstairs together. 'We know now that the people who are so interested in our friend have not settled down in his own hotel. That means that while they are, as we have seen, very anxious to watch him, they are equally anxious that he should not see them. Now, this is a most suggestive fact.'

'What does it suggest?'

'It suggests—hullo, my dear fellow, what on earth is the matter?'

As we came round the top of the stairs we had run up against Sir Henry Baskerville himself. His face was flushed with anger, and he held an old and dusty boot in one of his hands. So furious was he that he was hardly articulate, and when he did speak it was in a much broader and more Western dialect* than any which we had heard from him in the morning.

'Seems to me they are playing me for a sucker in this hotel,' he cried. 'They'll find they've started in to monkey with the wrong man unless they are careful. By thunder, if that chap can't find my missing boot there will be trouble. I can take a joke with the best, Mr Holmes, but they've got a bit over the mark this time.'

'Still looking for your boot?'

'Yes, sir, and mean to find it.'

'But surely, you said that it was a new brown boot?'

'So it was, sir. And now it's an old black one.'

'What! you don't mean to say—?'

'That's just what I do mean to say. I only had three pairs in the world—the new brown, the old black, and the patent leathers, which I am wearing. Last night they took one of my brown ones, and to-day they have sneaked one of the black. Well, have you got it? Speak out, man, and don't stand staring!'

An agitated German waiter had appeared upon the scene.

'No, sir; I have made inquiry all over the hotel, but I can hear no word of it.'

'Well, either that boot comes back before sundown or I'll see the manager and tell him that I go right straight out of this hotel.'

'It shall be found, sir—I promise you that if you will have a little patience it will be found.'

'Mind it is, for it's the last thing of mine that I'll lose in this den of thieves. Well, well, Mr Holmes, you'll excuse my troubling you about such a trifle—'

'I think it's well worth troubling about.'

'Why, you look very serious over it.'

'How do you explain it?'

'I just don't attempt to explain it. It seems the very maddest, queerest thing that ever happened to me.'

'The queerest, perhaps,' said Holmes, thoughtfully.

'What do you make of it yourself?'

'Well, I don't profess to understand it yet. This case of yours is very complex, Sir Henry. When taken in conjunction with your uncle's death I am not sure that of all the five hundred cases* of capital importance which I have handled there is one which cuts so deep. But we hold several threads in our hands, and the odds are that one or other of them guides us to the truth. We may waste time in following the wrong one, but sooner or later we must come upon the right.'

We had a pleasant luncheon in which little was said of the business which had brought us together. It was in the private sitting-room to which we afterwards repaired that Holmes asked Baskerville what were his intentions.

'To go to Baskerville Hall.'

'And when?'

'At the end of the week.'

'On the whole,' said Holmes, 'I think that your decision is a wise one. I have ample evidence that you are being dogged in London, and amid the millions of this great city* it is difficult to discover who these people are or what their object can be. If their intentions are evil they might do you a mischief, and we should be powerless to prevent it. You did not know, Dr Mortimer, that you were followed this morning from my house?'

Dr Mortimer started violently. 'Followed! By whom?'

'That, unfortunately, is what I cannot tell you. Have you among your neighbours or acquaintances on Dartmoor any man with a black, full beard?'

'No—or, let me see—why, yes. Barrymore, Sir Charles's butler, is a man with a full, black beard.'

'Ha! Where is Barrymore?'

'He is in charge of the Hall.'

'We had best ascertain if he is really there, or if by any possibility he might be in London.'

'How can you do that?'

'Give me a telegraph form. "Is all ready for Sir Henry?" That will do. Address to Mr Barrymore, Baskerville Hall. Which is the nearest telegraph-office? Grimpen. Very good, we will send a second wire to the postmaster, Grimpen: "Telegram to Mr Barrymore, to be delivered into his own hand. If absent, please return wire to Sir Henry Baskerville, Northumberland Hotel." That should let us know before evening whether Barrymore is at his post in Devonshire or not.'

'That's so,' said Baskerville. 'By the way, Dr Mortimer, who is this Barrymore, anyhow?'

'He is the son of the old caretaker, who is dead. They have looked after the Hall for four generations now. So far as I know, he and his wife are as respectable a couple as any in the county.'

'At the same time,' said Baskerville, 'it's clear enough that so long as there are none of the family at the Hall these people have a mighty fine home and nothing to do.'

'That is true.'

'Did Barrymore profit at all by Sir Charles's will?' asked Holmes.

'He and his wife had five hundred pounds each.'

'Ha! Did they know that they would receive this?'

'Yes; Sir Charles was very fond of talking about the provisions of his will.'

'That is very interesting.'

'I hope', said Dr Mortimer, 'that you do not look with suspicious eyes upon everyone who received a legacy from Sir Charles, for I also had a thousand pounds left to me.'

'Indeed! And anyone else?'

'There were many insignificant sums to individuals and a large number of public charities. The residue all went to Sir Henry.'

'And how much was the residue?'

'Seven hundred and forty thousand pounds.'

Holmes raised his eyebrows in surprise. 'I had no idea that so gigantic a sum was involved,' said he.

'Sir Charles had the reputation of being rich, but we did not know how very rich he was until we came to examine his securities. The total value of the estate was close on to a million.'*

'Dear me! It is a stake for which a man might well play a desperate game. And one more question, Dr Mortimer. Supposing that anything happened to our young friend here—you will forgive the unpleasant hypothesis!—who would inherit the estate?'

'Since Rodger Baskerville, Sir Charles's younger brother, died unmarried, the estate would descend to the Desmonds, who are distant cousins. James Desmond is an elderly clergyman in Westmorland.'*

'Thank you. These details are all of great interest. Have you met Mr James Desmond?'

'Yes; he once came down to visit Sir Charles. He is a man of venerable appearance and of saintly life. I remember that he refused to accept any settlement from Sir Charles, though he pressed it upon him.'

'And this man of simple tastes would be the heir to Sir Charles's thousands?'

'He would be the heir to the estate, because that is entailed.* He would also be the heir to the money unless it were willed otherwise by the present owner, who can, of course, do what he likes with it.'

'And have you made your will, Sir Henry?'

'No, Mr Holmes, I have not. I've had no time, for it was only yesterday that I learned how matters stood. But in any case I feel that the money should go with the title and estate. That was my poor uncle's idea. How is the owner going to restore the glories of the Baskervilles if he has not money enough to keep up the property? House, land, and dollars must go together.'

'Quite so. Well, Sir Henry, I am of one mind with you as to the advisability of your going down to Devonshire without delay. There is only one provision which I must make. You certainly must not go alone.'

'Dr Mortimer returns with me.'

'But Dr Mortimer has his practice to attend to, and his house is miles away from yours. With all the good will in the world, he may be unable to help you. No, Sir Henry, you must take with you someone, a trusty man, who will be always by your side.'

'Is it possible that you could come yourself, Mr Holmes?'

'If matters came to a crisis I should endeavour to be present in person; but you can understand that, with my extensive consulting practice and with the constant appeals which reach me from many quarters, it is impossible for me to be absent from London for an indefinite time. At the present instant one of the most revered names in England is being besmirched by a blackmailer, and only I can stop a disastrous scandal. You will see how impossible it is for me to go to Dartmoor.'

'Whom would you recommend, then?'

Holmes laid his hand upon my arm.

'If my friend would undertake it there is no man who is better worth having at your side when you are in a tight place. No one can say so more confidently than I.'

The proposition took me completely by surprise, but before I had time to answer Baskerville seized me by the hand and wrung it heartily.

'Well, now, that is real kind of you, Dr Watson,' said he. 'You see how it is with me, and you know just as much about the matter as I do. If you will come down to Baskerville Hall and see me through I'll never forget it.'

The promise of adventure had always a fascination for me, and I was complimented by the words of Holmes and by the eagerness with which the Baronet hailed me as a companion.

'I will come with pleasure,' said I. 'I do not know how I could employ my time better.'

'And you will report very carefully to me,' said Holmes. 'When a crisis comes, as it will do, I will direct how you shall act. I suppose that by Saturday all might be ready?'

'Would that suit Dr Watson?'

'Perfectly.'

'Then on Saturday, unless you hear to the contrary, we shall meet at the 10.30 train from Paddington.'*

We had risen to depart when Baskerville gave a cry of triumph, and diving into one of the corners of the room he drew a brown boot from under a cabinet.

'My missing boot!' he cried.

'May all our difficulties vanish as easily!' said Sherlock Holmes.

'But it is a very singular thing,' Dr Mortimer remarked. 'I searched this room carefully before lunch.'

'And so did I,' said Baskerville. 'Every inch of it.'

'There was certainly no boot in it then.'

'In that case the waiter must have placed it there while we were lunching.'

The German was sent for, but professed to know nothing of the matter, nor could any inquiry clear it up. Another item had been added to that constant and apparently purposeless series of small mysteries which had succeeded each other so rapidly. Setting aside the whole grim story of Sir Charles's death, we had a line of inexplicable incidents all within the limits of two days, which included the receipt of the printed letter, the black-bearded spy in the hansom, the loss of the new brown boot, the loss of the old black boot, and now the return of the new brown boot. Holmes sat in silence in the cab as we drove back to Baker Street, and I knew from his drawn brows and keen face that his mind, like my own, was busy in endeavouring to frame some scheme into which all these strange and apparently disconnected episodes could be fitted. All afternoon and late into the evening he sat lost in tobacco and thought.

Just before dinner two telegrams were handed in. The first ran:

Have just heard that Barrymore is at the Hall—BASKERVILLE.

The second:

Visited twenty-three hotels as directed, but sorry to report unable to trace cut sheet of *Times*—CARTWRIGHT.

'There go two of my threads, Watson. There is nothing more stimulating than a case where everything goes against you. We must cast round for another scent.'

'We have still the cabman who drove the spy.'

'Exactly. I have wired to get his name and address from the Official Registry. I should not be surprised if this were an answer to my question.'

The ring at the bell proved to be something even more satisfactory than an answer, however, for the door opened and a rough-looking fellow entered who was evidently the man himself.

'I got a message from the head office that a gent at this address had been inquiring for 2704,' said he. 'I've driven my cab this seven years and never a word of complaint. I came here straight from the Yard to ask you to your face what you had against me.'

'I have nothing in the world against you, my good man,' said Holmes. 'On the contrary, I have half a sovereign for you if you will give me a clear answer to my questions.'

'Well, I've had a good day and no mistake,' said the cabman, with a grin. 'What was it you wanted to ask, sir?'

'First of all your name and address, in case I want you again.'

'John Clayton, 3, Turpey Street, the Borough. My cab is out of Shipley's Yard, near Waterloo Station.'*

Sherlock Holmes made a note of it.

'Now, Clayton, tell me all about the fare who came and watched this house at ten o'clock this morning and afterwards followed the two gentlemen down Regent Street.'

The man looked surprised and a little embarrassed.

'Why, there's no good my telling you things, for you seem to know as much as I do already,' said he. 'The truth is that the gentleman told me that he was a detective, and that I was to say nothing about him to anyone.'

'My good fellow, this is a very serious business, and you may find yourself in a pretty bad position if you try to hide anything from me. You say that your fare told you that he was a detective?'

'Yes, he did.'

'When did he say this?'

'When he left me.'

'Did he say anything more?'

'He mentioned his name.'

Holmes cast a swift glance of triumph at me.

'Oh, he mentioned his name, did he? That was imprudent. What was the name that he mentioned?'

'His name', said the cabman, 'was Mr Sherlock Holmes.'

Never have I seen my friend more completely taken aback than by the cabman's reply. For an instant he sat in silent amazement. Then he burst into a hearty laugh.

'A touch, Watson—an undeniable touch!' said he. 'I feel a foil as quick and supple as my own. He got home* upon me very prettily that time. So his name was Sherlock Holmes, was it?'

'Yes, sir, that was the gentleman's name.'

'Excellent! Tell me where you picked him up and all that occurred.'

'He hailed me at half-past nine in Trafalgar Square. He said that he was a detective, and he offered me two guineas* if I would do exactly what he wanted all day and ask no questions. I was glad enough to agree. First we drove down to the Northumberland Hotel and waited there until two gentlemen came out and took a cab from the rank. We followed their cab until it pulled up somewhere near here.'

'This very door,' said Holmes.

'Well, I couldn't be sure of that, but I dare say my fare knew all about it. We pulled up half-way down the street and waited an hour and a half. Then the two gentlemen passed us, walking, and we followed down Baker Street and along—'

'I know,' said Holmes.

'Until we got three-quarters down Regent Street. Then my gentleman threw up the trap, and he cried that I should drive right away to Waterloo Station as hard as I could go. I whipped up the mare and we were there under the ten minutes. Then he paid up his two guineas, like a good one, and away he went into the station. Only just as he was leaving he turned round and said: "It might interest you to know that you have been driving Mr Sherlock Holmes." That's how I came to know the name.'

'I see. And you saw no more of him?'

'Not after he went into the station.'

'And how would you describe Mr Sherlock Holmes?'

The cabman scratched his head. 'Well, he wasn't altogether such an easy gentleman to describe. I'd put him at forty years of age, and he was of a middle height, two or three inches shorter than you, sir.* He was dressed like a toff,* and he had a black beard, cut square at the end, and a pale face. I don't know as I could say more than that.'

'Colour of his eyes?'

'No, I can't say that.'

'Nothing more that you can remember?'

'No, sir; nothing.'

'Well, then, here is your half-sovereign. There's another one wait-ing for you if you can bring any more information. Good-night!'

'Good-night, sir, and thank you!'

John Clayton departed, chuckling, and Holmes turned to me with a shrug of the shoulders and a rueful smile.

'Snap goes our third thread, and we end where we began,' said he. 'The cunning rascal! He knew our number, knew that Sir Henry Baskerville had consulted me, spotted who I was in Regent Street, conjectured that I had got the number of the cab and would lay my hands on the driver, and so sent back this audacious message. I tell you, Watson, this time we have got a foeman who is worthy of our steel.* I've been checkmated in London. I can only wish you better luck in Devonshire. But I'm not easy in my mind about it.'

'About what?'

'About sending you. It's an ugly business, Watson, an ugly, danger-ous business, and the more I see of it the less I like it. Yes, my dear fellow, you may laugh, but I give you my word that I shall be very glad to have you back safe and sound in Baker Street once more.'

CHAPTER 6

BASKERVILLE HALL

SIR HENRY BASKERVILLE and Dr Mortimer were ready upon the appointed day, and we started as arranged for Devonshire. Mr Sherlock Holmes drove with me to the station, and gave me his last parting injunctions and advice.

'I will not bias your mind by suggesting theories or suspicions, Watson,' said he; 'I wish you simply to report facts in the fullest pos-sible manner to me, and you can leave me to do the theorizing.'

'What sort of facts?' I asked.

'Anything which may seem to have a bearing, however indirect, upon the case, and especially the relations between young Baskerville and his neighbours, or any fresh particulars concerning the death of Sir Charles. I have made some inquiries myself in the last few days, but the results have, I fear, been negative. One thing only appears to be certain, and that is that Mr James Desmond, who is the next heir, is an elderly gentleman of a very amiable disposition, so that this persecution does not arise from him. I really think that we may eliminate him entirely from our calculations. There remain the people who will actually surround Sir Henry Baskerville upon the moor.'

'Would it not be well in the first place to get rid of this Barrymore couple?'

'By no means. You could not make a greater mistake. If they are innocent it would be a cruel injustice, and if they are guilty we should be giving up all chance of bringing it home to them. No, no, we will preserve them upon our list of suspects. Then there is a groom at the Hall, if I remember right. There are two moorland farmers. There is our friend Dr Mortimer, whom I believe to be entirely honest, and there is his wife, of whom we know nothing. There is this naturalist Stapleton, and there is his sister, who is said to be a young lady of attractions. There is Mr Frankland, of Lafter Hall, who is also an unknown factor, and there are one or two other neighbours. These are the folk who must be your very special study.'

'I will do my best.'

'You have arms, I suppose?'

'Yes, I thought it as well to take them.'

'Most certainly. Keep your revolver near you night and day, and never relax your precautions.'

Our friends had already secured a first-class carriage, and were waiting for us upon the platform.

'No, we have no news of any kind,' said Dr Mortimer, in answer to my friend's questions. 'I can swear to one thing, and that is that we have not been shadowed during the last two days. We have never gone out without keeping a sharp watch, and no one could have escaped our notice.'

'You have always kept together, I presume?'

'Except yesterday afternoon. I usually give up one day to pure amusement when I come to town, so I spent it at the Museum of the College of Surgeons.'*

'And I went to look at the folk in the park,' said Baskerville. 'But we had no trouble of any kind.'

'It was imprudent, all the same,' said Holmes, shaking his head and looking very grave. 'I beg, Sir Henry, that you will not go about alone. Some great misfortune will befall you if you do. Did you get your other boot?'

'No, sir, it is gone for ever.'

'Indeed. That is very interesting. Well, good-bye,' he added, as the train began to glide down the platform. 'Bear in mind, Sir Henry, one of the phrases in that queer old legend which Dr Mortimer has read to us, and avoid the moor in those hours of darkness when the powers of evil are exalted.'

I looked back at the platform when we had left it far behind, and saw the tall, austere figure of Holmes standing motionless and gazing after us.

The journey was a swift and pleasant one, and I spent it in making the more intimate acquaintance of my two companions, and in playing with Dr Mortimer's spaniel. In a very few hours the brown earth had become ruddy, the brick had changed to granite, and red cows grazed in well-hedged fields where the lush grasses and more luxuriant vegetation spoke of a richer, if a damper, climate. Young Baskerville stared eagerly out of the window, and cried aloud with delight as he recognized the familiar features of the Devon scenery.

'I've been over a good part of the world since I left it, Dr Watson,' said he; 'but I have never seen a place to compare with it.'

'I never saw a Devonshire man who did not swear by his county,' I remarked.

'It depends upon the breed of men quite as much as on the county,' said Dr Mortimer. 'A glance at our friend here reveals the rounded head of the Celt, which carries inside it the Celtic enthusiasm and power of attachment.* Poor Sir Charles's head was of a very rare type, half Gaelic, half Ivernian* in its characteristics. But you were very young when you last saw Baskerville Hall, were you not?'

'I was a boy in my teens at the time of my father's death, and had never seen the Hall, for he lived in a little cottage on the south coast. Thence I went straight to a friend in America. I tell you it is all as new to me as it is to Dr Watson, and I'm as keen as possible to see the moor.'

'Are you? Then your wish is easily granted, for there is your first sight of the moor,' said Dr Mortimer, pointing out of the carriage window.

Over the green squares of the fields and the low curve of a wood there rose in the distance a grey, melancholy hill, with a strange jagged summit, dim and vague in the distance, like some fantastic landscape in a dream. Baskerville sat for a long time, his eyes fixed upon it, and I read upon his eager face how much it meant to him, this first sight of that strange spot where the men of his blood had held sway so long and left their mark so deep. There he sat, with his tweed suit and his American accent, in the corner of a prosaic railway-carriage, and yet as I looked at his dark and expressive face I felt more than ever how true a descendant he was of that long line of high-blooded, fiery, and masterful men. There were pride, valour, and strength in his thick brows, his sensitive nostrils, and his large hazel eyes. If on that forbidding moor a difficult and dangerous quest should lie before us, this was at least a comrade for whom one might venture to take a risk with the certainty that he would bravely share it.

The train pulled up at a small wayside station, and we all descended. Outside, beyond the low, white fence, a wagonette with a pair of cobs* was waiting. Our coming was evidently a great event, for station-master and porters clustered round us to carry out our luggage. It was a sweet, simple country spot, but I was surprised to observe that by the gate there stood two soldierly men in dark uniforms, who leaned upon their short rifles and glanced keenly at us as we passed. The coachman, a hard-faced, gnarled little fellow, saluted Sir Henry Baskerville,* and in a few minutes we were flying swiftly down the broad, white road. Rolling pasture lands curved upwards on either side of us, and old gabled houses peeped out from amid the thick green foliage, but behind the peaceful and sunlit country-side there rose ever, dark against the evening sky, the long, gloomy curve of the moor, broken by the jagged and sinister hills.

The wagonette swung round into a side road, and we curved upwards through deep lanes worn by centuries of wheels, high banks on either side, heavy with dripping moss and fleshy hart's-tongue ferns.* Bronzing bracken and mottled bramble gleamed in the light of the sinking sun. Still steadily rising, we passed over a narrow granite bridge, and skirted a noisy stream, which gushed swiftly down, foam-ing and roaring amid the grey boulders. Both road and stream wound up through a valley dense with scrub oak and fir. At every turning Baskerville gave an exclamation of delight, looking eagerly about him and asking countless questions. To his eyes all seemed beautiful, but to me a tinge of melancholy lay upon the country-side, which bore so clearly the mark of the waning year. Yellow leaves carpeted the lanes and fluttered down upon us as we passed. The rattle of our wheels died away as we drove through drifts of rotting vegetation—sad

gifts, as it seemed to me, for Nature to throw before the carriage of the
returning heir of the Baskervilles.

'Hullo!' cried Dr Mortimer, 'what is this?'

A steep curve of heath-clad land, an outlying spur of the moor, lay
in front of us. On the summit, hard and clear like an equestrian statue
upon its pedestal, was a mounted soldier, dark and stern, his rifle
poised ready over his forearm. He was watching the road along which
we travelled.

'What is this, Perkins?' asked Dr Mortimer.

Our driver half turned in his seat.

'There's a convict escaped from Princetown, sir. He's been out
three days now, and the warders watch every road and every station,
but they've had no sight of him yet. The farmers about here don't like
it, sir, and that's a fact.'

'Well, I understand that they get five pounds if they can give
information.'

'Yes, sir, but the chance of five pounds is but a poor thing compared to the chance of having your throat cut. You see, it isn't like any
ordinary convict. This is a man that would stick at nothing.'

'Who is he, then?'

'It is Selden, the Notting Hill murderer.'*

I remembered the case well, for it was one in which Holmes had
taken an interest on account of the peculiar ferocity of the crime and
the wanton brutality which had marked all the actions of the assassin.
The commutation of his death sentence had been due to some doubts
as to his complete sanity, so atrocious was his conduct. Our wagonette
had topped a rise and in front of us rose the huge expanse of the
moor, mottled with gnarled and craggy cairns* and tors. A cold wind
swept down from it and set us shivering. Somewhere there, on that
desolate plain, was lurking this fiendish man, hiding in a burrow like
a wild beast, his heart full of malignancy against the whole race which
had cast him out. It needed but this to complete the grim suggestive-
ness of the barren waste, the chilling wind, and the darkling* sky.
Even Baskerville fell silent and pulled his overcoat more closely
around him.

We had left the fertile country behind and beneath us. We looked
back on it now, the slanting rays of a low sun turning the streams to
threads of gold and glowing on the red earth new turned by the
plough and the broad tangle of the woodlands. The road in front of us

grew bleaker and wilder over huge russet and olive slopes, sprinkled with giant boulders. Now and then we passed a moorland cottage, walled and roofed with stone, with no creeper to break its harsh outline. Suddenly we looked down into a cup-like depression, patched with stunted oaks and firs which had been twisted and bent by the fury of years of storm. Two high, narrow towers rose over the trees. The driver pointed with his whip.

'Baskerville Hall,' said he.

Its master had risen, and was staring with flushed cheeks and shining eyes. A few minutes later we had reached the lodge-gates, a maze of fantastic tracery in wrought iron, with weather-bitten pillars on either side, blotched with lichens, and surmounted by the boars' heads of the Baskervilles.* The lodge was a ruin of black granite and bared ribs of rafters, but facing it was a new building, half constructed, the first fruit of Sir Charles's South African gold.

Through the gateway we passed into the avenue, where the wheels were again hushed amid the leaves, and the old trees shot their branches in a sombre tunnel over our heads. Baskerville shuddered as he looked up the long, dark drive to where the house glimmered like a ghost at the farther end.

'Was it here?' he asked, in a low voice.

'No, no, the Yew Alley is on the other side.'

The young heir glanced round with a gloomy face.

'It's no wonder my uncle felt as if trouble were coming on him in such a place as this,' said he. 'It's enough to scare any man. I'll have a row of electric lamps up here inside of six months, and you won't know it again with a thousand-candle-power Swan and Edison* right here in front of the hall door.'

The avenue opened into a broad expanse of turf, and the house lay before us. In the fading light I could see that the centre was a heavy block of building from which a porch projected. The whole front was draped in ivy, with a patch clipped bare here and there where a window or a coat-of-arms broke through the dark veil. From this central block rose the twin towers, ancient, crenellated, and pierced with many loopholes. To right and left of the turrets were more modern wings of black granite. A dull light shone through heavy mullioned windows,* and from the high chimneys which rose from the steep, high-angled roof there sprang a single black column of smoke.

'Welcome, Sir Henry! Welcome, to Baskerville Hall!'

A tall man had stepped from the shadow of the porch to open the door of the wagonette. The figure of a woman was silhouetted against the yellow light of the hall. She came out and helped the man to hand down our bags.

'You don't mind my driving straight home, Sir Henry?' said Dr Mortimer. 'My wife is expecting me.'

'Surely you will stay and have some dinner?'

'No, I must go. I shall probably find some work awaiting me. I would stay to show you over the house, but Barrymore will be a better guide than I. Good-bye, and never hesitate night or day to send for me if I can be of service.'

The wheels died away down the drive while Sir Henry and I turned into the hall, and the door clanged heavily behind us. It was a fine apartment in which we found ourselves, large, lofty, and heavily raftered with huge balks of age-blackened oak. In the great old-fashioned fireplace behind the high iron dogs* a log-fire crackled and snapped. Sir Henry and I held out our hands to it, for we were numb from our long drive. Then we gazed round us at the high, thin window of old stained glass, the oak panelling, the stags' heads, the coats-of-arms upon the walls, all dim and sombre in the subdued light of the central lamp.

'It's just as I imagined it,' said Sir Henry. 'Is it not the very picture of an old family home? To think that this should be the same hall in which for five hundred years my people have lived! It strikes me solemn to think of it.'

I saw his dark face lit up with a boyish enthusiasm as he gazed about him. The light beat upon him where he stood, but long shadows trailed down the walls and hung like a black canopy above him. Barrymore had returned from taking our luggage to our rooms. He stood in front of us now with the subdued manner of a well-trained servant. He was a remarkable-looking man, tall, handsome, with a square black beard, and pale, distinguished features.

'Would you wish dinner to be served at once, sir?'

'Is it ready?'

'In a very few minutes, sir. You will find hot water in your rooms. My wife and I will be happy, Sir Henry, to stay with you until you have made your fresh arrangements, but you will understand that under the new conditions this house will require a considerable staff.'

'What new conditions?'

'I only meant, sir, that Sir Charles led a very retired life, and we were able to look after his wants. You would, naturally, wish to have more company, and so you will need changes in your household.'

'Do you mean that your wife and you wish to leave?'

'Only when it is quite convenient to you, sir.'

'But your family have been with us for several generations, have they not? I should be sorry to begin my life here by breaking an old family connection.'

I seemed to discern some signs of emotion upon the butler's white face.

'I feel that also, sir, and so does my wife. But to tell the truth, sir, we were both very much attached to Sir Charles, and his death gave us a shock and made these surroundings very painful to us. I fear that we shall never again be easy in our minds at Baskerville Hall.'

'But what do you intend to do?'

'I have no doubt, sir, that we shall succeed in establishing ourselves in some business. Sir Charles's generosity has given us the means to do so. And now, sir, perhaps I had best show you to your rooms.'

A square balustraded gallery* ran round the top of the old hall, approached by a double stair. From this central point two long corridors extended the whole length of the building, from which all the bedrooms opened. My own was in the same wing as Baskerville's and almost next door to it. These rooms appeared to be much more modern than the central part of the house, and the bright paper and numerous candles did something to remove the sombre impression which our arrival had left upon my mind.

But the dining-room which opened out of the hall was a place of shadow and gloom. It was a long chamber with a step separating the dais where the family sat from the lower portion reserved for their dependents. At one end a minstrels' gallery* overlooked it. Black beams shot across above our heads, with a smoke-darkened ceiling beyond them. With rows of flaring torches to light it up, and the colour and rude hilarity of an old-time banquet, it might have softened; but now, when two black-clothed gentlemen sat in the little circle of light thrown by a shaded lamp, one's voice became hushed and one's spirit subdued. A dim line of ancestors, in every variety of dress, from the Elizabethan knight to the buck of the Regency,* stared down upon us and daunted us by their silent company. We talked little, and I for one was glad when the meal was over and we were able to retire into the modern billiard-room and smoke a cigarette.

'My word, it isn't a very cheerful place,' said Sir Henry. 'I suppose one can tone down to it, but I feel a bit out of the picture at present. I don't wonder that my uncle got a little jumpy if he lived all alone in such a house as this. However, if it suits you, we will retire early tonight, and perhaps things may seem more cheerful in the morning.'

I drew aside my curtains before I went to bed and looked out from my window. It opened upon the grassy space which lay in front of the hall door. Beyond, two copses of trees moaned and swung in a rising wind. A half moon broke through the rifts of racing clouds. In its cold light I saw beyond the trees a broken fringe of rocks and the long, low curve of the melancholy moor. I closed the curtain, feeling that my last impression was in keeping with the rest.

And yet it was not quite the last. I found myself weary and yet wakeful, tossing restlessly from side to side, seeking for the sleep which would not come. Far away a chiming clock struck out the quarters of the hours, but otherwise a deathly silence lay upon the old house. And then suddenly, in the very dead of the night, there came a sound to my ears, clear, resonant, and unmistakable. It was the sob of a woman, the muffled, strangling gasp of one who is torn by an uncontrollable sorrow. I sat up in bed and listened intently. The noise could not have been far away, and was certainly in the house. For half an hour I waited with every nerve on the alert, but there came no other sound save the chiming clock and the rustle of the ivy on the wall.*

CHAPTER 7

THE STAPLETONS OF MERRIPIT HOUSE*

THE fresh beauty of the following morning did something to efface from our minds the grim and grey impression which had been left upon both of us by our first experience at Baskerville Hall. As Sir Henry and I sat at breakfast the sunlight flooded in through the high mullioned windows, throwing watery patches of colour from the coats-of-arms which covered them. The dark panelling glowed like bronze in the golden rays, and it was hard to realize that this was indeed the chamber which had struck such a gloom into our souls upon the evening before.

'I guess it is ourselves and not the house that we have to blame!' said the Baronet. 'We were tired with our journey and chilled by our drive, so we took a grey view of the place. Now we are fresh and well, so it is all cheerful once more.'

'And yet it was not entirely a question of imagination,' I answered. 'Did you, for example, happen to hear someone, a woman I think, sobbing in the night?'

'That is curious, for I did when I was half asleep fancy that I heard something of the sort. I waited quite a time, but there was no more of it, so I concluded that it was all a dream.'

'I heard it distinctly, and I am sure that it was really the sob of a woman.'

'We must ask about this right away.'

He rang the bell and asked Barrymore whether he could account for our experience. It seemed to me that the pallid features of the butler turned a shade paler still as he listened to his master's question.

'There are only two women in the house, Sir Henry,' he answered. 'One is the scullery-maid, who sleeps in the other wing. The other is my wife, and I can answer for it that the sound could not have come from her.'

And yet he lied as he said it, for it chanced that after breakfast I met Mrs Barrymore in the long corridor with the sun full upon her face. She was a large, impassive, heavy-featured woman with a stern, set expression of mouth. But her tell-tale eyes were red and glanced at me from between swollen lids. It was she, then, who wept in the night, and if she did so her husband must know it. Yet he had taken the obvious risk of discovery in declaring that it was not so. Why had he done this? And why did she weep so bitterly? Already round this pale-faced, handsome, black-bearded man there was gathering an atmosphere of mystery and of gloom. It was he who had been the first to discover the body of Sir Charles, and we had only his word for all the circumstances which led up to the old man's death. Was it possible that it was Barrymore, after all, whom we had seen in the cab in Regent Street? The beard might well have been the same. The cabman had described a somewhat shorter man, but such an impression might easily have been erroneous. How could I settle the point for ever? Obviously the first thing to do was to see the Grimpen postmaster, and find whether the test telegram had really been placed in Barrymore's own hands. Be the answer what it might, I should at least have something to report to Sherlock Holmes.

Sir Henry had numerous papers to examine after breakfast, so that the time was propitious for my excursion. It was a pleasant walk of four miles along the edge of the moor, leading me at last to a small grey hamlet, in which two larger buildings, which proved to be the inn and the house of Dr Mortimer, stood high above the rest. The postmaster, who was also the village grocer, had a clear recollection of the telegram.

'Certainly, sir,' said he, 'I had the telegram delivered to Mr Barrymore exactly as directed.'

'Who delivered it?'

'My boy here. James, you delivered that telegram to Mr Barrymore at the Hall last week, did you not?'

'Yes, father, I delivered it.'

'Into his own hands?' I asked.

'Well, he was up in the loft at the time, so that I could not put it into his own hands, but I gave it into Mrs Barrymore's hands, and she promised to deliver it at once.'

'Did you see Mr Barrymore?'

'No, sir; I tell you he was in the loft.'

'If you didn't see him, how do you know he was in the loft?'

'Well, surely his own wife ought to know where he is,' said the postmaster, testily. 'Didn't he get the telegram? If there is any mistake it is for Mr Barrymore himself to complain.'

It seemed hopeless to pursue the inquiry any further, but it was clear that in spite of Holmes's ruse we had no proof that Barrymore had not been in London all the time. Suppose that it were so—suppose that the same man had been the last who had seen Sir Charles alive, and the first to dog the new heir when he returned to England. What then? Was he the agent of others, or had he some sinister design of his own? What interest could he have in persecuting the Baskerville family? I thought of the strange warning clipped out of the leading article of *The Times*. Was that his work or was it possibly the doing of someone who was bent upon counteracting his schemes? The only conceivable motive was that which had been suggested by Sir Henry, that if the family could be scared away a comfortable and permanent home would be secured for the Barrymores. But surely such an explanation as that would be quite inadequate to account for the deep and subtle scheming which seemed to be weaving an invisible net round the young baronet. Holmes himself had said that no more complex case had come to him in all the long series of his sensational investigations. I prayed, as I walked back along the grey, lonely road, that my friend might soon be freed from his preoccupations and able to come down to take this heavy burden of responsibility from my shoulders.

Suddenly my thoughts were interrupted by the sound of running feet behind me and by a voice which called me by name. I turned, expecting to see Dr Mortimer, but to my surprise it was a stranger who was pursuing me. He was a small, slim, clean-shaven, prim-faced man, flaxen-haired and lean-jawed, between thirty and forty years of age, dressed in a grey suit and wearing a straw hat. A tin box for botanical specimens hung over his shoulder, and he carried a green butterfly-net in one of his hands.

'You will, I am sure, excuse my presumption, Dr Watson,' said he, as he came panting up to where I stood. 'Here on the moor we are homely folk, and do not wait for formal introductions. You may possibly have heard my name from our mutual friend,* Mortimer. I am Stapleton, of Merripit House.'

'Your net and box would have told me as much,' said I, 'for I knew that Mr Stapleton was a naturalist. But how did you know me?'

'I have been calling on Mortimer, and he pointed you out to me from the window of his surgery as you passed. As our road lay the same way I thought that I would overtake you and introduce myself. I trust that Sir Henry is none the worse for his journey?'

'He is very well, thank you.'

'We were all rather afraid that after the sad death of Sir Charles the new baronet might refuse to live here. It is asking much of a wealthy man to come down and bury himself in a place of this kind, but I need not tell you that it means a very great deal to the country-side. Sir Henry has, I suppose, no superstitious fears in the matter?'

'I do not think that it is likely.'

'Of course you know the legend of the fiend dog which haunts the family?'

'I have heard it.'

'It is extraordinary how credulous the peasants are about here! Any number of them are ready to swear that they have seen such a creature upon the moor.' He spoke with a smile, but I seemed to read in his eyes that he took the matter more seriously. 'The story took a great hold upon the imagination of Sir Charles, and I have no doubt that it led to his tragic end.'

'But how?'

'His nerves were so worked up that the appearance of any dog might have had a fatal effect upon his diseased heart. I fancy that he really did see something of the kind upon that last night in the Yew Alley. I feared that some disaster might occur, for I was very fond of the old man, and I knew that his heart was weak.'

'How did you know that?'

'My friend Mortimer told me.'

'You think then, that some dog pursued Sir Charles, and that he died of fright in consequence?'

'Have you any better explanation?'

'I have not come to any conclusion.'

'Has Mr Sherlock Holmes?'

The words took away my breath for an instant, but a glance at the placid face and steadfast eyes of my companion showed no surprise was intended.

'It is useless for us to pretend that we do not know you, Dr Watson,' said he. 'The records of your detective have reached us here,* and you could not celebrate him without being known yourself. When Mortimer told me your name he could not deny your identity. If you are here, then it follows that Mr Sherlock Holmes is interesting himself in the matter, and I am naturally curious to know what view he may take.'

'I am afraid that I cannot answer that question.'

'May I ask if he is going to honour us with a visit himself?'

'He cannot leave town at present. He has other cases which engage his attention.'

'What a pity! He might throw some light on that which is so dark to us. But as to your own researches, if there is any possible way in which I can be of service to you, I trust that you will command me. If I had any indication of the nature of your suspicions, or how you propose to investigate the case, I might perhaps even now give you some aid or advice.'

'I assure you that I am simply here upon a visit to my friend Sir Henry, and that I need no help of any kind.'

'Excellent!' said Stapleton. 'You are perfectly right to be wary and discreet. I am justly reproved for what I feel was an unjustifiable intrusion, and I promise you that I will not mention the matter again.'

We had come to a point where a narrow grassy path struck off from the road and wound away across the moor. A steep, boulder-sprinkled hill lay upon the right which had in bygone days been cut into a granite quarry. The face which was turned towards us formed a dark cliff, with ferns and brambles growing in its niches. From over a distant rise there floated a grey plume of smoke.

'A moderate walk along this moor-path brings us to Merripit House,' said he. 'Perhaps you will spare an hour that I may have the pleasure of introducing you to my sister.'

My first thought was that I should be by Sir Henry's side. But then I remembered the pile of papers and bills with which his study table was littered. It was certain that I could not help him with those. And Holmes had expressly said that I should study the neighbours upon the moor. I accepted Stapleton's invitation, and we turned together down the path.

'It is a wonderful place, the moor,' said he, looking round over the undulating downs, long green rollers, with crests of jagged granite foaming up into fantastic surges. 'You never tire of the moor. You cannot think the wonderful secrets which it contains. It is so vast, and so barren, and so mysterious.'

'You know it well, then?'

'I have only been here two years. The residents would call me a new-comer. We came shortly after Sir Charles settled. But my tastes led me to explore every part of the country round, and I should think that there are few men who know it better than I do.'

'Is it so hard to know?'

'Very hard. You see, for example, this great plain to the north here, with the queer hills breaking out of it. Do you observe anything remarkable about that?'

'It would be a rare place for a gallop.'

'You would naturally think so, and the thought has cost folk their lives before now. You notice those bright green spots scattered thickly over it?'

'Yes, they seem more fertile than the rest.'

Stapleton laughed. 'That is the great Grimpen Mire,'* said he. 'A false step yonder means death to man or beast. Only yesterday I saw one of the

moor ponies wander into it. He never came out. I saw his head for quite
a long time craning out of the bog-hole, but it sucked him down at last.*
Even in dry seasons it is a danger to cross it, but after these autumn rains
it is an awful place. And yet I can find my way to the very heart of it and
return alive. By George, there is another of those miserable ponies!'

Something brown was rolling and tossing among the green sedges.
Then a long, agonized, writhing neck shot upwards and a dreadful
cry echoed over the moor. It turned me cold with horror, but my companion's nerves seemed to be stronger than mine.

'It's gone!' said he. 'The Mire has him. Two in two days, and many
more, perhaps, for they get in the way of going there in the dry
weather, and never know the difference until the Mire has them in its
clutch. It's a bad place, the great Grimpen Mire.'

'And you say you can penetrate it?'

'Yes, there are one or two paths which a very active man can take.
I have found them out.'

'But why should you wish to go into so horrible a place?'

'Well, you see the hills beyond? They are really islands cut off on all
sides by the impassable Mire, which has crawled round them in the
course of years. That is where the rare plants and the butterflies are, if
you have the wit to reach them.'

'I shall try my luck some day.'

He looked at me with a surprised face. 'For God's sake put such an
idea out of your mind,' said he. 'Your blood would be upon my head.
I assure you that there would not be the least chance of your coming
back alive. It is only by remembering certain complex landmarks that
I am able to do it.'

'Hullo,' I cried. 'What is that?'

A long, low moan, indescribably sad, swept over the moor. It filled
the whole air, and yet it was impossible to say whence it came. From
a dull murmur it swelled into a deep roar and then sank back into
a melancholy, throbbing murmur once again. Stapleton looked at me
with a curious expression on his face.

'Queer place, the moor!' said he.

'But what is it?'

'The peasants say it is the Hound of the Baskervilles calling for its
prey. I've heard it once or twice before, but never quite so loud.'

I looked round, with a chill of fear in my heart, at the huge swelling
plain, mottled with the green patches of rushes. Nothing stirred over

the vast expanse save a pair of ravens, which croaked loudly from a tor behind us.

'You are an educated man. You don't believe such nonsense as that?' said I. 'What do you think is the cause of so strange a sound?'

'Bogs make queer noises sometimes. It's the mud settling, or the water rising, or something.'

'No, no, that was a living voice.'

'Well, perhaps it was. Did you ever hear a bittern booming?'

'No, I never did.'

'It's a very rare bird—practically extinct—in England now, but all things are possible upon the moor. Yes, I should not be surprised to learn that what we have heard is the cry of the last of the bitterns.'*

'It's the weirdest, strangest thing that ever I heard in my life.'

'Yes, it's rather an uncanny place altogether. Look at the hillside yonder. What do you make of those?'

The whole steep slope was covered with grey circular rings of stone, a score of them at least.

'What are they? Sheep-pens?'

'No, they are the homes of our worthy ancestors. Prehistoric man lived thickly on the moor, and as no one in particular has lived there since, we find all his little arrangements exactly as he left them. These are his wigwams with the roofs off.* You can even see his hearth and his couch if you have the curiosity to go inside.'

'But it is quite a town. When was it inhabited?'

'Neolithic man—no date.'*

'What did he do?'

'He grazed his cattle on these slopes, and he learned to dig for tin when the bronze sword began to supersede the stone axe. Look at the great trench in the opposite hill. That is his mark. Yes, you will find some very singular points about the moor, Dr Watson. Oh, excuse me an instant! It is surely Cyclopides.'*

A small fly or moth had fluttered across our path, and in an instant Stapleton was rushing with extraordinary energy and speed in pursuit of it. To my dismay the creature flew straight for the great Mire, but my acquaintance never paused for an instant, bounding from tuft to tuft behind it, his green net waving in the air. His grey clothes and jerky, zigzag, irregular progress made him not unlike some huge moth himself. I was standing watching his pursuit with a mixture of admiration for his extraordinary activity and fear lest he should lose his footing in the treacherous Mire, when I heard the sound of steps, and, turning round, found a woman near me upon the path. She had come from the direction in which the plume of smoke indicated the position of Merripit House, but the dip of the moor had hid her until she was quite close.

I could not doubt that this was the Miss Stapleton of whom I had been told, since ladies of any sort must be few upon the moor, and I remembered that I had heard someone describe her as being a beauty. The woman who approached me was certainly that, and of a most uncommon type. There could not have been a greater contrast between brother and sister, for Stapleton was neutral tinted, with light hair and grey eyes, while she was darker than any brunette whom I have seen in England—slim, elegant, and tall. She had a proud, finely cut face, so regular that it might have seemed impassive were it not for the sensitive mouth and the beautiful dark, eager eyes. With her perfect figure and elegant dress she was, indeed, a strange apparition upon a lonely moorland path. Her eyes were on her brother as I turned, and then she quickened her pace towards me. I had raised my hat, and was about to make some explanatory remark, when her own words turned all my thoughts into a new channel.

'Go back!' she said. 'Go straight back to London, instantly.'

I could only stare at her in stupid surprise. Her eyes blazed at me, and she tapped the ground impatiently with her foot.

'Why should I go back?' I asked.

'I cannot explain.' She spoke in a low, eager voice, with a curious lisp in her utterance. 'But for God's sake do what I ask you. Go back and never set foot upon the moor again.'

'But I have only just come.'

'Man, man!' she cried. 'Can you not tell when a warning is for your own good? Go back to London! Start to-night! Get away from this place at all costs! Hush, my brother is coming! Not a word of what I have said. Would you mind getting that orchid for me among the mare's-tails* yonder? We are very rich in orchids on the moor, though, of course, you are rather late to see the beauties of the place.'

Stapleton had abandoned the chase and came back to us breathing hard and flushed with his exertions.

'Hullo, Beryl!' said he, and it seemed to me that the tone of his greeting was not altogether a cordial one.

'Well, Jack, you are very hot.'

'Yes, I was chasing a Cyclopides. He is very rare, and seldom found in the late autumn. What a pity that I should have missed him!'

He spoke unconcernedly, but his small light eyes glanced incessantly from the girl to me.

'You have introduced yourselves, I can see.'

'Yes. I was telling Sir Henry that it was rather late for him to see the true beauties of the moor.'

'Why, who do you think this is?'

'I imagine that it must be Sir Henry Baskerville.'

'No, no,' said I. 'Only a humble commoner,* but his friend. My name is Dr Watson.'

A flush of vexation passed over her expressive face.

'We have been talking at cross purposes,' said she.

'Why, you had not very much time for talk,' her brother remarked, with the same questioning eyes.

'I talked as if Dr Watson were a resident instead of being merely a visitor,' said she. 'It cannot much matter to him whether it is early or late for the orchids. But you will come on, will you not, and see Merripit House?'

A short walk brought us to it, a bleak moorland house, once the farm of some grazier* in the old prosperous days, but now put into repair and turned into a modern dwelling. An orchard surrounded it, but the trees, as is usual upon the moor, were stunted and nipped, and the effect of the whole place was mean and melancholy. We were admitted by a strange, wizened, rusty-coated old manservant, who seemed in keeping with the house. Inside, however, there were large rooms furnished with an elegance in which I seemed to recognize the taste of the lady. As I looked from their windows at the interminable granite-flecked moor rolling unbroken to the farthest horizon I could not but marvel at what could have brought this highly educated man and this beautiful woman to live in such a place.

'Queer spot to choose, is it not?' said he, as if in answer to my thought. 'And yet we manage to make ourselves fairly happy, do we not, Beryl?'

'Quite happy,' said she, but there was no ring of conviction in her words.

'I had a school,' said Stapleton. 'It was in the north country. The work to a man of my temperament was mechanical and uninteresting, but the privilege of living with youth, of helping to mould those young minds and of impressing them with one's own character and ideals, was very dear to me. However, the fates were against us. A serious epidemic broke out in the school, and three of the boys died. It never recovered from the blow, and much of my capital was irretrievably swallowed up. And yet, if it were not for the loss of the charming companionship of the boys, I could rejoice over my own misfortune, for, with my strong tastes for botany and zoology, I find an unlimited field of work here, and my sister is as devoted to Nature as I am. All this, Dr Watson, has been brought upon your head by your expression as you surveyed the moor out of our window.'

'It certainly did cross my mind that it might be a little dull—less for you, perhaps, than for your sister.'

'No, no, I am never dull,' said she quickly.

'We have books, we have our studies, and we have interesting neighbours. Dr Mortimer is a most learned man in his own line. Poor Sir Charles was also an admirable companion. We knew him well, and miss him more than I can tell. Do you think that I should intrude if I were to call this afternoon and make the acquaintance of Sir Henry?'

'I am sure that he would be delighted.'

'Then perhaps you would mention that I propose to do so. We may in our humble way do something to make things more easy for him until he becomes accustomed to his new surroundings. Will you come upstairs, Dr Watson, and inspect my collection of Lepidoptera?* I think it is the most complete one in the south-west of England. By the time that you have looked through them lunch will be almost ready.'

But I was eager to get back to my charge. The melancholy of the moor, the death of the unfortunate pony, the weird sound which had been associated with the grim legend of the Baskervilles—all these things tinged my thoughts with sadness. Then on the top of these more or less vague impressions there had come the definite and distinct warning of Miss Stapleton, delivered with such intense earnestness that I could not doubt that some grave and deep reason lay behind it. I resisted all pressure to stay for lunch, and I set off at once upon my return journey, taking the grass-grown path by which we had come.

It seems, however, that there must have been some short cut for those who knew it, for before I had reached the road I was astounded to see Miss Stapleton sitting upon a rock by the side of the track. Her face was beautifully flushed with her exertions, and she held her hand to her side.

'I have run all the way in order to cut you off, Dr Watson,' said she. 'I had not even time to put on my hat. I must not stop, or my brother may miss me. I wanted to say to you how sorry I am about the stupid mistake I made in thinking that you were Sir Henry. Please forget the words I said, which have no application whatever to you.'

'But I can't forget them, Miss Stapleton,' said I. 'I am Sir Henry's friend, and his welfare is a very close concern of mine. Tell me why it was that you were so eager that Sir Henry should return to London.'

'A woman's whim, Dr Watson. When you know me better you will understand that I cannot always give reasons for what I say or do.'

'No, no. I remember the thrill in your voice. I remember the look in your eyes. Please, please, be frank with me, Miss Stapleton, for ever since I have been here I have been conscious of shadows all round me. Life has become like that great Grimpen Mire, with little green patches everywhere into which one may sink and with no guide to point the track. Tell me, then, what it was that you meant, and I will promise to convey your warning to Sir Henry.'

An expression of irresolution passed for an instant over her face, but her eyes had hardened again when she answered me.

'You make too much of it, Dr Watson,' said she. 'My brother and I were very much shocked by the death of Sir Charles. We knew him very intimately, for his favourite walk was over the moor to our house. He was deeply impressed with the curse which hung over his family, and when this tragedy came I naturally felt that there must be some grounds for the fears he had expressed. I was distressed, therefore, when another member of the family came down to live here, and I felt that he should be warned of the danger which he will run. That was all which I intended to convey.'

'But what is the danger?'

'You know the story of the hound?'

'I do not believe in such nonsense.'

'But I do. If you have any influence with Sir Henry, take him away from a place which has always been fatal to his family. The world is wide. Why should he wish to live at the place of danger?'

'Because it *is* the place of danger. That is Sir Henry's nature. I fear that unless you can give me some more definite information than this it would be impossible to get him to move.'

'I cannot say anything definite, for I do not know anything definite.'

'I would ask you one more question, Miss Stapleton. If you meant no more than this when you first spoke to me, why should you not wish your brother to overhear what you said? There is nothing to which he, or anyone else, could object.'

'My brother is very anxious to have the Hall inhabited, for he thinks that it is for the good of the poor folk upon the moor. He would be very angry if he knew that I had said anything which might induce Sir Henry to go away. But I have done my duty now and I will say no more. I must get back, or he will miss me and suspect that I have seen you. Good-bye!'

She turned, and had disappeared in a few minutes among the scattered boulders, while I, with my soul full of vague fears, pursued my way to Baskerville Hall.

CHAPTER 8

FIRST REPORT OF DR WATSON

FROM this point onwards I will follow the course of events by transcribing my own letters to Mr Sherlock Holmes which lie before me on the table. One page is missing,* but otherwise they are exactly as written, and show my feelings and suspicions of the moment more accurately than my memory, clear as it is upon these tragic events, can possibly do.

Baskerville Hall, Oct. 13th

My Dear Holmes,

My previous letters and telegrams have kept you pretty well up-to-date as to all that has occurred in this most God-forsaken corner of the world. The longer one stays here the more does the spirit of the moor sink into one's soul, its vastness, and also its grim charm. When you are once out upon its bosom you have left all traces of modern England behind you, but on the other hand you are conscious everywhere of the homes and the work of prehistoric people. On all sides of you as you walk are the houses of these forgotten folk, with their graves and the huge monoliths* which are supposed to have marked their temples. As you look at their grey stone huts against the scarred hillsides you leave your own age behind you, and if you were to see a skin-clad, hairy man crawl out from the low door, fitting a flint-tipped arrow on to the string of his bow, you would feel that his presence there was more natural than your own. The strange thing is that they should have lived so thickly on what must always have been most unfruitful soil. I am no antiquarian, but I could imagine that they were some unwarlike and harried race who were forced to accept that which none other would occupy.

All this, however, is foreign to the mission on which you sent me, and will probably be very uninteresting to your severely practical mind. I can still remember your complete indifference as to whether the sun moved round the earth or the earth round the sun.* Let me, therefore, return to the facts concerning Sir Henry Baskerville.

If you have not had any report within the last few days it is because up till to-day there was nothing of importance to relate. Then a very surprising circumstance occurred, which I shall tell you in due course. But, first of all, I must keep you in touch with some of the other factors in the situation.

One of these, concerning which I have said little, is the escaped convict upon the moor. There is strong reason now to believe that he has got right away, which is a considerable relief to the lonely householders of this district. A fortnight has passed since his flight, during which he has not been seen and nothing has been heard of him. It is surely inconceivable that he could have held out upon the moor during all that time. Of course, so far as his concealment goes there is no difficulty at all. Any one of these stone huts would give him a hiding-place. But there is nothing to eat unless he were to catch and slaughter one of the moor sheep. We think, therefore, that he has gone, and the outlying farmers sleep the better in consequence.

We are four able-bodied men in this household, so that we could take good care of ourselves, but I confess that I have had uneasy moments when I have thought of the Stapletons. They live miles from any help. There are one maid, an old manservant, the sister, and the brother, the latter not a very strong man. They would be helpless in the hands of a desperate fellow like this Notting Hill criminal, if he could once effect an entrance. Both Sir Henry and I were concerned at their situation, and it was suggested that Perkins the groom should go over to sleep there, but Stapleton would not hear of it.

The fact is that our friend the baronet begins to display a considerable interest in our fair neighbour. It is not to be wondered at, for time hangs heavily in this lonely spot to an active man like him, and she is a very fascinating and beautiful woman. There is something tropical and exotic about her which forms a singular contrast to her cool and unemotional brother. Yet he also gives the idea of hidden fires. He has certainly a very marked influence over her, for I have seen her continually glance at him as she talked as if seeking approbation for what she said. I trust that he is kind to her. There is a dry glitter in his eyes, and a firm set of his thin lips, which go with a positive and possibly a harsh nature. You would find him an interesting study.

He came over to call upon Baskerville on that first day, and the very next morning he took us both to show us the spot where the legend of the wicked Hugo is supposed to have had its origin.* It was an excursion of some miles across the moor to a place which is so dismal that it might have suggested the story. We found a short valley between rugged tors which led to an open, grassy space flecked over with the white cotton grass.* In the middle of it rose two great stones, worn and sharpened at the upper end, until they looked like the huge, corroding fangs of some monstrous beast. In every way it corresponded with the scene of the old tragedy. Sir Henry was much interested, and asked Stapleton more than once whether he did really believe in the possibility of the interference of the supernatural in the affairs of men. He spoke lightly, but it was evident that he was very much in earnest. Stapleton was guarded in his replies, but it was easy to see that he said less than he might, and that he would not express his whole opinion out of consideration for the feelings of the Baronet. He told us of similar cases where families had suffered from some evil influence, and he left us with the impression that he shared the popular view upon the matter.

On our way back we stayed for lunch at Merripit House, and it was there that Sir Henry made the acquaintance of Miss Stapleton. From the first moment that he saw her he appeared to be strongly attracted by her, and I am much mistaken if the feeling was not mutual. He referred to her again and again on our walk home, and since then hardly a day has passed that we have not seen something of the brother and sister. They dine here to-night, and there is some talk of our going to them next week. One would imagine that such a match would be very welcome to Stapleton, and yet I have more than once caught a look of the strongest disapprobation in his face when Sir Henry has been paying some attention to his sister. He is much attached to her, no doubt, and would lead a lonely life without her, but it would seem the height of selfishness, if he were to stand in the way of her making so brilliant a marriage. Yet I am certain that he does not wish their intimacy to ripen into love, and I have several times observed that he has taken pains to prevent them from being *tête-à-tête*. By the way, your instructions to me never to allow Sir Henry to go out alone will become very much more onerous if a love affair were to be added to our other difficulties. My popularity would soon suffer if I were to carry out your orders to the letter.

The other day—Thursday, to be more exact—Dr Mortimer lunched with us. He has been excavating a barrow at Long Down,* and has got a prehistoric skull which fills him with great joy. Never was there such a single-minded enthusiast as he! The Stapletons came in afterwards, and the good doctor took us all to the Yew Alley, at Sir Henry's request, to show us exactly how everything occurred upon that fatal night. It is a long, dismal walk, the Yew Alley, between two high walls of clipped hedge, with a narrow band of grass upon either side. At the far end is an old, tumble-down summer-house. Half-way down is the moor-gate, where the old gentleman left his cigar ash. It is a white wooden gate with a latch. Beyond it lies the wide moor. I remembered your theory of the affair and tried to picture all that had occurred. As the old man stood there he saw something coming across the moor, something which terrified him so that he lost his wits, and ran and ran until he died of sheer horror and exhaustion. There was the long, gloomy tunnel down which he fled. And from what? A sheep-dog of the moor? Or a spectral hound, black, silent, and monstrous? Was there a human agency in the matter? Did the pale, watchful Barrymore know more than he cared to say? It was all dim and vague, but always there is the dark shadow of crime behind it.

One other neighbour I have met since I wrote last. This is Mr Frankland, of Lafter Hall, who lives some four miles to the south of us. He is an elderly man, red-faced, white-haired, and choleric. His passion is for the British law, and he has spent a large fortune in litigation. He fights for the mere pleasure of fighting, and is equally ready to take up either side of a question, so that it is no wonder that he has found it a costly amusement. Sometimes he will shut up a right of way and defy the parish to make him open it. At others he will with his own hands tear down some other man's gate and declare that a path has existed there from time immemorial, defying the owner to prosecute him for trespass. He is learned in old manorial and communal rights, and he applies his knowledge sometimes in favour of the villagers of Fernworthy* and sometimes against them, so that he is periodically either carried in triumph down the village street or else burned in effigy, according to his latest exploit. He is said to have about seven lawsuits upon his hands at present, which will probably swallow up the remainder of his fortune, and so draw his sting and leave him harmless for the future. Apart from the law he seems a kindly, good-natured person, and I only mention him because you were particular that I should send some description of the people who surround us. He is curiously employed at present, for, being an amateur astronomer, he has an excellent telescope, with which he lies upon the roof of his own house and sweeps the moor all day in the hope of catching a glimpse of the escaped convict. If he would confine his energies to this all would be well, but there are rumours that he intends to prosecute Dr Mortimer for opening a grave without the consent of the next-of-kin, because he dug up the neolithic skull in the barrow on Long Down. He helps to keep our lives from being monotonous and gives a little comic relief where it is badly needed.

And now, having brought you up to date on the escaped convict,* the Stapletons, Dr Mortimer, and Frankland of Lafter Hall, let me end on that which is most important and tell you more about the Barrymores, and especially about the surprising development of last night.

First of all about the test telegram, which you sent from London in order to make sure that Barrymore was really here. I have already explained that the testimony of the postmaster shows that the test was worthless and that we have no proof one way or the other. I told Sir Henry how the matter stood, and he at once, in his downright fashion, had Barrymore up and asked him whether he had received the telegram himself. Barrymore said that he had.

'Did the boy deliver it into your own hands?' asked Sir Henry.

Barrymore looked surprised, and considered for a little time.

'No,' said he, 'I was in the box-room at the time, and my wife brought it up to me.'

'Did you answer it yourself?'

'No; I told my wife what to answer, and she went down to write it.'

In the evening he returned to the subject of his own accord.

'I could not quite understand the object of your questions this morning, Sir Henry,' said he. 'I trust that they do not mean that I have done anything to forfeit your confidence?'

Sir Henry had to assure him that it was not so and pacify him by giving him a considerable part of his old wardrobe, the London outfit having now all arrived.

Mrs Barrymore is of interest to me. She is a heavy, solid person, very limited, intensely respectable, and inclined to be puritanical. You could hardly conceive a less emotional subject. Yet I have told you how, on the first night here, I heard her sobbing bitterly, and since then I have more than once observed traces of tears upon her face. Some deep sorrow gnaws ever at her heart. Sometimes I wonder if she has a guilty memory which haunts her, and sometimes I suspect Barrymore of being a domestic tyrant. I have always felt that there was something singular and questionable in this man's character, but the adventure of last night brings all my suspicions to a head.

And yet it may seem a small matter in itself. You are aware that I am not a very sound sleeper, and since I have been on guard in this house my slumbers have been lighter than ever. Last night, about two in the morning, I was aroused by a stealthy step passing my room. I rose, opened my door, and peeped out. A long black shadow was trailing down the corridor. It was thrown by a man who walked softly down the passage with a candle held in his hand. He was in shirt and trousers, with no covering to his feet. I could merely see the outline, but his height told me that it was Barrymore. He walked very slowly and circumspectly, and there was something indescribably guilty and furtive in his whole appearance.

I have told you that the corridor is broken by the balcony which runs round the hall, but that it is resumed upon the farther side. I waited until he had passed out of sight, and then I followed him. When I came round the balcony he had reached the end of the farther corridor, and I could see from the glimmer of light through an open door that he had entered one of the rooms. Now, all these rooms are unfurnished and unoccupied, so that his expedition became more mysterious than ever. The light shone steadily, as if he were standing motionless. I crept down the passage as noiselessly as I could and peeped round the corner of the door.

Barrymore was crouching at the window with the candle held against the glass. His profile was half turned towards me, and his face seemed to be rigid with expectation as he stared out into the blackness of the moor. For some minutes he stood watching intently. Then he gave a deep groan and with an impatient gesture he put out the light. Instantly I made my way back to my room, and very shortly came the stealthy steps passing once more upon their return journey. Long afterwards when I had fallen into a light sleep I heard a key turn somewhere in a lock, but I could not tell whence the sound came. What it all means I cannot guess, but there is some secret business going on in this house of gloom which sooner or later we shall get to the bottom of. I do not trouble you with my theories, for you asked me to furnish you only with facts. I have had a long talk with Sir Henry this morning, and we have made a plan of campaign founded upon my observations of last night. I will not speak about it just now, but it should make my next report interesting reading.*

CHAPTER 9

THE LIGHT UPON THE MOOR

[*Second report of Dr Watson*]*

Baskerville Hall, Oct. 15th

MY Dear Holmes, If I was compelled to leave you without much news during the early days of my mission you must acknowledge that I am making up for lost time, and that events are now crowding thick and fast upon us. In my last report I ended upon my top note with Barrymore at the window, and now I have quite a budget* already which will, unless I am much mistaken, considerably surprise you. Things have taken a turn which I could not have anticipated. In some ways they have within the last forty-eight hours become much clearer and in some ways they have become more complicated. But I will tell you all and you shall judge for yourself.

Before breakfast on the morning following my adventure I went down the corridor and examined the room in which Barrymore had been on the night before. The western window through which he had stared so intently has, I noticed, one peculiarity above all other windows in the house—it commands the nearest outlook on to the moor. There is an opening between two trees which enables one from this point of view to look right down upon it, while from all the other windows it is only a distant glimpse which can be obtained. It follows, therefore, that Barrymore, since only this window would serve his purpose, must have been looking out for something or somebody upon the moor. The night was very dark, so that I can hardly imagine how he could have hoped to see anyone. It had struck me that it was possible that some love intrigue was on foot. That would have accounted for his stealthy movements and also for the uneasiness of his wife. The man is a striking-looking fellow, very well equipped to steal the heart of a country girl, so that this theory seemed to have something to support it. That opening of the door which I had heard after I had returned to my room might mean that he had gone out to keep some clandestine appointment. So I reasoned with myself in the morning, and I tell you the direction of my suspicions, however much the result may have shown that they were unfounded.

But whatever the true explanation of Barrymore's movements might be, I felt that the responsibility of keeping them to myself until I could explain them was more than I could bear. I had an interview with the baronet in his study after breakfast, and I told him all that I had seen. He was less surprised than I had expected.

'I knew that Barrymore walked about nights, and I had a mind to speak to him about it,' said he. 'Two or three times I have heard his steps in the passage, coming and going, just about the hour you name.'

'Perhaps, then, he pays a visit every night to that particular window,' I suggested.

'Perhaps he does. If so, we should be able to shadow him, and see what it is that he is after. I wonder what your friend Holmes would do if he were here?'

'I believe that he would do exactly what you now suggest,' said I. 'He would follow Barrymore and see what he did.'

'Then we shall do it together.'

'But surely he would hear us.'

'The man is rather deaf, and in any case we must take our chance of that. We'll sit up in my room tonight, and wait until he passes.' Sir Henry rubbed his hands with pleasure, and it was evident that he hailed the adventure as a relief to his somewhat quiet life upon the moor.

The baronet has been in communication with the architect who prepared the plans for Sir Charles, and with a contractor from London, so that we may expect great changes to begin here soon. There have been decorators and furnishers up from Plymouth,* and it is evident that our friend has large ideas, and means to spare no pains or expense to restore the grandeur of his family. When the house is renovated and refurnished, all that he will need will be a wife to make it complete. Between ourselves, there are pretty clear signs that this will not be wanting if the lady is willing, for I have seldom seen a man more infatuated with a woman than he is with our beautiful neighbour, Miss Stapleton. And yet the course of true love does not run quite as smoothly as one would under the circumstances expect. To-day, for example, its surface was broken by a very unexpected ripple, which has caused our friend considerable perplexity and annoyance.

After the conversation which I have quoted about Barrymore, Sir Henry put on his hat and prepared to go out. As a matter of course I did the same.

'What, are *you* coming, Watson?' he asked, looking at me in a curious way.

'That depends on whether you are going on the moor,' said I.

'Yes, I am.'

'Well, you know what my instructions are. I am sorry to intrude, but you heard how earnestly Holmes insisted that I should not leave you, and especially that you should not go alone upon the moor.'

Sir Henry put his hand upon my shoulder, with a pleasant smile.

'My dear fellow,' said he, 'Holmes, with all his wisdom, did not foresee some things which have happened since I have been on the moor. You understand me? I am sure that you are the last man in the world who would wish to be a spoil-sport. I must go out alone.'

It put me in a most awkward position. I was at a loss what to say or what to do, and before I had made up my mind he picked up his cane and was gone.

But when I came to think the matter over my conscience reproached me bitterly for having on any pretext allowed him to go out of my sight. I imagined what my feelings would be if I had to return to you and to confess that some misfortune had occurred through my disregard for your instructions. I assure you my cheeks flushed at the very thought. It might not even now be too late to overtake him, so I set off at once in the direction of Merripit House.

I hurried along the road at the top of my speed without seeing anything of Sir Henry, until I came to the point where the moor path branches off. There, fearing that perhaps I had come in the wrong direction, after all, I mounted a hill from which I could command a view—the same hill which is cut into the dark quarry. Then I saw him at once. He was on the moor path, about a quarter of a mile off, and a lady was by his side who could only be Miss Stapleton. It was clear that there was already an understanding between them and that they had met by appointment. They were walking slowly along in deep conversation, and I saw her making quick little movements of her hands as if she were very earnest in what she was saying, while he listened intently, and once or twice shook his head in strong dissent. I stood among the rocks watching them, very much puzzled as to what I should do next. To follow them and break into their intimate conversation seemed to be an outrage, and yet my clear duty was never for an instant to let him out of my sight. To act the spy upon a friend was a hateful task. Still, I could see no better course than to observe him from the hill, and to clear my conscience by confessing to him afterwards what I had done. It is true that if any sudden danger had threatened him I was too far away to be of use, and yet I am sure that you will agree with me that the position was very difficult, and that there was nothing more which I could do.

Our friend, Sir Henry, and the lady had halted on the path and were standing deeply absorbed in their conversation, when I was suddenly aware that I was not the only witness of their interview. A wisp of green floating in the air caught my eye, and another glance showed me that it was carried on a stick by a man who was moving among the broken ground. It was Stapleton with his butterfly-net. He was very much closer to the pair than I was, and he appeared to be moving in their direction. At this instant Sir Henry suddenly drew Miss Stapleton to his side. His arm was round her, but it seemed to me that she was straining away from him with her face averted. He stooped his head to hers, and she raised one hand as if in protest. Next moment I saw them spring apart and turn hurriedly round. Stapleton was the cause of the interruption. He was running wildly towards them, his absurd net dangling behind him. He gesticulated and almost danced with excitement in front of the lovers. What the scene meant I could not imagine, but it seemed to me that Stapleton was abusing Sir Henry, who offered explanations, which became more angry as the other refused to accept them. The lady stood by in haughty silence. Finally Stapleton turned upon his heel and beckoned in a peremptory way to his sister, who, after an irresolute glance at Sir Henry, walked off by the side of her brother. The naturalist's angry gestures showed that the lady was included in his displeasure. The baronet stood for a minute looking after them, and then he walked slowly back the way that he had come, his head hanging, the very picture of dejection.

What all this meant I could not imagine, but I was deeply ashamed to have witnessed so intimate a scene without my friend's knowledge. I ran down the hill, therefore, and met the baronet at the bottom. His face was flushed with anger and his brows were wrinkled, like one who is at his wits' ends what to do.

'Hullo, Watson! Where have you dropped from?' said he. 'You don't mean to say that you came after me in spite of all?'

I explained everything to him: how I had found it impossible to remain behind, how I had followed him, and how I had witnessed all that had occurred. For an instant his eyes blazed at me, but my frankness disarmed his anger, and he broke at last into a rather rueful laugh.

'You would have thought the middle of that prairie a fairly safe place for a man to be private,' said he, 'but, by thunder, the whole country-side seems to have been out to see me do my wooing—and a mighty poor wooing at that! Where had you engaged a seat?'

'I was on that hill.'

'Quite in the back row, eh? But her brother was well up to the front. Did you see him come out on us?'

'Yes, I did.'

'Did he ever strike you as being crazy—this brother of hers?'

'I can't say that he ever did.'

'I dare say not. I always thought him sane enough until to-day, but you can take it from me that either he or I ought to be in a strait-jacket. What's the matter with me, anyhow? You've lived near me for some weeks, Watson. Tell me straight, now! Is there anything that would prevent me from making a good husband to a woman that I loved?'

'I should say not.'

'He can't object to my worldly position, so it must be myself that he has this down on. What has he against me? I never hurt man or woman in my life that I know of. And yet he would not so much as let me touch the tips of her fingers.'

'Did he say so?'

'That, and a deal more. I tell you, Watson, I've only known her these few weeks, but from the first I just felt that she was made for me, and she, too—she was happy when she was with me, and that I'll swear. There's a light in a woman's eyes that speaks louder than words. But he has never let us get together, and it was only to-day for the first time that I saw a chance of having a few words with her alone. She was glad to meet me, but when she did it was not love that she would talk about, and she wouldn't let me talk about it either if she could have stopped it. She kept coming back to it that this was a place of danger, and that she would never be happy until I had left it. I told her that since I had seen her I was in no hurry to leave it, and that if she really wanted me to go, the only way to work it was for her to arrange to go with me. With that I offered in as many words to marry her, but before she could answer down came this brother of hers, running at us with a face on him like a madman. He was just white with rage, and those light eyes of his were blazing with fury. What was I doing with the lady? How darcd I offer her attentions which were distasteful to her? Did I think that because I was a baronet I could do what I liked? If he had not been her brother I should have known better how to answer him. As it was I told him that my feelings towards his sister were such as I was not ashamed of, and that I hoped that she might honour me by becoming my wife. That seemed to make the matter no better, so then I lost my temper too, and I answered him rather more hotly than I should, perhaps, considering that she was standing by. So it ended by his going off with her, as you saw, and here am I as badly puzzled a man as any in this county. Just tell me what it all means, Watson, and I'll owe you more than ever I can hope to pay.'

I tried one or two explanations, but, indeed, I was completely puzzled myself. Our friend's title, his fortune, his age, his character, and his appearance are all in his favour, and I know nothing against him, unless it be this dark fate which runs in his family. That his advances should be rejected so brusquely without any reference to the lady's own wishes, and that the lady should accept the situation without protest, is very amazing. However, our conjectures were set at rest by a visit from Stapleton himself that very afternoon. He had come to offer apologies for his rudeness of the morning, and after a long private interview with Sir Henry in his study the upshot of their conversation was that the breach is quite healed, and that we are to dine at Merripit House next Friday as a sign of it.

'I don't say now that he isn't a crazy man,' said Sir Henry; 'I can't forget the look in his eyes when he ran at me this morning, but I must allow that no man could make a more handsome apology than he has done.'

'Did he give any explanation of his conduct?'

'His sister is everything in his life, he says. That is natural enough, and I am glad that he should understand her value. They have always been together, and according to his account he has been a very lonely man with only her as a companion, so that the thought of losing her was really terrible to him. He had not understood, he said, that I was becoming attached to her, but when he saw with his own eyes that it was really so, and that she might be taken away from him, it gave him such a shock that for a time he was not responsible for what he said or did. He was very sorry for all that had passed, and he recognized how foolish and how selfish it was that he should imagine that he could hold a beautiful woman like his sister to himself for her whole life. If she had to leave him he had rather it was to a neighbour like myself than to anyone else. But in any case it was a blow to him, and it would take him some time before he could prepare himself to meet it. He would withdraw all opposition upon his part if I would promise for three months to let the matter rest, and to be content with cultivating the lady's friendship during that time without claiming her love. This I promised, and so the matter rests.'

So there is one of our small mysteries cleared up. It is something to have touched bottom anywhere in this bog in which we are floundering. We know now why Stapleton looked with disfavour upon his sister's suitor—even when that suitor was so eligible a one as Sir Henry. And now I pass on to another thread which I have extricated out of the tangled skein,* the mystery of the sobs in the night, of the tear-stained face of Mrs Barrymore, of the secret journey of the butler to the western lattice-window.* Congratulate me, my dear Holmes, and tell me that I have not disappointed you as an agent—that you do not regret the confidence which you showed in me when you sent me down. All these things have by one night's work been thoroughly cleared.

I have said 'by one night's work', but, in truth, it was by two nights' work, for on the first we drew entirely blank. I sat up with Sir Henry in his room until nearly three o'clock in the morning, but no sound of any sort did we hear except the chiming clock upon the stairs. It was a most melancholy vigil, and ended by each of us falling asleep in our chairs. Fortunately we were not discouraged, and we determined to try again. The next night we lowered the lamp and sat smoking cigarettes, without making the least sound. It was incredible how slowly the hours crawled by, and yet we were helped through it by the same sort of patient interest which the hunter must feel as he watches the trap into which he hopes the game may wander. One struck, and two, and we had almost for the second time given it up in despair, when in an instant we both sat bolt upright in our chairs, with all our weary senses keenly on the alert once more. We had heard the creak of a step in the passage.

Very stealthily we heard it pass along until it died away in the distance. Then the baronet gently opened his door, and we set out in pursuit. Already our man had gone round the gallery, and the corridor was all in darkness. Softly we stole along until we had come into the other wing. We were just in time to catch a glimpse of the tall, black-bearded figure, his shoulders rounded, as he tip-toed down the passage. Then he passed through the same door as before, and the light of the candle framed it in the darkness and shot one single yellow beam across the gloom of the corridor. We shuffled cautiously towards it, trying every plank before we dared to put our whole weight upon it. We had taken the precaution of leaving our boots behind us, but, even so, the old boards snapped and creaked beneath our tread. Sometimes it seemed impossible that he should fail to hear our approach. However, the man is fortunately rather deaf, and he was entirely preoccupied in that which he was doing. When at last we reached the door and peeped through we found him crouching at the window, candle in hand, his white, intent face pressed against the pane, exactly as I had seen him two nights before.

We had arranged no plan of campaign, but the baronet is a man to whom the most direct way is always the most natural. He walked into the room, and as he did so Barrymore sprang up from the window with a sharp hiss of his breath, and stood, livid and trembling, before us. His dark eyes, glaring out of the white mask of his face, were full of horror and astonishment as he gazed from Sir Henry to me.

'What are you doing here, Barrymore?'

'Nothing, sir.' His agitation was so great that he could hardly speak, and the shadows sprang up and down from the shaking of his candle. 'It was the window, sir. I go round at night to see that they are fastened.'

'On the second floor?'

'Yes, sir, all the windows.'

'Look here, Barrymore,' said Sir Henry, sternly, 'we have made up our minds to have the truth out of you, so it will save you trouble to tell it sooner rather than later. Come, now! No lies! What were you doing at that window?'

The fellow looked at us in a helpless way, and he wrung his hands together like one who is in the last extremity of doubt and misery.

'I was doing no harm, sir. I was holding a candle to the window.'

'And why were you holding a candle to the window?'

'Don't ask me, Sir Henry—don't ask me! I give you my word, sir, that it is not my secret, and that I cannot tell it. If it concerned no one but myself I would not try to keep it from you.'

A sudden idea occurred to me, and I took the candle from the window-sill, where the butler had placed it.

'He must have been holding it as a signal,' said I. 'Let us see if there is any answer.'

I held it as he had done, and stared out into the darkness of the night. Vaguely I could discern the black bank of the trees and the lighter expanse of the moor, for the moon was behind the clouds. And then I gave a cry of exultation, for a tiny pin-point of yellow light had suddenly transfixed the dark veil, and glowed steadily in the centre of the black square framed by the window.

'There it is!' I cried.

'No, no, sir, it is nothing—nothing at all,' the butler broke in; 'I assure you, sir—'

'Move your light across the window, Watson!' cried the baronet. 'See, the other moves also! Now, you rascal, do you deny that it is a signal? Come, speak up! Who is your confederate out yonder, and what is this conspiracy that is going on?'

The man's face became openly defiant.

'It is my business, and not yours. I will not tell.'

'Then you leave my employment right away.'

'Very good, sir. If I must, I must.'

'And you go in disgrace. By thunder, you may well be ashamed of yourself. Your family has lived with mine for over a hundred years under this roof, and here I find you deep in some dark plot against me.'

'No, no, sir; no, not against you!'

It was a woman's voice, and Mrs Barrymore, paler and more horror-struck than her husband, was standing at the door. Her bulky figure in a shawl and skirt might have been comic were it not for the intensity of feeling upon her face.

'We have to go, Eliza. This is the end of it. You can pack our things,' said the butler.

'Oh, John, John, have I brought you to this? It is my doing, Sir Henry—all mine. He has done nothing except for my sake, and because I asked him.'

'Speak out, then! What does it mean?'

'My unhappy brother is starving on the moor. We cannot let him perish at our very gates. The light is a signal to him that food is ready for him, and his light out yonder is to show the spot to which to bring it.'

'Then your brother is—'

'The escaped convict, sir—Selden, the criminal.'

'That's the truth, sir,' said Barrymore. 'I said that it was not my secret, and that I could not tell it to you. But now you have heard it, and you will see that if there was a plot it was not against you.'

This, then, was the explanation of the stealthy expeditions at night and the light at the window. Sir Henry and I both stared at the woman in amazement. Was it possible that this stolidly respectable person was of the same blood as one of the most notorious criminals in the country?

'Yes, sir, my name was Selden, and he is my younger brother. We humoured him too much when he was a lad, and gave him his own way in everything, until he came to think that the world was made for his pleasure, and that he could do what he liked in it. Then, as he grew older, he met wicked companions, and the devil entered into him until he broke my mother's heart and dragged our name in the dirt. From crime to crime he sank lower and lower, until it is only the mercy of God which has snatched him from the scaffold; but to me, sir, he was always the little curly-headed boy that I had nursed and played with, as an elder sister would. That was why he broke prison, sir. He knew that I was here, and that we could not refuse to help him. When he dragged himself here one night, weary and starving, with the warders hard at his heels, what could we do? We took him in and fed him and cared for him. Then you returned, sir, and my brother thought he would be safer on the moor than anywhere else until the hue and cry was over, so he lay in hiding there. But every second night we made sure if he was still there by putting a light in the window, and if there was an answer my husband took out some bread and meat to him. Every day we hoped that he was gone, but as long as he was there we could not desert him. That is the whole truth, as I am an honest Christian woman, and you will see that if there is blame in the matter it does not lie with my husband, but with me, for whose sake he has done all that he has.'

The woman's words came with an intense earnestness which carried conviction with them.

'Is this true, Barrymore?'

'Yes, Sir Henry. Every word of it.'

'Well, I cannot blame you for standing by your own wife. Forget what I have said. Go to your room, you two, and we shall talk further about this matter in the morning.'

When they were gone we looked out of the window again. Sir Henry had flung it open, and the cold night wind beat in upon our faces. Far away in the black distance there still glowed that one tiny point of yellow light.

'I wonder he dares,' said Sir Henry.

'It may be so placed as to be only visible from here.'

'Very likely. How far do you think it is?'

'Out by the Cleft Tor,* I think.'

'Not more than a mile or two off.'

'Hardly that.'

'Well, it cannot be far if Barrymore had to carry out the food to it. And he is waiting, this villain, beside that candle. By thunder, Watson, I am going out to take that man!'

The same thought had crossed my own mind. It was not as if the Barrymores had taken us into their confidence. Their secret had been forced from them. The man was a danger to the community, an unmitigated scoundrel for whom there was neither pity nor excuse. We were only doing our duty in taking this chance of putting him back where he could do no harm. With his brutal and violent nature, others would have to pay the price if we held our hands. Any night, for example, our neighbours the Stapletons might be attacked by him, and it may have been the thought of this which made Sir Henry so keen upon the adventure.

'I will come,' said I.

'Then get your revolver and put on your boots. The sooner we start the better, as the fellow may put out his light and be off.'

In five minutes we were outside the door, starting upon our expedition. We hurried through the dark shrubbery, amid the dull moaning of the autumn wind and the rustle of the falling leaves. The night-air was heavy with the smell of damp and decay. Now and again the moon peeped out for an instant, but clouds were driving over the face of the sky, and just as we came out on the moor a thin rain began to fall. The light still burned steadily in front.

'Are you armed?' I asked.

'I have a hunting-crop.'*

'We must close in on him rapidly, for he is said to be a desperate fellow. We shall take him by surprise and have him at our mercy before he can resist.'

'I say, Watson,' said the baronet, 'what would Holmes say to this? How about that hour of darkness in which the power of evil is exalted?'

As if in answer to his words there rose suddenly out of the vast gloom of the moor that strange cry which I had already heard upon the borders of the great Grimpen Mire. It came with the wind through the silence of the night, a long, deep mutter, then a rising howl, and then the sad moan in which it died away. Again and again it sounded, the whole air throbbing with it, strident, wild, and menacing. The baronet caught my sleeve, and his face glimmered white through the darkness.

'Good heavens, what's that, Watson?'

'I don't know. It's a sound they have on the moor. I heard it once before.'

It died away, and an absolute silence closed in upon us. We stood straining our ears, but nothing came.

'Watson,' said the baronet, 'it was the cry of a hound.'

My blood ran cold in my veins, for there was a break in his voice which told of the sudden horror which had seized him.

'What do they call this sound?' he asked.

'Who?'

'The folk on the country-side.'*

'Oh, they are ignorant people. Why should you mind what they call it?'

'Tell me, Watson. What do they say of it?'

I hesitated, but could not escape the question.

'They say it is the cry of the Hound of the Baskervilles.'

He groaned, and was silent for a few moments.

'A hound it was,' he said at last, 'but it seemed to come from miles away over yonder, I think.'

'It was hard to say whence it came.'

'It rose and fell with the wind. Isn't that the direction of the great Grimpen Mire?'

'Yes, it is.'

'Well, it was up there. Come now, Watson, didn't you think yourself that it was the cry of a hound? I am not a child. You need not fear to speak the truth.'

'Stapleton was with me when I heard it last. He said that it might be the calling of a strange bird.'

'No, no, it was a hound. My God, can there be some truth in all these stories? Is it possible that I am really in danger from so dark a cause? You don't believe it, do you, Watson?'

'No, no.'

'And yet it was one thing to laugh about it in London, and it is another to stand out here in the darkness of the moor and to hear such a cry as that. And my uncle! There was the footprint of the hound beside him as he lay. It all fits together. I don't think that I am a coward, Watson, but that sound seemed to freeze my very blood. Feel my hand!'

It was as cold as a block of marble.

'You'll be all right to-morrow.'

'I don't think I'll get that cry out of my head. What do you advise that we do now?'

'Shall we turn back?'

'No, by thunder; we have come out to get our man, and we will do it. We are after the convict, and a hell-hound, as likely as not, after us. Come on. We'll see it through if all the fiends of the pit were loose upon the moor.'

We stumbled slowly along in the darkness, with the black loom of the craggy hills around us, and the yellow speck of light burning steadily in front. There is nothing so deceptive as the distance of a light upon a pitch-dark night, and sometimes the glimmer seemed to be far away upon the horizon and sometimes it might have been within a few yards of us. But at last we could see whence it came, and then we knew that we were indeed very close. A guttering candle was stuck in a crevice of the rocks which flanked it on each side so as to keep the wind from it, and also to prevent it from being visible, save in the direction of Baskerville Hall. A boulder of granite concealed our approach, and crouching behind it we gazed over it at the signal light. It was strange to see this single candle burning there in the middle of the moor, with no sign of life near it—just the one straight yellow flame and the gleam of the rock on each side of it.

'What shall we do now?' whispered Sir Henry.

'Wait here. He must be near his light. Let us see if we can get a glimpse of him.'

The words were hardly out of my mouth when we both saw him. Over the rocks, in the crevice of which the candle burned, there was thrust out an evil yellow face, a terrible animal face, all seamed and scored with vile passions. Foul with mire, with a bristling beard, and hung with matted hair, it might well have belonged to one of those old savages* who dwelt in the burrows on the hill-sides. The light beneath him was reflected in his small, cunning eyes, which peered fiercely to right and left through the darkness, like a crafty and savage animal who has heard the steps of the hunters.

Something had evidently aroused his suspicions. It may have been that Barrymore had some private signal which we had neglected to give, or the fellow may have had some other reason for thinking that all was not well, but I could read his fears upon his wicked face. Any instant he might dash out the light and vanish in the darkness. I sprang forward, therefore, and Sir Henry did the same. At the same moment the convict screamed out a curse at us and hurled a rock which splintered up against the boulder which had sheltered us. I caught one glimpse of his short, squat, strongly-built figure as he sprang to his feet and turned to run. At the same moment by a lucky chance the moon broke through the clouds. We rushed over the brow of the hill, and there was our man running with great speed down the other side, springing over the stones in his way with the activity of a mountain goat. A lucky long shot of my revolver might have crippled him, but I had brought it only to defend myself if attacked, and not to shoot an unarmed man who was running away.

We were both fair runners and in good condition,* but we soon found that we had no chance of overtaking him. We saw him for a long time in the moonlight until he was only a small speck moving swiftly among the boulders upon the side of a distant hill. We ran and ran until we were completely blown, but the space between us grew ever wider. Finally we stopped and sat panting on two rocks, while we watched him disappearing in the distance.

And it was at this moment that there occurred a most strange and unexpected thing. We had risen from our rocks and were turning to go home, having abandoned the hopeless chase. The moon was low upon the right, and the jagged pinnacle of a granite tor stood up against the lower curve of its silver disc. There, outlined as black as an ebony statue on that shining background, I saw the figure of a man upon the tor. Do not think that it was a delusion, Holmes. I assure you that I have never in my life seen anything more clearly. As far as I could judge, the figure was that of a tall, thin man. He stood with his legs a little separated, his arms folded, his head bowed, as if he were brooding over that enormous wilderness of peat and granite which lay behind him. He might have been the very spirit of that terrible place. It was not the convict. This man was far from the place where the latter had disappeared. Besides, he was a much taller man. With a cry of surprise I pointed him out to the baronet, but in the instant during which I had turned to grasp his arm the man was gone. There was the sharp pinnacle of granite still cutting the lower edge of the moon, but its peak bore no trace of that silent and motionless figure.

I wished to go in that direction and to search the tor, but it was some distance away. The Baronet's nerves were still quivering from that cry, which recalled the dark story of his family, and he was not in the mood for fresh adventures. He had not seen this lonely man upon the tor, and could not feel the thrill which his strange presence and his commanding attitude had given to me. 'A warder, no doubt,' said he. 'The moor has been thick with them since this fellow escaped.' Well, perhaps his explanation may be the right one, but I should like to have some further proof of it. To-day we mean to communicate to the Princetown people where they should look for their missing man, but it is hard lines that we have not actually had the triumph of bringing him back as our own prisoner. Such are the adventures of last night, and you must acknowledge, my dear Holmes, that I have done you very well in the matter of a report. Much of what I tell you is no doubt quite irrelevant, but still I feel that it is best that I should let you have all the facts and leave you to select for yourself those which will be of most service to you in helping you to your conclusions. We are certainly making some progress. So far as the Barrymores go, we have found the motive of their actions, and that has cleared up the situation very much. But the moor with its mysteries and its strange inhabitants remains as inscrutable as ever. Perhaps in my next I may be able to throw some light upon this also. Best of all would it be if you could come down to us.* [In any case you will hear from me again in the course of the next few days.]*

CHAPTER 10

EXTRACT FROM THE DIARY OF DR WATSON

So far I have been able to quote from the reports which I have forwarded during these early days to Sherlock Holmes. Now, however, I have arrived at a point in my narrative where I am compelled to abandon this method and to trust once more to my recollections, aided by the diary which I kept at the time. A few extracts from the latter will carry me on to those scenes which are indelibly fixed in every detail upon my memory. I proceed, then, from the morning which followed our abortive chase of the convict and our other strange experiences upon the moor.

October 16th—A dull and foggy day, with a drizzle of rain. The house is banked in with rolling clouds, which rise now and then to show the dreary curves of the moor, with thin, silver veins upon the sides of the hills, and the distant boulders gleaming where the light strikes upon their wet faces. It is melancholy outside and in. The baronet is in a black reaction after the excitements of the night. I am conscious myself of a weight at my heart and a feeling of impending danger—ever-present, which is the more terrible because I am unable to define it.

And have I not cause for such a feeling? Consider the long sequence of incidents which have all pointed to some sinister influence which is at work around us. There is the death of the last occupant of the Hall, fulfilling so exactly the conditions of the family legend, and there are* the repeated reports from peasants of the appearance of a strange creature upon the moor. Twice I have with my own ears heard the sound which resembled the distant baying of a hound. It is incredible, impossible, that it should really be outside the ordinary laws of Nature. A spectral hound which leaves material footmarks and fills the air with its howling is surely not to be thought of. Stapleton may fall in with such a superstition, and Mortimer also; but if I have one quality upon earth it is common sense, and nothing will persuade me to believe in such a thing. To do so would be to descend to the level of these poor peasants who are not content with a mere fiend-dog,* but must needs describe him with hell-fire shooting from his mouth and eyes. Holmes would not listen to such fancies, and I am his agent. But facts are facts, and I have twice heard this crying upon the moor. Suppose that there were really some huge hound loose upon it; that would go far to explain everything. But where could such a hound lie concealed, where did it get its food,* where did it come from, how was it that no one saw it by day?

It must be confessed that the natural explanation offers almost as many difficulties as the other. And always, apart from the hound, there was the fact of the human agency in London, the man in the cab, and the letter which warned Sir Henry against the moor. This at least was real, but it might have been the work of a protecting friend as easily as an enemy. Where was that friend or enemy now? Had he remained in London, or had he followed us down here? Could he—could he be the stranger whom I had seen upon the Tor?

It is true that I have had only the one glance at him, and yet there are some things to which I am ready to swear. He is no one whom I have seen down here, and I have now met all the neighbours. The figure was far taller than that of Stapleton, far thinner than that of Frankland. Barrymore it might possibly have been, but we had left him behind us, and I am certain that he could not have followed us. A stranger then is still dogging us, just as a stranger had dogged us in London. We have never shaken him off. If I could lay my hands upon that man, then at last we might find ourselves at the end of all our difficulties. To this one purpose I must now devote all my energies.

My first impulse was to tell Sir Henry all my plans. My second and wisest one is to play my own game and speak as little as possible to anyone. He is silent and distrait.* His nerves have been strangely shaken by that sound upon the moor. I will say nothing to add to his anxieties, but I will take my own steps to attain my own end.

We had a small scene this morning after breakfast. Barrymore asked leave to speak with Sir Henry, and they were closeted in his study some little time. Sitting in the billiard-room, I more than once heard the sound of voices raised, and I had a pretty good idea what the point was which was under discussion. After a time the Baronet opened his door and called for me.

'Barrymore considers that he has a grievance,' he said. 'He thinks that it was unfair on our part to hunt his brother-in-law down when he, of his own free will, had told us the secret.'

The butler was standing, very pale but very collected, before us.

'I may have spoken too warmly, sir,' said he, 'and if I have I am sure that I beg your pardon. At the same time, I was very much surprised when I heard you two gentlemen come back this morning and learned that you had been chasing Selden. The poor fellow has enough to fight against without my putting more upon his track.'

'If you had told us of your own free will it would have been a different thing,' said the baronet. 'You only told us, or rather your wife only told us, when it was forced from you and you could not help yourself.'

'I didn't think you would have taken advantage of it, Sir Henry—indeed I didn't.'

'The man is a public danger. There are lonely houses scattered over the moor, and he is a fellow who would stick at nothing. You only want to get a glimpse of his face to see that. Look at Mr Stapleton's house, for example, with no one but himself to defend it. There's no safety for anyone until he is under lock and key.'

'He'll break into no house, sir. I give you my solemn word upon that. And* he will never trouble anyone in this country again. I assure you, Sir Henry, that in a very few days the necessary arrangements will have been made and he will be on his way to South America. For God's sake, sir, I beg of you not to let the police know that he is still on the moor. They have given up the chase there, and he can lie quiet until the ship is ready for him. You can't tell on him without getting my wife and me into trouble. I beg you, sir, to say nothing to the police.'

'What do you say, Watson?'

I shrugged my shoulders. 'If he were safely out of the country it would relieve the taxpayer of a burden.'

'But how about the chance of his holding someone up before he goes?'

'He would not do anything so mad, sir. We have provided him with all that he can want. To commit a crime would be to show where he was hiding.'

'That is true,' said Sir Henry. 'Well, Barrymore—'

'God bless you, sir, and thank you from my heart! It would have killed my poor wife had he been taken again.'

'I guess we are aiding and abetting a felony, Watson? But, after what we have heard, I don't feel as if I could give the man up, so there is an end of it. All right, Barrymore, you can go.'

With a few broken words of gratitude the man turned, but he hesitated and then came back.

'You've been so kind to us, sir, that I should like to do the best I can for you in return. I know something, Sir Henry, and perhaps I should have said it before, but it was long after the inquest that I found it out. I've never breathed a word about it yet to a mortal man. It's about poor Sir Charles's death.'

The baronet and I were both upon our feet.

'Do you know how he died?'

'No, sir, I don't know that.'

'What, then?'

'I know why he was at the gate at that hour. It was to meet a woman.'

'To meet a woman! He?'

'Yes, sir.'

'And the woman's name?'

'I can't give you the name, sir, but I can give you the initials. Her initials were L.L.'

'How do you know this, Barrymore?'

'Well, Sir Henry, your uncle had a letter that morning. He had usually a great many letters, for he was a public man and well known for his kind heart, so that everyone who was in trouble was glad to turn to him. But that morning, as it chanced, there was only this one letter, so I took the more notice of it. It was from Coombe Tracey,* and it was addressed in a woman's hand.'

'Well?'

'Well, sir, I thought no more of the matter, and never would have done had it not been for my wife. Only a few weeks ago she was cleaning out Sir Charles's study—it had never been touched since his death—and she found the ashes of a burned letter in the back of the grate. The greater part of it was charred to pieces, but one little slip, the end of a page, hung together, and the writing could still be read, though it was grey on a black ground. It seemed to us to be a post-script at the end of the letter, and it said: "Please, please, as you are a gentleman, burn this letter, and be at the gate by ten o'clock." Beneath it were signed the initials L.L.'

'Have you got that slip?'

'No, sir, it crumbled all to bits after we moved it.'

'Had Sir Charles received any other letters in the same writing?'

'Well, sir, I took no particular notice of his letters. I should not have noticed this one only it happened to come alone.'

'And you have no idea who L.L. is?'

'No, sir. No more than you have. But I expect if we could lay our hands upon that lady we should know more about Sir Charles's death.'

'I cannot understand, Barrymore, how you came to conceal this important information.'

'Well, sir, it was immediately after that our own trouble came to us. And then again, sir, we were both of us very fond of Sir Charles, as we well might be considering all that he has done for us. To rake this up couldn't help our poor master, and it's well to go carefully when there's a lady in the case. Even the best of us—'

'You thought it might injure his reputation?'

'Well, sir, I thought no good could come of it. But now you have been kind to us, and I feel as if it would be treating you unfairly not to tell you all that I know about the matter.'

'Very good, Barrymore; you can go.'

When the butler had left us, Sir Henry turned to me. 'Well, Watson, what do you think of this new light?'

'It seems to leave the darkness rather blacker than before.'

'So I think. But if we can only trace L.L. it should clear up the whole business. We have gained that much. We know that there is someone who has the facts if we can only find her. What do you think we should do?'

'Let Holmes know all about it at once. It will give him the clue for which he has been seeking. I am much mistaken if it does not bring him down.'

I went at once to my room and drew up my report of the morning's conversation for Holmes.* It was evident to me that he had been very busy of late, for the notes which I had from Baker Street were few and short, with no comments upon the information which I had supplied, and hardly any reference to my mission. No doubt his blackmailing case is absorbing all his faculties. And yet this new factor must surely arrest his attention and renew his interest. I wish that he were here.

October 17th—All day to-day the rain poured down, rustling on the ivy and dripping from the eaves. I thought of the convict out upon the bleak, cold, shelterless moor. Poor fellow! Whatever his crimes, he has suffered something to atone for them. And then I thought of that other one—the face in the cab, the figure against the moon. Was he also out in that deluge—the unseen watcher, the man of darkness? In the evening I put on my waterproof and I walked far upon the sodden moor, full of dark imaginings, the rain beating upon my face and the wind whistling about my ears. God help those who wander into the Great Mire now, for even the firm uplands are becoming a morass. I found the Black Tor* upon which I had seen the solitary watcher, and from its craggy summit I looked out myself across the melancholy downs. Rain squalls drifted across their russet face, and the heavy, slate-coloured clouds hung low over the landscape, trailing in grey wreaths down the sides of the fantastic hills. In the distant hollow on the left, half hidden by the mist, the two thin towers of Baskerville Hall rose above the trees. They were the only signs of human life which I could see, save only those prehistoric huts which lay thickly upon the slopes of the hills. Nowhere was there any trace of that lonely man whom I had seen on the same spot two nights before.

As I walked back I was overtaken by Dr Mortimer driving in his dog-cart* over a rough moorland track, which led from the outlying farmhouse of Foulmire. He has been very attentive to us, and hardly a day has passed that he has not called at the Hall to see how we were getting on. He insisted upon my climbing into his dog-cart and he gave me a lift homewards. I found him much troubled over the disappearance of his little spaniel. It had wandered on to the moor and had never come back. I gave him such consolation as I might, but I thought of the pony on the Grimpen Mire, and I do not fancy that he will see his little dog again.

'By the way, Mortimer,' said I, as we jolted along the rough road, 'I suppose there are few people living within driving distance of this whom you do not know?'

'Hardly any, I think.'

'Can you, then, tell me the name of any woman whose initials are L.L.?'

He thought for a few minutes. 'No,' said he. 'There are a few gipsies and labouring folk for whom I can't answer, but among the farmers or gentry there is no one whose initials are those. Wait a bit, though,' he added, after a pause. 'There is Laura Lyons—her initials are L.L.—but she lives in Coombe Tracey.'

'Who is she?' I asked.

'She is Frankland's daughter.'

'What? Old Frankland the crank?'

'Exactly. She married an artist named Lyons, who came sketching on the moor. He proved to be a blackguard and deserted her. The fault, from what I hear, may not have been entirely on one side. Her father refused to have anything to do with her, because she had married without his consent, and perhaps for one or two other reasons as well. So, between the old sinner and the young one the girl has had a pretty bad time.'

'How does she live?'

'I fancy old Frankland allows her a pittance, but it cannot be more, for his own affairs are considerably involved.* Whatever she may have deserved one could not allow her to go hopelessly to the bad. Her story got about, and several of the people here did something to enable her to earn an honest living. Stapleton did for one, and Sir Charles for another. I gave a trifle myself. It was to set her up in a typewriting business.'

He wanted to know the object of my inquiries, but I managed to satisfy his curiosity without telling him too much, for there is no reason why we should take anyone into our confidence. Tomorrow morning I shall find my way to Coombe Tracey, and if I can see this Mrs Laura Lyons, of equivocal reputation, a long step will have been made towards clearing one incident in this chain of mysteries. I am certainly developing the wisdom of the serpent, for when Mortimer pressed his questions to an inconvenient extent I asked him casually to what type Frankland's skull belonged, and so heard nothing but craniology* for the rest of our drive. I have not lived for years with Sherlock Holmes for nothing.

I have only one other incident to record upon this tempestuous and melancholy day. This was my conversation with Barrymore just now, which gives me one more strong card which I can play in due time.

Mortimer had stayed to dinner, and he and the Baronet played écarté* afterwards. The butler brought me my coffee into the library, and I took the chance to ask him a few questions.

'Well,' said I, 'has this precious relation of yours departed, or is he still lurking out yonder?'

'I don't know, sir. I hope to Heaven that he has gone, for he has brought nothing but trouble here! I've not heard of him since I left out food for him last, and that was three days ago.'

'Did you see him then?'

'No, sir; but the food was gone when next I went that way.'

'Then he was certainly there?'

'So you would think, sir, unless it was the other man who took it.'

I sat with my coffee-cup half-way to my lips, and stared at Barrymore.

'You know that there is another man, then?'

'Yes, sir; there is another man upon the moor.'

'Have you seen him?'

'No, sir.'

'How do you know of him, then?'

'Selden told me of him, sir, a week ago or more.* He's in hiding, too, but he's not a convict, so far as I can make out. I don't like it, Dr Watson—I tell you straight, sir, that I don't like it.' He spoke with a sudden passion of earnestness.

'Now, listen to me, Barrymore! I have no interest in this matter but that of your master. I have come here with no object except to help him. Tell me, frankly, what it is that you don't like.'

Barrymore hesitated for a moment, as if he regretted his outburst, or found it difficult to express his own feelings in words.

'It's all these goings-on, sir,' he cried, at last, waving his hand towards the rain-lashed window which faced the moor. 'There's foul play somewhere, and there's black villainy brewing, to that I'll swear! Very glad I should be, sir, to see Sir Henry on his way back to London again!'

'But what is it that alarms you?'

'Look at Sir Charles's death! That was bad enough, for all that the coroner said. Look at the noises on the moor at night. There's not a man would cross it after sundown if he was paid for it. Look at this stranger hiding out yonder, and watching and waiting! What's he waiting for? What does it mean? It means no good to anyone of the name of Baskerville, and very glad I shall be to be quit of it all on the day that Sir Henry's new servants are ready to take over the Hall.'

'But about this stranger,' said I. 'Can you tell me anything about him? What did Selden say? Did he find out where he hid or what he was doing?'

'He saw him once or twice, but he is a deep one, and gives nothing away. At first he thought that he was the police, but soon he found that he had some lay of his own.* A kind of gentleman he was, as far as he could see, but what he was doing he could not make out.'

'And where did he say that he lived?'

'Among the old houses on the hillside—the stone huts where the old folk used to live.'

'But how about his food?'

'Selden found out that he has got a lad who works for him and brings him all he needs. I dare say he goes to Coombe Tracey for what he wants.'

'Very good, Barrymore. We may talk further of this some other time.'

When the butler had gone I walked over to the black window, and I looked through a blurred pane at the driving clouds and at the tossing outline of the wind-swept trees. It is a wild night indoors, and what must it be in a stone hut upon the moor? What passion of hatred can it be which leads a man to lurk in such a place at such a time? And what deep and earnest purpose can he have which calls for such a trial? There, in that hut upon the moor, seems to lie the very centre of that problem which has vexed me so sorely. I swear that another day shall not have passed before I have done all that man can do to reach the heart of the mystery.

CHAPTER 11

THE MAN ON THE TOR

THE extract from my private diary which forms the last chapter has brought my narrative up to the 18th of October, a time when these strange events began to move swiftly towards their terrible conclusion. The incidents of the next few days are indelibly graven upon my recollection, and I can tell them without reference to the notes made at the time. I start, then, from the day which succeeded that upon which I had established two facts of great importance, the one that Mrs Laura Lyons of Coombe Tracey* had written to Sir Charles Baskerville and made an appointment with him at the very place and hour that he met his death, the other that the lurking man upon the moor was to be found among the stone huts upon the hillside. With these two facts in my possession I felt that either my intelligence or my courage must be deficient if I could not throw some further light upon these dark places.

I had no opportunity to tell the baronet what I had learned about Mrs Lyons upon the evening before, for Dr Mortimer remained with him at cards until it was very late. At breakfast, however, I informed him about my discovery, and asked him whether he would care to accompany me to Coombe Tracey. At first he was very eager to come, but on second thoughts it seemed to both of us that if I went alone the results might be better. The more formal we made the visit the less information we might obtain. I left Sir Henry behind, therefore, not without some prickings of conscience, and drove off upon my new quest.

When I reached Coombe Tracey I told Perkins to put up the horses, and I made inquiries for the lady whom I had come to interrogate. I had no difficulty in finding her rooms, which were central and well appointed. A maid showed me in without ceremony,* and as I entered the sitting-room a lady who was sitting before a Remington type-writer* sprang up with a pleasant smile of welcome. Her face fell, however, when she saw that I was a stranger, and she sat down again and asked me the object of my visit.

The first impression left by Mrs Lyons was one of extreme beauty. Her eyes and hair were of the same rich hazel colour, and her cheeks, though considerably freckled, were flushed with the exquisite bloom of the brunette, the dainty pink which lurks at the heart of the sulphur rose.* Admiration was, I repeat, the first impression. But the second was criticism. There was something subtly wrong with the face, some coarseness of expression, some hardness, perhaps, of eye, some loose-ness of lip* which marred its perfect beauty. But these, of course, are after-thoughts. At the moment I was simply conscious that I was in the presence of a very handsome woman, and that she was asking me the reasons for my visit. I had not quite understood until that instant how delicate my mission was.

'I have the pleasure', said I, 'of knowing your father.'

It was a clumsy introduction, and the lady made me feel it.

'There is nothing in common between my father and me,' she said. 'I owe him nothing, and his friends are not mine. If it were not for the late Sir Charles Baskerville and some other kind hearts I might have starved for all that my father cared.'

'It was about the late Sir Charles Baskerville that I have come here to see you.'

The freckles started out on the lady's face.

'What can I tell you about him?' she asked, and her fingers played nervously over the stops* of her typewriter.

'You knew him, did you not?'

'I have already said that I owe a great deal to his kindness. If I am able to support myself it is largely due to the interest which he took in my unhappy situation.'

'Did you correspond with him?'

The lady looked quickly up, with an angry gleam in her hazel eyes.

'What is the object of these questions?' she asked, sharply.

'The object is to avoid a public scandal. It is better that I should ask them here than that the matter should pass outside our control.'

She was silent and her face was very pale. At last she looked up with something reckless and defiant in her manner.

'Well, I'll answer,' she said. 'What are your questions?'

'Did you correspond with Sir Charles?'

'I certainly wrote to him once or twice to acknowledge his delicacy and his generosity.'

'Have you the dates of those letters?'

'No.'

'Have you ever met him?'

'Yes, once or twice, when he came into Coombe Tracey. He was a very retiring man, and he preferred to do good by stealth.'

'But if you saw him so seldom and wrote so seldom, how did he know enough about your affairs to be able to help you, as you say that he has done?'

She met my difficulty with the utmost readiness.

'There were several gentlemen who knew my sad history and united to help me. One was Mr Stapleton, a neighbour and intimate friend of Sir Charles. He was exceedingly kind, and it was through him that Sir Charles learned about my affairs.'

I knew already that Sir Charles Baskerville had made Stapleton his almoner* upon several occasions, so the lady's statement bore the impress of truth upon it.

'Did you ever write to Sir Charles asking him to meet you?' I continued.

Mrs Lyons flushed with anger again.

'Really, sir, this is a very extraordinary question.'

'I am sorry, madam, but I must repeat it.'

'Then I answer—certainly not.'

'Not on the very day of Sir Charles's death?'

The flush had faded in an instant, and a deathly face was before me. Her dry lips could not speak the 'No' which I saw rather than heard.

'Surely your memory deceives you,' said I. 'I could even quote a passage of your letter.* It ran "Please, please, as you are a gentleman, burn this letter, and be at the gate by ten o'clock."'

I thought that she had fainted, but she recovered herself by a supreme effort.

'Is there no such thing as a gentleman?' she gasped.

'You do Sir Charles an injustice. He *did* burn the letter. But sometimes a letter may be legible even when burned. You acknowledge now that you wrote it?'*

'Yes, I did write it,' she cried, pouring out her soul in a torrent of words. 'I did write it. Why should I deny it? I have no reason to be ashamed of it. I wished him to help me. I believed that if I had an interview I could gain his help, so I asked him to meet me.'

'But why at such an hour?'

'Because I had only just learned that he was going to London next day and might be away for months. There were reasons why I could not get there earlier.'

'But why a rendezvous in the garden instead of a visit to the house?'

'Do you think a woman could go alone at that hour to a bachelor's house?'

'Well, what happened when you did get there?'

'I never went.'

'Mrs Lyons!'

'No, I swear it to you on all I hold sacred. I never went. Something intervened to prevent my going.'

'What was that?'

'That is a private matter. I cannot tell it.'

'You acknowledge then, that you made an appointment with Sir Charles at the very hour and place at which he met his death, but you deny that you kept the appointment?'

'That is the truth.'

Again and again I cross-questioned her, but I could never get past that point.

'Mrs Lyons,' said I, as I rose from this long and inconclusive interview, 'you are taking a very great responsibility and putting yourself in a very false position by not making an absolutely clean breast of all that you know. If I have to call in the aid of the police you will find how seriously you are compromised. If your position is innocent, why did you in the first instance deny having written to Sir Charles upon that date?'

'Because I feared that some false conclusion might be drawn from it, and that I might find myself involved in a scandal.'

'And why were you so pressing that Sir Charles should destroy your letter?'

'If you have read the letter you will know.'

'I did not say that I had read all the letter.'

'You quoted some of it.'

'I quoted the postscript. The letter had, as I said, been burned, and it was not all legible. I ask you once again why it was that you were so pressing that Sir Charles should destroy this letter which he received on the day of his death.'

'The matter is a very private one.'

'The more reason why you should avoid a public investigation.'

'I will tell you, then. If you have heard anything of my unhappy history you will know that I made a rash marriage and had reason to regret it.'

'I have heard so much.'

'My life has been one incessant persecution from a husband whom I abhor. The law is upon his side, and every day I am faced by the possibility that he may force me to live with him.* At the time that I wrote this letter to Sir Charles I had learned that there was a prospect of my regaining my freedom if certain expenses could be met.* It meant everything to me—peace of mind, happiness, self-respect—everything. I knew Sir Charles's generosity, and I thought that if he heard the story from my own lips he would help me.'

'Then how is it that you did not go?'

'Because I received help in the interval from another source.'

'Why, then, did you not write to Sir Charles and explain this?'

'So I should have done had I not seen his death in the paper next morning.'

The woman's story hung coherently together, and all my questions were unable to shake it. I could only check it by finding if she had, indeed, instituted divorce proceedings against her husband at or about the time of the tragedy.

It was unlikely that she would dare to say that she had not been to Baskerville Hall if she really had been, for a trap* would be necessary to take her there, and could not have returned to Coombe Tracey until the early hours of the morning. Such an excursion could not be kept secret. The probability was, therefore, that she was telling the truth, or, at least, a part of the truth. I came away baffled and disheartened. Once again I had reached that dead wall which seemed to be built across every path by which I tried to get at the object of my mission. And yet the more I thought of the lady's face and of her manner the more I felt that something was being held back from me. Why should she turn so pale? Why should she fight against every admission until it was forced from her? Why should she have been so reticent at the time of the tragedy? Surely the explanation of all this could not be as innocent as she would have me believe. For the moment I could proceed no farther in that direction, but must turn back to that other clue which was to be sought for among the stone huts upon the moor.*

And that was a most vague direction. I realized it as I drove back and noted how hill after hill showed traces of the ancient people. Barrymore's only indication had been that the stranger lived in one of these abandoned huts, and many hundreds of them are scattered throughout the length and breadth of the moor. But I had my own experience for a guide, since it had shown me the man himself standing upon the summit of the Black Tor. That, then, should be the centre of my search. From there I should explore every hut upon the moor until I lighted upon the right one. If this man were inside it I should find out from his own lips, at the point of my revolver if necessary, who he was and why he had dogged us so long. He might slip away from us in the crowd of Regent Street, but it would puzzle him to do so upon the lonely moor. On the other hand, if I should find the hut, and its tenant should not be within it, I must remain there, however long the vigil, until he returned. Holmes had missed him in London. It would indeed be a triumph for me if I could run him to earth* where my master had failed.

Luck had been against us again and again in this inquiry, but now at last it came to my aid. And the messenger of good fortune was none other than Mr Frankland, who was standing, grey-whiskered and red-faced,* outside the gate of his garden, which opened on to the high road along which I travelled.

'Good-day, Dr Watson,' cried he, with unwonted good humour, 'you must really give your horses a rest, and come in to have a glass of wine and to congratulate me.'

My feelings towards him were far from being friendly after what I had heard of his treatment of his daughter, but I was anxious to send Perkins and the wagonette* home, and the opportunity was a good one. I alighted and sent a message to Sir Henry that I should walk over in time for dinner. Then I followed Frankland into his dining-room.

'It is a great day for me, sir—one of the red-letter days of my life,' he cried, with many chuckles. 'I have brought off a double event. I mean to teach them in these parts that law is law, and that there is a man here who does not fear to invoke it. I have established a right of way through the centre of old Middleton's park, slap across it, sir, within a hundred yards of his own front door. What do you think of that? We'll teach these magnates* that they cannot ride rough-shod over the rights of the commoners, confound them! And I've closed the wood where the Fernworthy folk used to picnic. These infernal people seem to think that there are no rights of property, and that they can swarm where they like with their papers and their bottles. Both cases decided, Dr Watson, and both in my favour. I haven't had such a day since I had Sir John Morland* for trespass, because he shot in his own warren.'

'How on earth did you do that?'

'Look it up in the books, sir. It will repay reading—Frankland *v.* Morland, Court of Queen's Bench. It cost me £200, but I got my verdict.'

'Did it do you any good?'

'None, sir, none. I am proud to say that I had no interest in the matter. I act entirely from a sense of public duty. I have no doubt, for example, that the Fernworthy people will burn me in effigy to-night. I told the police last time they did it that they should stop these disgraceful exhibitions. The county constabulary is in a scandalous state, sir, and it has not afforded me the protection to which I am entitled. The case of Frankland *v.* Regina* will bring the matter before the attention of the public. I told them that they would have occasion to regret their treatment of me, and already my words have come true.'

'How so?' I asked.

The old man put on a very knowing expression.

'Because I could tell them what they are dying to know; but nothing would induce me to help the rascals in any way.'

I had been casting round for some excuse by which I could get away from his gossip, but now I began to wish to hear more of it. I had seen enough of the contrary nature of the old sinner to understand that any strong sign of interest would be the surest way to stop his confidences.

'Some poaching case, no doubt?' said I, with an indifferent manner.

'Ha, ha, my boy, a very much more important matter than that! What about the convict on the moor?'

I started. 'You don't mean that you know where he is?' said I.

'I may not know exactly where he is, but I am quite sure that I could help the police to lay their hands on him. Has it never struck you that the way to catch that man was to find out where he got his food, and so trace it to him?'

He certainly seemed to be getting uncomfortably near the truth. 'No doubt,' said I; 'but how do you know that he is anywhere upon the moor?'

'I know it because I have seen with my own eyes the messenger who takes him his food.'

My heart sank for Barrymore. It was a serious thing to be in the power of this spiteful old busybody. But his next remark took a weight from my mind.

'You'll be surprised to hear that his food is taken to him by a child. I see him every day through my telescope upon the roof. He passes along the same path at the same hour, and to whom should he be going except to the convict?'

Here was luck indeed! And yet I suppressed all appearance of interest. A child! Barrymore had said that our unknown was supplied by a boy. It was on his track, and not upon the convict's, that Frankland had stumbled. If I could get his knowledge it might save me a long and weary hunt. But incredulity and indifference were evidently my strongest cards.

'I should say that it was much more likely that it was the son of one of the moorland shepherds taking out his father's dinner.'

The least appearance of opposition struck fire out of the old autocrat. His eyes looked malignantly at me, and his grey whiskers bristled like those of an angry cat.

'Indeed, sir!' said he, pointing out over the wide-stretching moor. 'Do you see that Black Tor over yonder? Well, do you see the low hill beyond with the thorn-bush upon it? It is the stoniest part of the whole moor. Is that a place where a shepherd would be likely to take his station? Your suggestion, sir, is a most absurd one.'

I meekly answered that I had spoken without knowing all the facts. My submission pleased him and led him to further confidences.

'You may be sure, sir, that I have very good grounds before I come to an opinion. I have seen the boy again and again with his bundle. Every day, and sometimes twice a day, I have been able—but wait a moment, Dr Watson. Do my eyes deceive me, or is there at the present moment something moving upon that hillside?'

It was several miles off, but I could distinctly see a small dark dot against the dull green and grey.

'Come, sir, come!' cried Frankland, rushing upstairs. 'You will see with your own eyes and judge for yourself.'

The telescope, a formidable instrument mounted upon a tripod, stood upon the flat leads of the house.* Frankland clapped his eye to it and gave a cry of satisfaction.

'Quick, Dr Watson, quick, before he passes over the hill!'

There he was, sure enough, a small urchin with a little bundle upon his shoulder, toiling slowly up the hill. When he reached the crest I saw the ragged, uncouth figure outlined for an instant against the cold blue sky. He looked round him, with a furtive and stealthy air, as one who dreads pursuit. Then he vanished over the hill.

'Well! Am I right?'

'Certainly, there is a boy who seems to have some secret errand.'

'And what the errand is even a county constable could guess. But not one word shall they have from me, and I bind you to secrecy also, Dr Watson. Not a word! You understand?'

'Just as you wish.'

'They have treated me shamefully—shamefully. When the facts come out in Frankland *v.* Regina I venture to think that a thrill of indignation will run through the country. Nothing would induce me to help the police in any way. For all they cared it might have been me, instead of my effigy, which these rascals burned at the stake. Surely you are not going! You will help me to empty the decanter in honour of this great occasion!'

But I resisted all his solicitations and succeeded in dissuading him from his announced intention of walking home with me. I kept the road as long as his eye was on me, and then I struck off across the moor and made for the stony hill over which the boy had disappeared. Everything was working in my favour, and I swore that it should not be through lack of energy or perseverance that I should miss the chance which Fortune had thrown in my way.

The sun was already sinking when I reached the summit of the hill, and the long slopes beneath me were all golden-green on one side and grey shadow on the other. A haze lay low upon the farthest sky-line, out of which jutted the fantastic shapes of Belliver and Vixen Tor.* Over the wide expanse there was no sound and no movement. One great grey bird, a gull or curlew,* soared aloft in the blue heaven. He and I seemed to be the only living things between the huge arch of the sky and the desert beneath it. The barren scene, the sense of loneliness, and the mystery and urgency of my task all struck a chill into my heart. The boy was nowhere to be seen. But down beneath me in a cleft of the hills there was a circle of the old stone huts, and in the middle of them there was one which retained sufficient roof to act as a screen against the weather. My heart leaped within me as I saw it. This must be the burrow where the stranger lurked. At last my foot was on the threshold of his hiding-place—his secret was within my grasp.

As I approached the hut, walking as warily as Stapleton would do when with poised net he drew near the settled butterfly, I satisfied myself that the place had indeed been used as a habitation. A vague pathway among the boulders led to the dilapidated opening which served as a door. All was silent within. The unknown might be lurking there, or he might be prowling on the moor. My nerves tingled with the sense of adventure. Throwing aside my cigarette, I closed my hand upon the butt of my revolver, and, walking swiftly up to the door, I looked in. The place was empty.

But there were ample signs that I had not come upon a false scent. This was certainly where the man lived. Some blankets rolled in a waterproof lay upon that very stone slab upon which neolithic man had once slumbered. The ashes of a fire were heaped in a rude grate. Beside it lay some cooking utensils and a bucket half-full of water. A litter of empty tins showed that the place had been occupied for some time, and I saw, as my eyes became accustomed to the chequered light,* a pannikin* and a half-full bottle of spirits standing in the corner. In the middle of the hut a flat stone served the purpose of a table, and upon this stood a small cloth bundle—the same, no doubt, which I had seen through the telescope upon the shoulder of the boy. It contained a loaf of bread, a tinned tongue, and two tins of preserved peaches. As I set it down again, after having examined it, my heart leaped to see that beneath it there lay a sheet of paper with writing upon it. I raised it, and this was what I read, roughly scrawled in pencil:

'Dr Watson has gone to Coombe Tracey.'

For a minute I stood there with the paper in my hands thinking out the meaning of this curt message. It was I, then, and not Sir Henry, who was being dogged by this secret man. He had not followed me himself, but he had set an agent—the boy, perhaps—upon my track, and this was his report. Possibly I had taken no step since I had been upon the moor which had not been observed and repeated. Always there was this feeling of an unseen force, a fine net drawn round us with infinite skill and delicacy, holding us so lightly that it was only at some supreme moment that one realized that one was indeed entangled in its meshes.

If there was one report there might be others, so I looked round the hut in search of them. There was no trace, however, of anything of the kind, nor could I discover any sign which might indicate the character or intentions of the man who lived in this singular place, save that he must be of Spartan habits,* and cared little for the comforts of life. When I thought of the heavy rains and looked at the gaping roof I understood how strong and immutable must be the purpose which had kept him in that inhospitable abode. Was he our malignant enemy, or was he by chance our guardian angel? I swore that I would not leave the hut until I knew.

Outside the sun was sinking low and the west was blazing with scarlet and gold. Its reflection was shot back in ruddy patches by the distant pools which lay amid the Great Grimpen Mire. There were the two towers of Baskerville Hall, and there a distant blur of smoke which marked the village of Grimpen. Between the two, behind the hill, was the house of the Stapletons. All was sweet and mellow and peaceful in the golden evening light, and yet as I looked at them my soul shared none of the peace of Nature, but quivered at the vagueness and the terror of that interview which every instant was bringing nearer.* With tingling nerves, but a fixed purpose, I sat in the dark recess of the hut and waited with sombre patience for the coming of its tenant.

And then at last I heard him. Far away came the sharp clink of a boot striking upon a stone. Then another and yet another, coming nearer and nearer. I shrank back into the darkest corner, and cocked the pistol in my pocket, determined not to discover myself until I had an opportunity of seeing something of the stranger. There was a long pause, which showed that he had stopped. Then once more the footsteps approached and a shadow fell across the opening of the hut.

'It is a lovely evening, my dear Watson,' said a well-known voice. 'I really think that you will be more comfortable outside than in.'*

CHAPTER 12

DEATH ON THE MOOR

FOR a moment or two I sat breathless, hardly able to believe my ears. Then my senses and my voice came back to me, while a crushing weight of responsibility seemed in an instant to be lifted from my soul. That cold, incisive, ironical voice could belong to but one man in all the world.

'Holmes!' I cried—'Holmes!'

'Come out,' said he, 'and please be careful with the revolver.'

I stooped under the rude lintel, and there he sat upon a stone outside, his grey eyes dancing with amusement as they fell upon my astonished features. He was thin and worn, but clear and alert, his keen face bronzed by the sun and roughened by the wind. In his tweed suit and cloth cap he looked like any other tourist upon the moor, and he had contrived, with that cat-like love of personal cleanliness which was one of his characteristics, that his chin should be as smooth and his linen as perfect as if he were in Baker Street.

'I never was more glad to see anyone in my life,' said I, as I wrung him by the hand.

'Or more astonished, eh?'

'Well, I must confess to it.'

'The surprise was not all on one side, I assure you. I had no idea that you found my occasional retreat, still less that you were inside it, until I was within twenty paces of the door.'

'My footprint, I presume?'

'No, Watson; I fear that I could not undertake to recognize your footprint amid all the footprints of the world. If you seriously desire to deceive me you must change your tobacconist; for when I see the stub of a cigarette marked Bradley, Oxford Street,* I know that my friend Watson is in the neighbourhood. You will see it there beside the path. You threw it down, no doubt, at that supreme moment when you charged into the empty hut.'

'Exactly.'

'I thought as much—and knowing your admirable tenacity, I was convinced that you were sitting in ambush, a weapon within reach, waiting for the tenant to return. So you actually thought that I was the criminal?'

'I did not know who you were, but I was determined to find out.'

'Excellent, Watson! And how did you localize me? You saw me, perhaps, on the night of the convict hunt, when I was so imprudent as to allow the moon to rise behind me?'

'Yes, I saw you then.'

'And have, no doubt, searched all the huts until you came to this one?'

'No, your boy had been observed, and that gave me a guide where to look.'

'The old gentleman with the telescope, no doubt. I could not make it out when first I saw the light flashing upon the lens.' He rose and peeped into the hut. 'Ha, I see that Cartwright has brought up some supplies. What's this paper? So you have been to Coombe Tracey, have you?'

'Yes.'

'To see Mrs Laura Lyons?'

'Exactly.'

'Well done! Our researches have evidently been running on parallel lines, and when we unite our results I expect we shall have a fairly full knowledge of the case.'

'Well, I am glad from my heart that you are here, for indeed the responsibility and the mystery were both becoming too much for my nerves. But how in the name of wonder did you come here, and what have you been doing? I thought that you were in Baker Street working out that case of blackmailing.'

'That was what I wished you to think.'

'Then you use me, and yet do not trust me!' I cried, with some bitterness. 'I think that I have deserved better at your hands, Holmes.'

'My dear fellow, you have been invaluable to me in this as in many other cases, and I beg that you will forgive me if I have seemed to play a trick upon you. In truth, it was partly for your own sake that I did it, and it was my appreciation of the danger which you ran which led me to come down and examine the matter for myself. Had I been with Sir Henry and you it is evident that my point of view would have been the same as yours, and my presence would have warned our very formidable opponents to be on their guard. As it is, I have been able to get about as I could not possibly have done had I been living at the Hall, and I remain an unknown factor in the business, ready to throw in all my weight at a critical moment.'

'But why keep me in the dark?'

'For you to know could not have helped us, and might possibly have led to my discovery. You would have wished to tell me something, or in your kindness you would have brought me out some comfort or other, and so an unnecessary risk would be run. I brought Cartwright down with me—you remember the little chap at the Express office—and he has seen after my simple wants: a loaf of bread and a clean collar. What does man want more? He has given me an extra pair of eyes upon a very active pair of feet, and both have been invaluable.'

'Then my reports have all been wasted!' My voice trembled as I recalled the pains and the pride with which I had composed them.

Holmes took a bundle of papers from his pocket.

'Here are your reports, my dear fellow, and very well thumbed, I assure you. I made excellent arrangements, and they are only delayed one day upon their way. I must compliment you exceedingly upon the zeal and the intelligence which you have shown over an extraordinarily difficult case.'

I was still rather raw over the deception which had been practised upon me, but the warmth of Holmes's praise drove my anger from my mind. I felt also in my heart that he was right in what he said, and that it was really best for our purpose that I should not have known that he was upon the moor.

'That's better,' said he, seeing the shadow rise from my face. 'And now tell me the result of your visit to Mrs Laura Lyons—it was not difficult for me to guess that it was to see her that you had gone, for I am already aware that she is the one person in Coombe Tracey who might be of service to us in the matter. In fact, if you had not gone to-day it is exceedingly probable that I should have gone to-morrow.'

The sun had set and dusk was settling over the moor. The air had turned chill, and we withdrew into the hut for warmth. There, sitting together in the twilight, I told Holmes of my conversation with the lady. So interested was he that I had to repeat some of it twice before he was satisfied.

'This is most important,' said he, when I had concluded. 'It fills up a gap which I had been unable to bridge, in this most complex affair. You are aware, perhaps, that a close intimacy exists between this lady and the man Stapleton?'

'I did not know of a close intimacy.'

'There can be no doubt about the matter. They meet, they write, there is a complete understanding between them. Now, this puts a very powerful weapon into our hands. If I could use it to detach his wife—'

'His wife?'

'I am giving you some information now, in return for all that you have given me. The lady who has passed here as Miss Stapleton is in reality his wife.'

'Good heavens, Holmes! Are you sure of what you say? How could he have permitted Sir Henry to fall in love with her?'

'Sir Henry's falling in love could do no harm to anyone except Sir Henry. He took particular care that Sir Henry did not *make* love to her,* as you have yourself observed. I repeat that the lady is his wife and not his sister.'

'But why this elaborate deception?'

'Because he foresaw that she would be very much more useful to him in the character of a free woman.'

All my unspoken instincts, my vague suspicions, suddenly took shape and centred upon the naturalist. In that impassive, colourless man, with his straw hat and his butterfly-net, I seemed to see something terrible—a creature of infinite patience and craft, with a smiling face and a murderous heart.

'It is he, then, who is our enemy—it is he who dogged us in London?'

'So I read the riddle.'

'And the warning—it must have come from her!'

'Exactly.'

The shape of some monstrous villainy, half seen, half guessed, loomed through the darkness which had girt me so long.

'But are you sure of this, Holmes? How do you know that the woman is his wife?'

'Because he so far forgot himself as to tell you a true piece of auto-biography upon the occasion when he first met you, and I dare say he has many a time regretted it since. He *was* once a schoolmaster in the North of England. Now, there is no one more easy to trace than a schoolmaster. There are scholastic agencies by which one may iden-tify any man who has been in the profession. A little investigation showed me that a school had come to grief under atrocious circum-stances, and that the man who had owned it—the name was different—had disappeared with his wife. The description agreed. When I learned that the missing man was devoted to entomology the identi-fication was complete.'

The darkness was rising, but much was still hidden by the shadows.

'If this woman is in truth his wife, where does Mrs Laura Lyons come in?' I asked.

'That is one of the points upon which your own researches have shed a light. Your interview with the lady has cleared the situation very much. I did not know about a projected divorce between herself and her husband. In that case, regarding Stapleton as an unmarried man, she counted no doubt upon becoming his wife.'

'And when she is undeceived?'

'Why, then we may find the lady of service. It must be our first duty to see her—both of us—tomorrow. Don't you think, Watson, that you are away from your charge rather long? Your place should be at Baskerville Hall.'

The last red streaks had faded away in the west and night had set-tled upon the moor. A few faint stars were gleaming in a violet sky.

'One last question, Holmes,' I said, as I rose. 'Surely there is no need of secrecy between you and me. What is the meaning of it all? What is he after?'

Holmes's voice sank as he answered—'It is murder, Watson—refined, cold-blooded, deliberate murder. Do not ask me for par-ticulars. My nets are closing upon him, even as his are upon Sir Henry, and with your help he is already almost at my mercy. There is but one danger which can threaten us. It is that he should strike before we are ready to do so. Another day—two at the most—and I have my case complete, but until then guard your charge as closely as ever a fond mother watched her ailing child. Your mission to-day has justified itself, and yet I could almost wish that you had not left his side—Hark!'

A terrible scream—a prolonged yell of horror and anguish burst out of the silence of the moor. That frightful cry turned the blood to ice in my veins.

'Oh, my God!' I gasped. 'What is it? What does it mean?'

Holmes had sprung to his feet, and I saw his dark, athletic outline at the door of the hut, his shoulders stooping, his head thrust forward, his face peering into the darkness.

'Hush!' he whispered. 'Hush!'

The cry had been loud on account of its vehemence, but it had pealed out from somewhere far off on the shadowy plain. Now it burst upon our ears, nearer, louder, more urgent than before.

'Where is it?' Holmes whispered; and I knew from the thrill of his voice that he, the man of iron, was shaken to the soul. 'Where is it, Watson?'

'There, I think.' I pointed into the darkness.

'No, there!'

Again the agonized cry swept through the silent night, louder and much nearer than ever. And a new sound mingled with it, a deep, muttered rumble, musical and yet menacing, rising and falling like the low, constant murmur of the sea.

'The hound!' cried Holmes. 'Come, Watson, come! Great heavens, if we are too late!'

He had started running swiftly over the moor, and I had followed at his heels. But now from somewhere among the broken ground immediately in front of us there came one last despairing yell, and then a dull, heavy thud. We halted and listened. Not another sound broke the heavy silence of the windless night.

I saw Holmes put his hand to his forehead, like a man distracted. He stamped his feet upon the ground.

'He has beaten us, Watson. We are too late.'

'No, no, surely not!'

'Fool that I was to hold my hand. And you, Watson, see what comes of abandoning your charge! But, by Heaven, if the worst has happened, we'll avenge him!'

Blindly we ran through the gloom, blundering against boulders, forcing our way through gorse bushes, panting up hills and rushing down slopes, heading always in the direction whence those dreadful sounds had come. At every rise Holmes looked eagerly round him, but the shadows were thick upon the moor and nothing moved upon its dreary face.

'Can you see anything?'

'Nothing.'

'But hark, what is that?'

A low moan had fallen upon our ears. There it was again upon our left! On that side a ridge of rocks ended in a sheer cliff, which overlooked a stone-strewn slope. On its jagged face was spread-eagled some dark, irregular object. As we ran towards it the vague outline hardened into a definite shape. It was a prostrate man face downwards upon the ground, the head doubled under him at a horrible angle, the shoulders rounded and the body hunched together as if in the act of throwing a somersault. So grotesque was the attitude that I could not for the instant realize that that moan had been the passing of his soul. Not a whisper, not a rustle, rose now from the dark figure over which we stooped. Holmes laid his hand upon him, and held it up again, with an exclamation of horror. The gleam of the match which he struck shone upon his clotted fingers and upon the ghastly pool which widened slowly from the crushed skull of the victim. And it shone upon something else which turned our hearts sick and faint within us—the body of Sir Henry Baskerville!

There was no chance of either of us forgetting that peculiar ruddy tweed suit—the very one which he had worn on the first morning that we had seen him in Baker Street. We caught the one clear glimpse of it, and then the match flickered and went out, even as the hope had gone out of our souls. Holmes groaned, and his face glimmered white through the darkness.

'The brute! the brute!' I cried, with clenched hands. 'Oh, Holmes, I shall never forgive myself for having left him to his fate.'

'I am more to blame than you, Watson. In order to have my case well rounded and complete, I have thrown away the life of my client. It is the greatest blow which has befallen me in my career. But how could I know—how *could* I know—that he would risk his life alone upon the moor in the face of all my warnings?'

'That we should have heard his screams—my God, those screams!—and yet have been unable to save him! Where is this brute of a hound which drove him to his death? It may be lurking among these rocks at this instant. And Stapleton, where is he? He shall answer for this deed.'

'He shall. I will see to that. Uncle and nephew have been murdered—the one frightened to death by the very sight of a beast which he thought to be supernatural, the other driven to his end in his wild flight to escape from it. But now we have to prove the connection between the man and the beast. Save from what we heard, we cannot even swear to the existence of the latter, since Sir Henry has evidently died from the fall. But, by heavens, cunning as he is, the fellow shall be in my power before another day is past!'

We stood with bitter hearts on either side of the mangled body, overwhelmed by this sudden and irrevocable disaster which had brought all our long and weary labours to so piteous an end. Then, as the moon rose, we climbed to the top of the rocks over which our poor friend had fallen, and from the summit we gazed out over the shadowy moor, half silver and half gloom. Far away, miles off, in the direction of Grimpen, a single steady yellow light was shining. It could only come from the lonely abode of the Stapletons. With a bitter curse I shook my fist at it as I gazed.

'Why should we not seize him at once?'

'Our case is not complete. The fellow is wary and cunning to the last degree. It is not what we know, but what we can prove. If we make one false move the villain may escape us yet.'

'What can we do?'

'There will be plenty for us to do to-morrow. To-night we can only perform the last offices to our poor friend.'

Together we made our way down the precipitous slope and approached the body, black and clear against the silver stones. The agony of those contorted limbs struck me with a spasm of pain and blurred my eyes with tears.

'We must send for help, Holmes! We cannot carry him all the way to the Hall. Good heavens, are you mad?'

He had uttered a cry and bent over the body. Now he was dancing and laughing and wringing my hand. Could this be my stern, self-contained friend? These were hidden fires, indeed!

'A beard! A beard! The man has a beard!'

'A beard?'

'It is not the Baronet—it is—why, it is my neighbour, the convict!'

With feverish haste we had turned the body over, and that dripping beard was pointing up to the cold, clear moon. There could be no doubt about the beetling forehead,* the sunken animal eyes. It was indeed the same face which had glared upon me in the light of the candle from over the rock—the face of Selden, the criminal.

Then in an instant it was all clear to me. I remembered how the Baronet had told me that he had handed his old wardrobe to Barrymore. Barrymore had passed it on in order to help Selden in his escape. Boots, shirt, cap—it was all Sir Henry's. The tragedy was still black enough, but this man had at least deserved death by the laws of his country.* I told Holmes how the matter stood, my heart bubbling over with thankfulness and joy.

'Then the clothes have been the poor fellow's death,' said he. 'It is clear enough that the hound has been laid on from some article of Sir Henry's—the boot which was abstracted in the hotel, in all probability—and so ran this man down. There is one very singular thing, however: How came Selden, in the darkness, to know that the hound was on his trail?'

'He heard him.'

'To hear a hound upon the moor would not work a hard man like this convict into such a paroxysm of terror that he would risk recapture by screaming wildly for help. By his cries he must have run a long way after he knew the animal was on his track. How did he know?'

'A greater mystery to me is why this hound, presuming that all our conjectures are correct—'

'I presume nothing.'

'Well, then, why this hound should be loose to-night. I suppose that it does not always run loose upon the moor. Stapleton would not let it go unless he had reason to think that Sir Henry would be there.'

'My difficulty is the more formidable of the two, for I think that we shall very shortly get an explanation of yours, while mine may remain for ever a mystery. The question now is, what shall we do with this poor wretch's body? We cannot leave it here to the foxes and the ravens.'

'I suggest that we put it in one of the huts until we can communicate with the police.'

'Exactly. I have no doubt that you and I could carry it so far. Hullo, Watson, what's this? It's the man himself, by all that's wonderful* and audacious! Not a word to show your suspicions—not a word, or my plans crumble to the ground.'

A figure was approaching us over the moor, and I saw the dull red glow of a cigar. The moon shone upon him, and I could distinguish the dapper shape and jaunty walk of the naturalist. He stopped when he saw us, and then came on again.

'Why, Dr Watson, that's not you, is it? You are the last man that I should have expected to see out on the moor at this time of night. But, dear me, what's this? Somebody hurt? Not—don't tell me that is our friend Sir Henry!'

He hurried past me and stooped over the dead man. I heard a sharp intake of his breath and the cigar fell from his fingers.

'Who—who's this?' he stammered.

'It is Selden, the man who escaped from Princetown.'

Stapleton turned a ghastly face upon us, but by a supreme effort he had overcome his amazement and his disappointment. He looked sharply from Holmes to me.

'Dear me! What a very shocking affair! How did he die?'

'He appears to have broken his neck by falling over these rocks. My friend and I were strolling on the moor when we heard a cry.'

'I heard a cry also. That was what brought me out. I was uneasy about Sir Henry.'

'Why about Sir Henry in particular?' I could not help asking.

'Because I had suggested that he should come over. When he did not come I was surprised, and I naturally became alarmed for his safety when I heard cries upon the moor. By the way'—his eyes darted again from my face to Holmes's—'did you hear anything else besides a cry?'

'No,' said Holmes; 'did you?'

'No.'

'What do you mean then?'

'Oh, you know the stories that the peasants tell about a phantom hound, and so on. It is said to be heard at night upon the moor. I was wondering if there were any evidence of such a sound to-night.'

'We heard nothing of the kind,' said I.

'And what is your theory of this poor fellow's death?'

'I have no doubt that anxiety and exposure have driven him off his head. He has rushed about the moor in a crazy state and eventually fallen over here and broken his neck.'

'That seems the most reasonable theory,' said Stapleton, and he gave a sigh which I took to indicate his relief. 'What do you think about it, Mr Sherlock Holmes?'

My friend bowed his compliments.

'You are quick at identification,' said he.

'We have been expecting you in these parts since Dr Watson came down. You are in time to see a tragedy.'

'Yes, indeed. I have no doubt that my friend's explanation will cover the facts. I will take an unpleasant remembrance back to London with me to-morrow.'

'Oh, you return to-morrow?'

'That is my intention.'

'I hope your visit has cast some light upon those occurrences which have puzzled us?'

Holmes shrugged his shoulders. 'One cannot always have the success for which one hopes. An investigator needs facts, and not legends or rumours. It has not been a satisfactory case.'

My friend spoke in his frankest and most unconcerned manner. Stapleton still looked hard at him. Then he turned to me.

'I would suggest carrying this poor fellow to my house, but it would give my sister such a fright that I do not feel justified in doing it. I think that if we put something over his face he will be safe until morning.'

And so it was arranged. Resisting Stapleton's offer of hospitality, Holmes and I set off to Baskerville Hall, leaving the naturalist to return alone. Looking back we saw the figure moving slowly away over the broad moor, and behind him that one black smudge on the silvered slope which showed where the man was lying who had come so horribly to his end.

'We're at close grips at last,' said Holmes, as we walked together across the moor. 'What a nerve the fellow has! How he pulled himself together in the face of what must have been a paralysing shock when he found that the wrong man had fallen a victim to his plot. I told you in London, Watson, and I will tell you now again, that we have never had a foeman more worthy of our steel.'

'I am sorry that he has seen you.'

'And so was I at first. But there was no getting out of it.'

'What effect do you think it will have upon his plans, now that he knows you are here?'

'It may cause him to be more cautious, or it may drive him to desperate measures at once. Like most clever criminals, he may be too confident in his own cleverness and imagine that he has completely deceived us.'

'Why should we not arrest him at once?'

'My dear Watson, you were born to be a man of action. Your instinct is always to do something energetic. But supposing, for argument's sake, that we had him arrested to-night, what on earth the better off should we be for that? We could prove nothing against him. There's the devilish cunning of it! If he were acting through a human agent we could get some evidence, but if we were to drag this great dog to the light of day it would not help in putting a rope round the neck of its master.'

'Surely we have a case.'

'Not a shadow of one—only surmise and conjecture. We should be laughed out of court if we came with such a story and such evidence.'

'There is Sir Charles's death.'

'Found dead without a mark upon him. You and I know that he died of sheer fright, and we know also what frightened him; but how are we to get twelve stolid jurymen to know it? What signs are there of a hound? Where are the marks of its fangs? Of course, we know that a hound does not bite a dead body,* and that Sir Charles was dead before ever the brute overtook him. But we have to *prove* all this, and we are not in a position to do it.'

'Well, then, to-night?'

'We are not much better off to-night. Again, there was no direct connection between the hound and the man's death. We never saw the hound. We heard it; but we could not prove that it was running upon this man's trail. There is a complete absence of motive. No, my dear fellow; we must reconcile ourselves to the fact that we have no case at present, and that it is worth our while to run any risk in order to establish one.'

'And how do you propose to do so?'

'I have great hopes of what Mrs Laura Lyons may do for us when the position of affairs is made clear to her. And I have my own plan as well. Sufficient for to-morrow is the evil thereof;* but I hope before the day is past to have the upper hand at last.'

I could draw nothing further from him, and he walked, lost in thought, as far as the Baskerville gates.

'Are you coming up?'

'Yes; I see no reason for further concealment. But one last word, Watson. Say nothing of the hound to Sir Henry. Let him think that Selden's death was as Stapleton would have us believe. He will have a better nerve for the ordeal which he will have to undergo to-morrow, when he is engaged, if I remember your report aright, to dine with these people.'

'And so am I.'

'Then you must excuse yourself, and he must go alone. That will be easily arranged. And now, if we are too late for dinner, I think that we are both ready for our suppers.'*

CHAPTER 13

FIXING THE NETS

SIR HENRY was more pleased than surprised to see Sherlock Holmes, for he had for some days been expecting that recent events would bring him down from London. He did raise his eyebrows, however, when he found that my friend had neither any luggage nor any explanations for its absence. Between us we soon supplied his wants, and then over a belated supper we explained to the Baronet as much of our experience as it seemed desirable that he should know. But first I had the unpleasant duty of breaking the news of Selden's death to Barrymore and his wife. To him it may have been an unmitigated relief, but she wept bitterly in her apron. To all the world he was the man of violence, half animal and half demon; but to her he always remained the little wilful boy of her own girlhood, the child who had clung to her hand. Evil indeed is the man who has not one woman to mourn him.

'I've been moping in the house all day since Watson went off in the morning,' said the baronet. 'I guess I should have some credit, for I have kept my promise. If I hadn't sworn not to go about alone I might have had a more lively evening, for I had a message from Stapleton asking me over there.'

'I have no doubt that you would have had a more lively evening,' said Holmes, drily. 'By the way, I don't suppose you appreciate that we have been mourning over you as having broken your neck?'

Sir Henry opened his eyes. 'How was that?'

'This poor wretch was dressed in your clothes. I fear your servant who gave them to him may get into trouble with the police.'

'That is unlikely. There was no mark on any of them, so far as I know.'

'That's lucky for him—in fact, it's lucky for all of you, since you are all on the wrong side of the law in this matter. I am not sure that as a conscientious detective my first duty is not to arrest the whole household. Watson's reports are most incriminating documents.'

'But how about the case?' asked the baronet. 'Have you made anything out of the tangle? I don't know that Watson and I are much the wiser since we came down.'

'I think that I shall be in a position to make the situation rather more clear to you before long. It has been an exceedingly difficult and most complicated business. There are several points upon which we still want light—but it is coming, all the same.'

'We've had one experience, as Watson has no doubt told you. We heard the hound on the moor, so I can swear that it is not all empty superstition. I had something to do with dogs when I was out West, and I know one when I hear one. If you can muzzle that one and put him on a chain I'll be ready to swear you are the greatest detective of all time.'

'I think I will muzzle him and chain him all right if you will give me your help.'

'Whatever you tell me to do I will do.'

'Very good; and I will ask you also to do it blindly, without always asking the reason.'

'Just as you like.'

'If you will do this I think the chances are that our little problem will soon be solved. I have no doubt—'

He stopped suddenly and stared fixedly up over my head into the air. The lamp beat upon his face, and so intent was it and so still that it might have been that of a clear-cut classical statue, a personification of alertness and expectation.

'What is it?' we both cried.

I could see as he looked down that he was repressing some internal emotion. His features were still composed, but his eyes shone with amused exultation.

'Excuse the admiration of a connoisseur,' said he, as he waved his hand towards the line of portraits which covered the opposite wall. 'Watson won't allow that I know anything of art, but that is mere jealousy, because our views upon the subject differ.* Now, these are a really very fine series of portraits.'

'Well, I'm glad to hear you say so,' said Sir Henry, glancing with some surprise at my friend. 'I don't pretend to know much about these things, and I'd be a better judge of a horse or a steer* than of a picture. I didn't know that you found time for such things.'

'I know what is good when I see it, and I see it now. That's a Kneller,* I'll swear, that lady in the blue silk over yonder, and the stout gentleman with the wig ought to be a Reynolds.* They are all family portraits, I presume?'

'Every one.'

'Do you know the names?'

'Barrymore has been coaching me in them, and I think I can say my lessons fairly well.'

'Who is the gentleman with the telescope?'

'That is Rear-Admiral Baskerville, who served under Rodney in the West Indies.* The man with the blue coat and the roll of paper is Sir William Baskerville, who was Chairman of Committees of the House of Commons under Pitt.'*

'And this Cavalier* opposite to me—the one with the black velvet and the lace?'

'Ah, you have a right to know about him. That is the cause of all the mischief, the wicked Hugo, who started the Hound of the Baskervilles. We're not likely to forget him.'

I gazed with interest and some surprise upon the portrait.

'Dear me!' said Holmes, 'he seems a quiet, meek-mannered man enough, but I dare say that there was a lurking devil in his eyes. I had pictured him as a more robust and ruffianly person.'

'There's no doubt about the authenticity, for the name and the date, 1647, are on the back of the canvas.'

Holmes said little more, but the picture of the old roysterer* seemed to have a fascination for him, and his eyes were continually fixed upon it during supper. It was not until later, when Sir Henry had gone to his room, that I was able to follow the trend of his thoughts. He led me back into the banqueting-hall, his bedroom candle in his hand, and he held it up against the time-stained portrait on the wall.

'Do you see anything there?'

I looked at the broad plumed hat, the curling love-locks,* the white lace collar, and the straight severe face which was framed between them. It was not a brutal countenance, but it was prim, hard, and stern, with a firm-set, thin-lipped mouth, and a coldly intolerant eye.

'Is it like anyone you know?'

'There is something of Sir Henry about the jaw.'

'Just a suggestion, perhaps. But wait an instant!'

He stood upon a chair, and holding up the light in his left hand, he curved his right arm over the broad hat and round the long ringlets.

'Good heavens!' I cried, in amazement.

The face of Stapleton had sprung out of the canvas.

'Ha, you see it now. My eyes have been trained to examine faces and not their trimmings. It is the first quality of a criminal investigator that he should see through a disguise.'

'But this is marvellous. It might be his portrait.'

'Yes, it is an interesting instance of a throw-back,* which appears to be both physical and spiritual. A study of family portraits is enough to convert a man to the doctrine of reincarnation.* The fellow is a Baskerville—that is evident.'

'With designs upon the succession.'

'Exactly. This chance of the picture has supplied us with one of our most obvious missing links. We have him, Watson, we have him, and I dare swear that before to-morrow night he will be fluttering in our net as helpless as one of his own butterflies. A pin, a cork, and a card, and we add him to the Baker Street collection!' He burst into one of his rare fits of laughter as he turned away from the picture. I have not heard him laugh often, and it has always boded ill to somebody.

I was up betimes in the morning, but Holmes was afoot earlier still, for I saw him as I dressed coming up the drive.

'Yes, we should have a full day to-day,' he remarked, and he rubbed his hands with the joy of action. 'The nets are all in place, and the drag is about to begin. We'll know before the day is out whether we have caught our big, lean-jawed pike, or whether he has got through the meshes.'

'Have you been on the moor already?'

'I have sent a report from Grimpen to Princetown as to the death of Selden. I think I can promise that none of you will be troubled in the matter. And I have also communicated with my faithful Cartwright, who would certainly have pined away at the door of my hut as a dog does at his master's grave if I had not set his mind at rest about my safety.'

'What is the next move?'

'To see Sir Henry. Ah, here he is!'

'Good morning, Holmes,' said the baronet. 'You look like a general who is planning a battle with his chief of the staff.'

'That is the exact situation. Watson was asking for orders.'

'And so do I.'

'Very good. You are engaged, as I understand, to dine with our friends the Stapletons to-night.'

'I hope that you will come also. They are very hospitable people, and I am sure that they would be very glad to see you.'

'I fear that Watson and I must go to London.'

'To London?'

'Yes, I think that we should be more useful there at the present juncture.'

The baronet's face perceptibly lengthened. 'I hoped that you were going to see me through this business. The Hall and the moor are not very pleasant places when one is alone.'

'My dear fellow, you must trust me implicitly and do exactly what I tell you. You can tell your friends that we should have been happy to have come with you, but that urgent business required us to be in town. We hope very soon to return to Devonshire. Will you remember to give them that message?'

'If you insist upon it.'

'There is no alternative, I assure you.'

I saw by the Baronet's clouded brow that he was deeply hurt by what he regarded as our desertion.

'When do you desire to go?' he asked, coldly.

'Immediately after breakfast. We will drive in to Coombe Tracey, but Watson will leave his things as a pledge that he will come back to you. Watson, you will send a note to Stapleton to tell him that you regret that you cannot come.'

'I have a good mind to go to London with you,' said the Baronet. 'Why should I stay here alone?'

'Because it is your post of duty. Because you gave me your word that you would do as you were told, and I tell you to stay.'

'All right, then, I'll stay.'

'One more direction! I wish you to drive to Merripit House. Send back your trap, however, and let them know that you intend to walk home.'

'To walk across the moor?'

'Yes.'

'But that is the very thing which you have so often cautioned me not to do.'

'This time you may do it with safety. If I had not every confidence in your nerve and courage I would not suggest it, but it is essential that you should do it.'

'Then I will do it.'

'And as you value your life do not go across the moor in any direction save along the straight path which leads from Merripit House to the Grimpen Road, and is your natural way home.'

'I will do just what you say.'

'Very good. I should be glad to get away as soon after breakfast as possible, so as to reach London in the afternoon.'

I was much astounded by this programme, though I remembered that Holmes had said to Stapleton on the night before that his visit would terminate next day. It had not crossed my mind, however, that he would wish me to go with him, nor could I understand how we could both be absent at a moment which he himself declared to be critical. There was nothing for it, however, but implicit obedience; so we bade good-bye to our rueful friend, and a couple of hours afterwards we were at the station of Coombe Tracey and had dispatched the trap upon its return journey. A small boy was waiting upon the platform.

'Any orders, sir?'

'You will take this train to town, Cartwright. The moment you arrive you will send a wire to Sir Henry Baskerville, in my name, to say that if he finds the pocket-book which I have dropped he is to send it by registered post to Baker Street.'

'Yes, sir.'

'And ask at the station office if there is a message for me.'

The boy returned with a telegram, which Holmes handed to me. It ran:

Wire received. Coming down with unsigned warrant. Arrive five-forty—LESTRADE.

'That is in answer to mine of this morning. He is the best of the professionals,* I think, and we may need his assistance. Now, Watson, I think that we cannot employ our time better than by calling upon your acquaintance, Mrs Laura Lyons.'

His plan of campaign was beginning to be evident. He would use the baronet in order to convince the Stapletons that we were really gone, while we would actually return at the instant when we were likely to be needed. That telegram from London, if mentioned by Sir Henry to the Stapletons, must remove the last suspicions from their minds. Already I seemed to see our nets drawing close round that lean-jawed pike.

Mrs Laura Lyons was in her office, and Sherlock Holmes opened his interview with a frankness and directness which considerably amazed her.

'I am investigating the circumstances which attended the death of the late Sir Charles Baskerville,' said he. 'My friend here, Dr Watson, has informed me of what you have communicated, and also of what you have withheld in connection with that matter.'

'What have I withheld?' she asked defiantly.

'You have confessed that you asked Sir Charles to be at the gate at ten o'clock. We know that that was the place and hour of his death. You have withheld what the connection is between these events.'

'There is no connection.'

'In that case the coincidence must indeed be an extraordinary one. But I think that we shall succeed in establishing a connection after all. I wish to be perfectly frank with you, Mrs Lyons. We regard this case as one of murder, and the evidence may implicate not only your friend Mr Stapleton, but his wife as well.'

The lady sprang from her chair. 'His wife!' she cried.

'The fact is no longer a secret. The person who has passed for his sister is really his wife.'

Mrs Lyons had resumed her seat. Her hands were grasping the arms of her chair, and I saw that the pink nails had turned white with the pressure of her grip.

'His wife!' she said, again. 'His wife! He was not a married man.'

Sherlock Holmes shrugged his shoulders.

'Prove it to me! Prove it to me! And if you can do so—!' The fierce flash of her eyes said more than any words.

'I have come prepared to do so,' said Holmes, drawing several papers from his pocket. 'Here is a photograph of the couple taken in York* four years ago. It is endorsed "Mr and Mrs Vandeleur", but you will have no difficulty in recognising him, and her also, if you know her by sight. Here are three written descriptions by trustworthy witnesses of Mr and Mrs Vandeleur, who at that time kept St Oliver's private school. Read them, and see if you can doubt the identity of these people.'

She glanced at them, and then looked up at us with the set, rigid face of a desperate woman.

'Mr Holmes,' she said, 'this man had offered me marriage on condition that I could get a divorce from my husband. He has lied to me, the villain, in every conceivable way. Not one word of truth has he ever told me. And why—why? I imagined that all was for my own sake. But now I see that I was never anything but a tool in his hands. Why should I preserve faith with him who never kept any with me? Why should I try to shield him from the consequences of his own wicked acts? Ask me what you like, and there is nothing which I shall hold back. One thing I swear to you, and that is, that when I wrote the letter I never dreamed of any harm to the old gentleman, who had been my kindest friend.'

'I entirely believe you, madam,' said Sherlock Holmes. 'The recital of these events must be very painful to you, and perhaps it will make it easier if I tell you what occurred, and you can check me if I make any material mistake. The sending of this letter was suggested to you by Stapleton?'

'He dictated it.'

'I presume that the reason he gave was that you would receive help from Sir Charles for the legal expenses connected with your divorce?'

'Exactly.'

'And then after you had sent the letter he dissuaded you from keeping the appointment?'

'He told me that it would hurt his self-respect that any other man should find the money for such an object, and that though he was a poor man himself he would devote his last penny to removing the obstacles which divided us.'

'He appears to be a very consistent character. And then you heard nothing until you read the reports of the death in the paper?'

'No.'

'And he made you swear to say nothing about your appointment with Sir Charles?'

'He did. He said that the death was a very mysterious one, and that I should certainly be suspected if the facts came out. He frightened me into remaining silent.'

'Quite so. But you had your suspicions?'

She hesitated and looked down.

'I knew him,' she said. 'But if he had kept faith with me I should always have done so with him.'

'I think that on the whole you have had a fortunate escape,' said Sherlock Holmes. 'You have had him in your power and he knew it, and yet you are alive. You have been walking for some months very near to the edge of a precipice. We must wish you good morning now, Mrs Lyons, and it is probable that you will very shortly hear from us again.'

'Our case becomes rounded off, and difficulty after difficulty thins away in front of us,' said Holmes as we stood waiting for the arrival of the express from town. 'I shall soon be in the position of being able to put into a single connected narrative one of the most singular and sensational crimes of modern times. Students of criminology will remember the analogous incidents in Grodno, in Little Russia,* in the year '66, and of course there are the Anderson murders in North Carolina, but this case possesses some features which are entirely its own. Even now we have no clear case against this very wily man. But I shall be very much surprised if it is not clear enough before we go to bed this night.'

The London express came roaring into the station, and a small, wiry bulldog of a man* had sprung from a first-class carriage. We all three shook hands, and I saw at once from the reverential way in which Lestrade gazed at my companion that he had learned a good deal since the days when they had first worked together. I could well remember the scorn which the theories of the reasoner used then to excite in the practical man.*

'Anything good?' he asked.

'The biggest thing for years,' said Holmes. 'We have two hours before we need think of starting. I think we might employ it in getting some dinner, and then, Lestrade, we will take the London fog out of your throat by giving you a breath of the pure night air of Dartmoor. Never been there? Ah, well, I don't suppose you will forget your first visit.'

CHAPTER 14

THE HOUND OF THE BASKERVILLES

ONE of Sherlock Holmes's defects—if, indeed, one may call it a defect—was that he was exceedingly loth to communicate his full plans to any other person until the instant of their fulfilment. Partly it came no doubt from his own masterful nature, which loved to dominate and surprise those who were around him. Partly also from his professional caution, which urged him never to take any chances. The result, however, was very trying for those who were acting as his agents and assistants. I had often suffered under it, but never more so than during that long drive in the darkness. The great ordeal was in front of us; at last we were about to make our final effort, and yet Holmes had said nothing, and I could only surmise what his course of action would be. My nerves thrilled with anticipation when at last the cold wind upon our faces and the dark, void spaces on either side of the narrow road told me that we were back upon the moor once again. Every stride of the horses and every turn of the wheels was taking us nearer to our supreme adventure.

Our conversation was hampered by the presence of the driver of the hired wagonette, so that we were forced to talk of trivial matters when our nerves were tense with emotion and anticipation. It was a relief to me, after that unnatural restraint, when we at last passed Frankland's house and knew that we were drawing near to the Hall and to the scene of action. We did not drive up to the door, but got down near the gate of the avenue. The wagonette was paid off and ordered to return to Coombe Tracey* forthwith, while we started to walk to Merripit House.

'Are you armed, Lestrade?'

The little detective smiled. 'As long as I have my trousers I have a hip-pocket, and as long as I have my hip-pocket I have something in it.'

'Good! My friend and I are also ready for emergencies.'

'You're mighty close about this affair, Mr Holmes. What's the game now?'

'A waiting game.'

'My word, it does not seem a very cheerful place,' said the detective, with a shiver, glancing round him at the gloomy slopes of the hill and at the huge lake of fog which lay over the Grimpen Mire. 'I see the lights of a house ahead of us.'

'That is Merripit House and the end of our journey. I must request you to walk on tip-toe and not to talk above a whisper.'

We moved cautiously along the track as if we were bound for the house, but Holmes halted us when we were about two hundred yards from it.

'This will do,' said he. 'These rocks upon the right make an admirable screen.'

'We are to wait here?'

'Yes, we shall make our little ambush here. Get into this hollow, Lestrade. You have been inside the house, have you not, Watson? Can you tell the position of the rooms? What are those latticed windows at this end?'

'I think they are the kitchen windows.'

'And the one beyond, which shines so brightly?'

'That is certainly the dining-room.'

'The blinds are up. You know the lie of the land best. Creep forward quietly and see what they are doing—but for Heaven's sake don't let them know that they are watched!'

I tip-toed down the path and stooped behind the low wall which surrounded the stunted orchard. Creeping in its shadow, I reached a point whence I could look straight through the uncurtained window.

There were only two men in the room, Sir Henry and Stapleton. They sat with their profiles towards me on either side of the round table. Both of them were smoking cigars, and coffee and wine were in front of them. Stapleton was talking with animation, but the Baronet looked pale and distrait. Perhaps the thought of that lonely walk across the ill-omened moor was weighing heavily upon his mind.

As I watched them Stapleton rose and left the room, while Sir Henry filled his glass again and leaned back in his chair, puffing at his cigar. I heard the creak of a door and the crisp sound of boots upon gravel. The steps passed along the path on the other side of the wall under which I crouched. Looking over, I saw the naturalist pause at the door of an out-house in the corner of the orchard. A key turned in a lock, and as he passed in there was a curious scuffling noise from within. He was only a minute or so inside, and then I heard the key turn once more, and he passed me and re-entered the house. I saw him rejoin his guest and I crept quietly back to where my companions were waiting to tell them what I had seen.

'You say, Watson, that the lady is not there?' Holmes asked, when I had finished my report.

'No.'

'Where can she be, then, since there is no light in any other room except the kitchen?'

'I cannot think where she is.'

I have said that over the great Grimpen Mire there hung a dense, white fog. It was drifting slowly in our direction and banked itself up like a wall on that side of us, low, but thick and well defined. The moon shone on it, and it looked like a great shimmering ice-field, with the heads of the distant tors as rocks borne upon its surface. Holmes's face was turned towards it, and he muttered impatiently as he watched its sluggish drift.

'It's moving towards us, Watson.'

'Is that serious?'

'Very serious, indeed—the one thing upon earth which could have disarranged my plans. He can't be very long now. It is already ten o'clock. Our success and even his life may depend upon his coming out before the fog is over the path.'

The night was clear and fine above us. The stars shone cold and bright, while a half-moon bathed the whole scene in a soft, uncertain light. Before us lay the dark bulk of the house, its serrated roof and bristling chimneys hard outlined against the silver-spangled sky. Broad bars of golden light from the lower windows stretched across the orchard and the moor. One of them was suddenly shut off. The servants had left the kitchen. There only remained the lamp in the dining-room where the two men, the murderous host and the unconscious guest, still chatted over their cigars.

Every minute that white woolly plain which covered one half of the moor was drifting closer and closer to the house. Already the first thin wisps of it were curling across the golden square of the lighted window. The farther wall of the orchard was already invisible, and the trees were standing out of a swirl of white vapour. As we watched it the fog-wreaths came crawling round both corners of the house and rolled slowly into one dense bank, on which the upper floor and the roof floated like a strange ship upon a shadowy sea. Holmes struck his hand passionately upon the rock in front of us, and stamped his feet in his impatience.

'If he isn't out in a quarter of an hour the path will be covered. In half an hour we won't be able to see our hands in front of us.'

'Shall we move farther back upon higher ground?'

'Yes, I think it would be as well.'

So as the fog-bank flowed onwards we fell back before it until we were half a mile from the house, and still that dense white sea, with the moon silvering its upper edge, swept slowly and inexorably on.

'We are going too far,' said Holmes. 'We dare not take the chance of his being overtaken before he can reach us. At all costs we must hold our ground where we are.' He dropped on his knees and clapped his ear to the ground. 'Thank God,* I think that I hear him coming.'

A sound of quick steps broke the silence of the moor. Crouching among the stones, we stared intently at the silver-tipped bank in front of us. The steps grew louder, and through the fog, as through a curtain, there stepped the man whom we were awaiting. He looked round him in surprise as he emerged into the clear, star-lit night. Then he came swiftly along the path, passed close to where we lay, and went on up the long slope behind us. As he walked he glanced continually over either shoulder, like a man who is ill at ease.

'Hist!' cried Holmes, and I heard the sharp click of a cocking pistol. 'Look out! It's coming!'

There was a thin, crisp, continuous patter from somewhere in the heart of that crawling bank. The cloud was within fifty yards of where we lay, and we glared at it, all three, uncertain what horror was about to break from the heart of it. I was at Holmes's elbow, and I glanced for an instant at his face. It was pale and exultant, his eyes shining brightly in the moonlight. But suddenly they started forward in a rigid, fixed stare, and his lips parted in amazement. At the same instant Lestrade gave a yell of terror and threw himself face downwards upon the ground. I sprang to my feet, my inert hand grasping my pistol, my mind paralysed by the dreadful shape which had sprung out upon us from the shadows of the fog. A hound it was, an enormous coal-black hound, but not such a hound as mortal eyes have ever seen. Fire burst from its open mouth, its eyes glowed with a smouldering glare, its muzzle and hackles and dewlap* were outlined in flickering flame. Never in the delirious dream of a disordered brain could anything more savage, more appalling, more hellish, be conceived than that dark form and savage face which broke upon us out of the wall of fog.*

With long bounds the huge black creature was leaping down the track, following hard upon the footsteps of our friend. So paralysed were we by the apparition that we allowed him to pass before we had recovered our nerve. Then Holmes and I both fired together, and the creature gave a hideous howl, which showed that one at least had hit him. He did not pause, however, but bounded onwards. Far away on the path we saw Sir Henry looking back, his face white in the moonlight, his hands raised in horror, glaring helplessly at the frightful thing which was hunting him down.

But that cry of pain from the hound had blown all our fears to the winds. If he was vulnerable he was mortal, and if we could wound him we could kill him. Never have I seen a man run as Holmes ran that night. I am reckoned fleet of foot, but he outpaced me as much as I outpaced the little professional. In front of us as we flew up the track we heard scream after scream from Sir Henry and the deep roar of the hound. I was in time to see the beast spring upon its victim, hurl him to the ground and worry at his throat. But the next instant Holmes had emptied five barrels* of his revolver into the creature's flank. With a last howl of agony and a vicious snap in the air it rolled upon its back, four feet pawing furiously, and then fell limp upon its side. I stooped, panting, and pressed my pistol to the dreadful, shimmering head, but it was useless to press the trigger. The giant hound was dead.

Sir Henry lay insensible where he had fallen. We tore away his collar, and Holmes breathed a prayer of gratitude when we saw that there was no sign of a wound and that the rescue had been in time. Already our friend's eyelids shivered and he made a feeble effort to move. Lestrade thrust his brandy-flask between the Baronet's teeth, and two frightened eyes were looking up at us.

'My God!' he whispered. 'What was it? What, in Heaven's name, was it?'

'It's dead, whatever it is,' said Holmes. 'We've laid the family ghost once and for ever.'

In mere size and strength it was a terrible creature which was lying stretched before us. It was not a pure bloodhound and it was not a pure mastiff; but it appeared to be a combination of the two*—gaunt, savage, and as large as a small lioness. Even now, in the stillness of death, the huge jaws seemed to be dripping with a bluish flame, and the small, deep-set, cruel eyes were ringed with fire. I placed my hand upon the glowing muzzle, and as I held them up my own fingers smouldered and gleamed in the darkness.

'Phosphorus,' I said.

'A cunning preparation of it,'* said Holmes, sniffing at the dead animal. 'There is no smell which might have interfered with his power of scent. We owe you a deep apology, Sir Henry, for having exposed you to this fright. I was prepared for a hound, but not for such a creature as this. And the fog gave us little time to receive him.'

'You have saved my life.'

'Having first endangered it. Are you strong enough to stand?'

'Give me another mouthful of that brandy, and I shall be ready for anything. So! Now, if you will help me up. What do you propose to do?'

'To leave you here. You are not fit for further adventures to-night. If you will wait, one or other of us will go back with you to the Hall.'

He tried to stagger to his feet; but he was still ghastly pale and trembling in every limb. We helped him to a rock, where he sat shivering with his face buried in his hands.

'We must leave you now,' said Holmes. 'The rest of our work must be done, and every moment is of importance. We have our case, and now we only want our man.

'It's a thousand to one against our finding him at the house,' he continued, as we retraced our steps swiftly down the path. 'Those shots must have told him that the game was up.'

'We were some distance off, and this fog may have deadened them.'

'He followed the hound to call him off—of that you may be certain. No, no, he's gone by this time! But we'll search the house and make sure.'

The front door was open, so we rushed in and hurried from room to room, to the amazement of a doddering old manservant, who met us in the passage. There was no light save in the dining-room, but Holmes caught up the lamp, and left no corner of the house unexplored. No sign could we see of the man whom we were chasing. On the upper floor, however, one of the bed-room doors was locked.

'There's someone in here!' cried Lestrade. 'I can hear a movement. Open this door!'

A faint moaning and rustling came from within. Holmes struck the door just over the lock with the flat of his foot, and it flew open. Pistol in hand, we all three rushed into the room.

But there was no sign within it of that desperate and defiant villain whom we expected to see. Instead we were faced by an object so strange and so unexpected that we stood for a moment staring at it in amazement.

The room had been fashioned into a small museum, and the walls were lined by a number of glass-topped cases full of that collection of butterflies and moths the formation of which had been the relaxation of this complex and dangerous man. In the centre of this room there was an upright beam, which had been placed at some period as a support for the old worm-eaten balk of timber which spanned the roof. To this post a figure was tied, so swathed and muffled in sheets which had been used to secure it that one could not for the moment tell whether it was that of a man or a woman. One towel passed round the throat, and was secured at the back of the pillar. Another covered the lower part of the face and over it two dark eyes—eyes full of grief and shame and a dreadful questioning—stared back at us. In a minute we had torn off the gag, unswathed the bonds, and Mrs Stapleton sank upon the floor in front of us. As her beautiful head fell upon her chest I saw the clear red weal of a whiplash across her neck.

'The brute!' cried Holmes. 'Here, Lestrade, your brandy-bottle! Put her in the chair! She has fainted from ill-usage and exhaustion.'

She opened her eyes again. 'Is he safe?' she asked. 'Has he escaped?'

'He cannot escape us, madam.'

'No, no, I did not mean my husband. Sir Henry? Is he safe?'

'Yes.'

'And the hound?'

'It is dead.'

She gave a long sigh of satisfaction. 'Thank God! Thank God! Oh, this villain! See how he has treated me!' She shot her arms out from her sleeves, and we saw with horror that they were all mottled with bruises. 'But this is nothing—nothing! It is my mind and soul that he has tortured and defiled. I could endure it all, ill-usage, solitude, a life of deception, everything, as long as I could still cling to the hope that I had his love, but now I know that in this also I have been his dupe and his tool.' She broke into passionate sobbing as she spoke.

'You bear him no good will, madam,' said Holmes. 'Tell us, then, where we shall find him. If you have ever aided him in evil, help us now and so atone.'

'There is but one place where he can have fled,' she answered. 'There is an old tin mine* on an island in the heart of the Mire. It was there that he kept his hound and there also he had made preparations so that he might have a refuge. That is where he would fly.'

The fog-bank lay like white wool against the window. Holmes held the lamp towards it.

'See,' said he. 'No one could find his way into the Grimpen Mire tonight.'

She laughed and clapped her hands. Her eyes and teeth gleamed with fierce merriment.

'He may find his way in, but never out,' she cried. 'How can he see the guiding wands to-night? We planted them together, he and I, to mark the pathway through the Mire. Oh, if I could only have plucked them out to-day! Then indeed you would have had him at your mercy!'

It was evident to us that all pursuit was in vain until the fog had lifted. Meanwhile we left Lestrade in possession of the house, while Holmes and I went back with the baronet to Baskerville Hall. The story of the Stapletons could no longer be withheld from him, but he took the blow bravely when he learned the truth about the woman whom he had loved. But the shock of the night's adventures had shattered his nerves, and before morning he lay delirious in a high fever, under the care of Dr Mortimer. The two of them were destined to travel together round the world before Sir Henry had become once more the hale, hearty man that he had been before he became master of that ill-omened estate.

And now I come rapidly to the conclusion of this singular narrative, in which I have tried to make the reader share those dark fears and vague surmises which clouded our lives so long, and ended in so tragic a manner. On the morning after the death of the hound the fog had lifted and we were guided by Mrs Stapleton to the point where they had found a pathway through the bog. It helped us to realize the horror of this woman's life when we saw the eagerness and joy with which she laid us on her husband's track. We left her standing upon the thin peninsula of firm, peaty soil which tapered out into the widespread bog. From the end of it a small wand planted here and there showed where the path zig-zagged from tuft to tuft of rushes among those green-scummed pits and foul quagmires which barred the way to the stranger. Rank reeds and lush, slimy water-plants sent an odour of decay and a heavy miasmatic* vapour into our faces, while a false step plunged us more than once thigh-deep into the dark, quivering mire, which shook for yards in soft undulations around our feet. Its tenacious grip plucked at our heels as we walked, and when we sank into it it was as if some malignant hand was tugging us down into those obscene depths, so grim and purposeful was the clutch in which it held us. Once only we saw a trace that someone had passed that perilous way before us. From amid a tuft of cotton-grass which bore it up out of the slime some dark thing was projecting. Holmes sank to his waist as he stepped from the path to seize it, and had we not been there to drag him out he could never have set his foot upon firm land again. He held an old black boot in the air. 'Meyers, Toronto', was printed on the leather inside.

'It is worth a mud bath,' said he. 'It is our friend Sir Henry's missing boot.'

'Thrown there by Stapleton in his flight.'

'Exactly. He retained it in his hand after using it to set the hound upon his track. He fled when he knew the game was up, still clutching it. And he hurled it away at this point of his flight. We know at least that he came so far in safety.'

But more than that we were never destined to know, though there was much which we might surmise. There was no chance of finding footsteps in the mire, for the rising mud oozed swiftly in upon them, but as we at last reached firmer ground beyond the morass we all looked eagerly for them. But no slightest sign of them ever met our eyes. If the earth told a true story, then Stapleton never reached that island of refuge towards which he struggled through the fog upon that last night. Somewhere in the heart of the great Grimpen Mire, down in the foul slime of the huge morass which had sucked him in, this cold and cruel-hearted man is for ever buried.

Many traces we found of him in the bog-girt island where he had hid his savage ally. A huge driving-wheel and a shaft half-filled with rubbish showed the position of an abandoned mine. Beside it were the crumbling remains of the cottages of the miners, driven away, no doubt, by the foul reek of the surrounding swamp. In one of these a staple and chain, with a quantity of gnawed bones, showed where the animal had been confined. A skeleton with a tangle of brown hair adhering to it lay among the *débris*.

'A dog!' said Holmes. 'By Jove, a curly-haired spaniel. Poor Mortimer will never see his pet again. Well, I do not know that this place contains any secret which we have not already fathomed. He could hide his hound, but he could not hush its voice, and hence came those cries which even in daylight were not pleasant to hear. On an emergency he could keep the hound in the outhouse at Merripit, but it was always a risk, and it was only on the supreme day, which he regarded as the end of all his efforts, that he dared do it. This paste in the tin is no doubt the luminous mixture with which the creature was daubed. It was suggested, of course, by the story of the family hell-hound, and by the desire to frighten old Sir Charles to death. No wonder the poor devil of a convict ran and screamed, even as our friend did, and as we ourselves might have done, when he saw such a creature bounding through the darkness of the moor upon his track. It was a cunning device, for, apart from the chance of driving your victim to his death, what peasant would venture to inquire too closely into such a creature should he get sight of it, as many have done, upon the moor? I said it in London, Watson, and I say it again now, that never yet have we helped to hunt down a more dangerous man than he who is lying yonder'—he swept his long arm towards the huge mottled expanse of green-splotched bog which stretched away until it merged into the russet slopes of the moor.

CHAPTER 15

A RETROSPECTION

It was the end of November, and Holmes and I sat, upon a raw and foggy night, on either side of a blazing fire in our sitting-room in Baker Street. Since the tragic upshot of our visit to Devonshire he had been engaged in two affairs of the utmost importance, in the first of which he had exposed the atrocious conduct of Colonel Upwood in connection with the famous card scandal* of the Nonpareil Club, while in the second he had defended the unfortunate Mme Montpensier from the charge of murder, which hung over her in connection with the death of her step-daughter, Mlle Carère, the young lady who, as it will be remembered, was found six months later alive and married in New York.* My friend was in excellent spirits over the success which had attended a succession of difficult and important cases, so that I was able to induce him to discuss the details of the Baskerville mystery. I had waited patiently for the opportunity, for I was aware that he would never permit cases to overlap,* and that his clear and logical mind would not be drawn from its present work to dwell upon memories of the past. Sir Henry and Dr Mortimer were, however, in London, on their way to that long voyage which had been recommended for the restoration of his shattered nerves. They had called upon us that very afternoon, so that it was natural that the subject should come up for discussion.

'The whole course of events,' said Holmes, 'from the point of view of the man who called himself Stapleton, was simple and direct, although to us, who had no means in the beginning of knowing the motives of his actions and could only learn part of the facts, it all appeared exceedingly complex. I have had the advantage of two conversations with Mrs Stapleton, and the case has now been so entirely cleared up that I am not aware that there is anything which has remained a secret to us. You will find a few notes upon the matter under the heading B in my indexed list of cases.'

'Perhaps you would kindly give me a sketch of the course of events from memory.'

'Certainly, though I cannot guarantee that I carry all the facts in my mind. Intense mental concentration has a curious way of blotting out what has passed. The barrister who has his case at his fingers' end, and is able to argue with an expert upon his own subject, finds that a week or two of the courts will drive it all out of his head once more. So each of my cases displaces the last, and Mlle Carère has blurred my recollection of Baskerville Hall. To-morrow some other little problem may be submitted to my notice, which will in turn dispossess the fair French lady and the infamous Upwood.* So far as the case of the Hound goes, however, I will give you the course of events as nearly as I can, and you will suggest anything which I may have forgotten.

'My inquiries show beyond all question that the family portrait did not lie, and that this fellow was indeed a Baskerville. He was a son of that Rodger Baskerville, the younger brother of Sir Charles, who fled with a sinister reputation to South America, where he was said to have died unmarried. He did, as a matter of fact, marry, and had one child, this fellow, whose real name is the same as his father. He married Beryl Garcia, one of the beauties of Costa Rica,* and, having purloined a considerable sum of public money, he changed his name to Vandeleur and fled to England, where he established a school in the east of Yorkshire.* His reason for attempting this special line of business was that he had struck up an acquaintance with a consumptive tutor upon the voyage home, and that he had used this man's ability to make the undertaking a success. Fraser, the tutor, died, however, and the school which had begun well, sank from disrepute into infamy. The Vandeleurs found it convenient to change their name to Stapleton, and he brought the remains of his fortune, his schemes for the future, and his taste for entomology to the south of England.

I learn at the British Museum that he was a recognized authority upon the subject, and that the name of Vandeleur has been permanently attached to a certain moth which he had, in his Yorkshire days, been the first to describe.

'We now come to that portion of his life which has proved to be of such intense interest to us. The fellow had evidently made inquiry, and found that only two lives intervened between him and a valuable estate. When he went to Devonshire his plans were, I believe, exceedingly hazy, but that he meant mischief from the first is evident from the way in which he took his wife with him in the character of his sister. The idea of using her as a decoy was clearly already in his mind, though he may not have been certain how the details of his plot were to be arranged. He meant in the end to have the estate, and he was ready to use any tool or run any risk for that end. His first act was to establish himself as near to his ancestral home as he could, and his second was to cultivate a friendship with Sir Charles Baskerville and with the neighbours.

'The Baronet himself told him about the family hound, and so prepared the way for his own death. Stapleton, as I will continue to call him, knew that the old man's heart was weak and that a shock would kill him. So much he had learned from Dr Mortimer. He had heard also that Sir Charles was superstitious and had taken this grim legend very seriously. His ingenious mind instantly suggested a way by which the Baronet could be done to death, and yet it would be hardly possible to bring home the guilt to the real murderer.

'Having conceived the idea, he proceeded to carry it out with considerable finesse. An ordinary schemer would have been content to work with a savage hound. The use of artificial means to make the creature diabolical was a flash of genius upon his part. The dog he bought in London from Ross and Mangles the dealers in Fulham Road.* It was the strongest and most savage in their possession. He brought it down by the North Devon line,* and walked a great distance over the moor, so as to get it home without exciting any remarks. He had already on his insect hunts learned to penetrate the Grimpen Mire, and so had found a safe hiding-place for the creature. Here he kennelled it and waited his chance.

'But it was some time coming. The old gentleman could not be decoyed outside of his grounds at night. Several times Stapleton lurked about with his hound, but without avail. It was during these fruitless quests that he, or rather his ally, was seen by peasants, and that the legend of the demon dog received a new confirmation. He had hoped that his wife might lure Sir Charles to his ruin, but here she proved unexpectedly independent. She would not endeavour to entangle the old gentleman in a sentimental attachment which might deliver him over to his enemy. Threats and even, I am sorry to say, blows failed to move her. She would have nothing to do with it, and for a time Stapleton was at a deadlock.

'He found a way out of his difficulties through the chance that Sir Charles, who had conceived a friendship with him, made him the minister of his charity in the case of this unfortunate woman, Mrs Laura Lyons. By representing himself as a single man, he acquired complete influence over her, and he gave her to understand that in the event of her obtaining a divorce from her husband he would marry her. His plans were suddenly brought to a head by his knowledge that Sir Charles was about to leave the Hall on the advice of Dr Mortimer, with whose opinion he himself pretended to coincide. He must act at once, or his victim might get beyond his power. He therefore put pressure upon Mrs Lyons to write this letter, imploring the old man to give her an interview on the evening before his departure for London. He then, by a specious argument, prevented her from going, and so had the chance for which he had waited.

'Driving back in the evening from Coombe Tracey, he was in time to get his hound, to treat it with his infernal paint, and to bring the beast round to the gate at which he had reason to expect that he would find the old gentleman waiting. The dog, incited by its master, sprang over the wicket-gate and pursued the unfortunate Baronet, who fled screaming down the Yew Alley. In that gloomy tunnel it must indeed have been a dreadful sight to see that huge black creature, with its flaming jaws and blazing eyes, bounding after its victim. He fell dead at the end of the alley from heart disease and terror. The hound had kept upon the grassy border while the baronet had run down the path, so that no track but the man's was visible. On seeing him lying still the creature had probably approached to sniff at him, but, finding him dead, had turned away again.* It was then that it left the print which was actually observed by Dr Mortimer. The hound was called off and hurried away to its lair in the Grimpen Mire, and a mystery was left which puzzled the authorities, alarmed the country-side, and finally brought the case within the scope of our observation.

'So much for the death of Sir Charles Baskerville. You perceive the devilish cunning of it, for really it would be almost impossible to make a case against the real murderer. His only accomplice was one who could never give him away, and the grotesque, inconceivable nature of the device only served to make it more effective. Both of the women concerned in the case, Mrs Stapleton and Mrs Laura Lyons, were left with a strong suspicion against Stapleton. Mrs Stapleton knew that he had designs upon the old man, and also of the existence of the hound. Mrs Lyons knew neither of these things, but had been impressed by the death occurring at the time of an uncancelled appointment which was only known to him. However, both of them were under his influence, and he had nothing to fear from them. The first half of his task was successfully accomplished, but the more difficult still remained.

'It is possible that Stapleton did not know of the existence of an heir in Canada. In any case he would very soon learn it from his friend Dr Mortimer, and he was told by the latter all details about the arrival of Henry Baskerville. Stapleton's first idea was that this young stranger from Canada might possibly be done to death in London without coming down to Devonshire at all. He distrusted his wife ever since she had refused to help him in laying a trap for the old man, and he dared not leave her long out of his sight for fear he should lose his influence over her. It was for this reason that he took her to London with him. They lodged, I find, at the Mexborough Private Hotel, in Craven Street,* which was actually one of those called upon by my agent in search of evidence. Here he kept his wife imprisoned in her room while he, disguised in a beard, followed Dr Mortimer to Baker Street, and afterwards to the station and to the Northumberland Hotel. His wife had some inkling of his plans; but she had such a fear of her husband—a fear founded upon brutal ill-treatment—that she dare not write to warn the man whom she knew to be in danger. If the letter should fall into Stapleton's hands her own life would not be safe. Eventually, as we know, she adopted the expedient of cutting out the words which would form the message, and addressing the letter in a disguised hand. It reached the Baronet, and gave him the first warning of his danger.

'It was very essential for Stapleton to get some article of Sir Henry's attire, so that, in case he was driven to use the dog, he might always have the means of setting him upon his track. With characteristic promptness and audacity he set about this at once, and we cannot doubt that the boots* or chambermaid of the hotel was well bribed to help him in his design. By chance, however, the first boot which was procured for him was a new one, and, therefore, useless for his purpose. He then had it returned and obtained another—a most instructive incident, since it proved conclusively to my mind that we were dealing with a real hound, as no other supposition could explain this anxiety to obtain an old boot and this indifference to a new one. The more *outré** and grotesque an incident is the more carefully it deserves to be examined, and the very point which appears to complicate a case is, when duly considered and scientifically handled, the one which is most likely to elucidate it.

'Then we had the visit from our friends next morning, shadowed always by Stapleton in the cab. From his knowledge of our rooms and of my appearance, as well as from his general conduct, I am inclined to think that Stapleton's career of crime has been by no means limited to this single Baskerville affair. It is suggestive that during the last three years there have been four considerable burglaries in the West Country, for none of which was any criminal ever arrested. The last of these, at Folkestone Court,* in May, was remarkable for the cold-blooded pistolling of the page, who surprised the masked and solitary burglar. I cannot doubt that Stapleton recruited his waning resources in this fashion, and that for years he has been a desperate and dangerous man.

'We had an example of his readiness of resource that morning when he got away from us so successfully, and also of his audacity in sending back my own name to me through the cabman. From that moment he understood that I had taken over the case in London, and that therefore there was no chance for him there. He returned to Dartmoor and awaited the arrival of the Baronet.'

'One moment!' said I. 'You have, no doubt, described the sequence of events correctly, but there is one point which you have left unexplained. What became of the hound when its master was in London?'

'I have given some attention to this matter, and it is undoubtedly of importance. There can be no question that Stapleton had a confidant, though it is unlikely that he ever placed himself in his power by sharing all his plans with him. There was an old manservant at Merripit House, whose name was Anthony. His connection with the Stapletons can be traced for several years, as far back as the schoolmastering days, so that he must have been aware that his master and mistress were really husband and wife. This man has disappeared and has escaped from the country. It is suggestive that Anthony is not a common name in England, while Antonio is so in all Spanish or Spanish-American countries.* The man, like Mrs Stapleton herself, spoke good English, but with a curious lisping accent. I have myself seen this old man cross the Grimpen Mire by the path which Stapleton had marked out. It is very probable, therefore, that in the absence of his master it was he who cared for the hound, though he may never have known the purpose for which the beast was used.

'The Stapletons then went down to Devonshire, whither they were soon followed by Sir Henry and you. One word now as to how I stood myself at that time. It may possibly recur to your memory that when I examined the paper upon which the printed words were fastened I made a close inspection for the water-mark. In doing so I held it within a few inches of my eyes, and was conscious of a faint smell of the scent known as white jessamine.* There are seventy-five perfumes, which it is very necessary that the criminal expert should be able to distinguish from each other, and cases have more than once within my own experience depended upon their prompt recognition. The scent suggested the presence of a lady, and already my thoughts began to turn towards the Stapletons. Thus I had made certain of the hound, and had guessed at the criminal before ever we went to the West Country.

'It was my game to watch Stapleton. It was evident, however, that I could not do this if I were with you, since he would be keenly on his guard. I deceived everybody, therefore, yourself included, and I came down secretly when I was supposed to be in London. My hardships were not so great as you imagine, though such trifling details must never interfere with the investigation of a case. I stayed for the most part at Coombe Tracey, and only used the hut upon the moor when it was necessary to be near the scene of action. Cartwright had come down with me, and in his disguise as a country boy he was of great assistance to me. I was dependent upon him for food and clean linen. When I was watching Stapleton, Cartwright was frequently watching you, so that I was able to keep my hand upon all the strings.

'I have already told you that your reports reached me rapidly, being forwarded instantly from Baker Street to Coombe Tracey. They were of great service to me, and especially that one incidentally truthful piece of biography of Stapleton's. I was able to establish the identity of the man and the woman, and knew at last exactly how I stood. The case had been considerably complicated through the incident of the escaped convict and the relations between him and the Barrymores. This also you cleared up in a very effective way, though I had already come to the same conclusions from my own observations.

'By the time that you discovered me upon the moor I had a complete knowledge of the whole business, but I had not a case which could go to a jury. Even Stapleton's attempt upon Sir Henry that night, which ended in the death of the unfortunate convict, did not help us much in proving murder against our man. There seemed to be no alternative but to catch him red-handed, and to do so we had to use Sir Henry, alone and apparently unprotected, as a bait. We did so, and at the cost of a severe shock to our client we succeeded in completing our case and driving Stapleton to his destruction. That Sir Henry should have been exposed to this is, I must confess, a reproach to my management of the case, but we had no means of foreseeing the terrible and paralysing spectacle which the beast presented, nor could we predict the fog which enabled him to burst upon us at short notice. We succeeded in our object at a cost which both the specialist and Dr Mortimer assure me will be a temporary one. A long journey may enable our friend to recover not only from his shattered nerves but also from his wounded feelings. His love for the lady was deep and sincere, and to him the saddest part of all this black business was that he should have been deceived by her.

'It only remains now to indicate the part which she had played throughout. There can be no doubt that Stapleton exercised an influence over her which may have been love or may have been fear, or very possibly both, since they are by no means incompatible emotions. It was, at least, absolutely effective. At his command she consented to pass as his sister, though he found the limits of his power over her when he endeavoured to make her the direct accessory to murder. She was ready to warn Sir Henry so far as she could without implicating her husband, and again and again she tried to do so. Stapleton himself seems to have been capable of jealousy, and when he saw the baronet paying court to the lady, even though it was part of his own plan, still he could not help interrupting with a passionate outburst which revealed the fiery soul which his self-contained manner so cleverly concealed. By encouraging the intimacy he made it certain that Sir Henry would frequently come to Merripit House, and that he would sooner or later get the opportunity which he desired. On the day of the crisis, however, his wife turned suddenly against him. She had learned something of the death of the convict, and she knew that the hound was being kept in the out-house on the evening that Sir Henry was coming to dinner. She taxed her husband with his intended crime and a furious scene followed, in which he showed her for the first time that she had a rival in his love. Her fidelity turned in an instant to bitter hatred, and he saw that she would betray him. He tied her up, therefore, that she might have no chance of warning Sir Henry, and he hoped, no doubt, that when the whole country-side put down the baronet's death to the curse of his family, as they certainly would do, he could win his wife back to accept an accomplished fact, and to keep silent upon what she knew. In this I fancy that in any case he made a miscalculation, and that, if we had not been there, his doom would none the less have been sealed. A woman of Spanish blood does not condone such an injury so lightly. And now, my dear Watson, without referring to my notes, I cannot give you a more detailed account of this curious case. I do not know that anything essential has been left unexplained.'

'He could not hope to frighten Sir Henry to death, as he had done the old uncle, with his bogie hound.'*

'The beast was savage and half-starved. If its appearance did not frighten its victim to death, at least it would paralyse the resistance which might be offered.'

'No doubt. There only remains one difficulty. If Stapleton came into the succession, how could he explain the fact that he, the heir, had been living unannounced under another name so close to the property? How could he claim it without causing suspicion and inquiry?'

'It is a formidable difficulty, and I fear that you ask too much when you expect me to solve it. The past and the present are within the field of my inquiry, but what a man may do in the future is a hard question to answer. Mrs Stapleton has heard her husband discuss the problem on several occasions. There were three possible courses. He might claim the property from South America, establish his identity before the British authorities there, and so obtain the fortune without ever coming to England at all; or he might adopt an elaborate disguise during the short time that he need be in London; or, again, he might furnish an accomplice with the proofs and papers, putting him in as heir, and retaining a claim upon some proportion of his income. We cannot doubt, from what we know of him, that he would have found some way out of the difficulty. And now, my dear Watson, we have had some weeks of severe work, and for one evening, I think, we may turn our thoughts into more pleasant channels. I have a box for *Les Huguenots*.* Have you heard the De Reszkes?* Might I trouble you then to be ready in half an hour, and we can stop at Marcini's* for a little dinner on the way?'

EXPLANATORY NOTES

ABBREVIATIONS

ACD   Arthur Conan Doyle

Baring-Gould   *The Annotated Sherlock Holmes*, 2 vols, ed. William S. Baring-Gould (London: John Murray, 1968).

BD   Sabine Baring-Gould, *A Book of Dartmoor* (London: Methuen, 1900).

Frayling   *The Hound of the Baskervilles*, edited with an introduction and notes by Christopher Frayling (London: Penguin, 2001).

Klinger   *The New Annotated Sherlock Holmes: The Novels*, edited with annotations by Leslie S. Klinger (New York: W. W. Norton, 2006).

Lycett   Andrew Lycett, *Conan Doyle: The Man who Created Sherlock Holmes* (London: Phoenix, 2007).

McClure   *The Hound of the Baskervilles* (New York: McClure, Phillips & Co., 1902). First US edition.

Newnes   *The Hound of the Baskervilles* (London: George Newnes, 1902). First edition in book form.

O'Gorman   *The Hound of the Baskervilles and 'The Adventure of the Speckled Band'*, ed. Francis O'Gorman (Peterborough, Ontario: Broadview, 2006).

OED   *Oxford English Dictionary*

Robson   *The Hound of the Baskervilles*, edited with an Introduction and Notes by W. W. Robson (Oxford: Oxford University Press, 1993).

SHCLS   *Sherlock Holmes: The Complete Long Stories* (London: John Murray, 1929).

SHCSS   *Sherlock Holmes: The Complete Short Stories* (London: John Murray, 1929).

Strand   *The Hound of the Baskervilles—Another Adventure of Sherlock Holmes, The Strand Magazine*, Aug. 1901–April 1902.

Weller   Philip Weller, *The Hound of the Baskervilles: Hunting the Dartmoor Legend* (Tiverton: Devon Books, 2001).

All Biblical quotations are from the King James Version.

DEDICATION PAGE

xlix *This story , , , A.C.D.*: dedication in *Strand*, Aug. 1901, p. 123.

xlix *MY DEAR ROBINSON . . . Haslemere*: dedication to Newnes. This
dedication is reproduced in *SHCLS*, where ACD adds the following gloss:
'Then came "The Hound of the Baskervilles." It arose from a remark by
that fine fellow, whose premature death was a loss to the world, Fletcher
Robinson, that there was a spectral dog near his home on Dartmoor. That
remark was the inception of the book, but I should add that the plot and
every word of the actual narrative was my own.'

MY DEAR ROBINSON . . . A. CONAN DOYLE: dedication to McClure.

3 *when he stayed up all night*: *Strand* has 'when he was up all night'. In
A Study in Scarlet, one of the first things that Watson observes about
Holmes is that 'his habits were regular. It was rare for him to be in bed
after ten at night' (*SHCLS*, 14).

'*Penang lawyer*': otherwise known as a Malacca cane; a walking-stick
made from a palm stem growing in the Penang district of the Malay
Peninsula, on the straits of Malacca in what is modern-day Malaysia.
Penang was under the control of the British East India Company from
1786, and formally a part of the British Empire from 1826. The implication of the phrase 'Penang lawyer' is that the cane could be used as
a weapon, to mete out summary justice in a remote and lawless corner of
the empire. In the Holmes story 'Silver Blaze' (1892), which is also set on
Dartmoor, Fitzroy Simpson carries 'a Penang lawyer, weighted with
lead', which is thought to be a murder weapon: ACD, 'Silver Blaze', in
SHCSS, 305–33.

MRCS: Member of the Royal College of Surgeons. Klinger (389) suggests
that this implies that Mortimer is a surgeon with no formal qualifications
to practise medicine, hence the description of him as a 'house-surgeon'
rather than a 'house-doctor' at Charing Cross Hospital, and as 'Medical
Officer' for Grimpen (p. 6), a role which usually, but not invariably, pre-
supposed a medical qualification.

ferrule: 'A ring or cap strengthening the end of a stick, tube, umbrella, etc.,
usually made of metal and used to prevent splitting of wearing' (*OED*).

4 '*Interesting, though elementary*': nowhere in ACD's stories does Holmes
utter the phrase 'Elementary, my dear Watson', though he says both
'elementary', and 'my dear Watson' on numerous occasions. William
Gillette's play *Sherlock Holmes* (1899) contained the line 'Elementary, my
dear fellow!' (at least, in some versions of the text). As Mattias Boström
writes, 'Despite its murky origins, "Elementary, my dear Watson" was so
well known in conjunction with Sherlock Holmes that by 1901 a parodist
had written a newspaper story in which his detective, Shylock Combs, said
to his colleague, "Elementary, my dear Potson": *The Life and Death of
Sherlock Holmes* (London: Head of Zeus, 2017), 182. It is therefore
entirely possible that ACD was aware of this catchphrase by the time he
wrote *Baskervilles*.

5 "*Charing Cross Hospital*": originally a hospital in Suffolk Street, near
Charing Cross, Central London. Founded in 1818 as the West London

Infirmary and Dispensary, its name was changed in 1827; it was formally incorporated into the University of London in 1911, and is now a part of Imperial College. In 1973, Charing Cross Hospital moved several miles west, to Fulham.

he could not have . . . the hospital: he did not hold a permanent position on the staff.

a house-surgeon or a house-physician: a junior doctor.

Medical Directory: *The British Medical Directory for England, Scotland and Wales* was founded in 1853, initially under the auspices of *The Lancet* (see note to p. 6).

6 *Grimpen*: fictitious Dartmoor village, though ACD likely derived the name from Grimspound, a notable Bronze Age settlement on Dartmoor, a few miles from Widecombe-on-the-Moor. Weller proposes the village of Hexworthy as the most likely real-life counterpart for Grimpen, though the novel's links to real-life places are as much suggestive as conclusive.

Jackson Prize for Comparative Pathology: 'the Jacksonian Prize of the Royal College of Surgeons in England . . . was founded in the year 1800, one of the conditions being that it should be open to competition only to the Fellows and members of the College': 'The Jacksonian Prize: A Retrospect', *British Medical Journal*, 1:1996 (1 April 1899), 818. The prize was named in honour of Col. Samuel Jackson, FRS, MRCS, and was awarded annually for a dissertation on a practical subject in surgery. Pathology is 'the branch of science that deals with the causes and nature of diseases and abnormal anatomical and physiological conditions' (*OED*).

'Is Disease a Reversion?': in a biological context, 'reversion' is 'The action or process of reverting to or towards an earlier type or form, esp. one that is less developed' (*OED*). Mortimer has a strong interest in Victorian physiognomical theories, and more generally in the science of human classification.

Corresponding member of the Swedish Pathological Society: a corresponding member of a society is one who lives far from its headquarters, and thus communicates by letter. The Swedish Pathological Society was (and remains) a genuine scientific body.

Atavism: in pathological terms, 'Recurrence of the disease or constitutional symptoms of an ancestor after the intermission of one or more generations' (*OED*). More generally, the return or revival of ancestral characteristics.

Lancet: major British medical journal, established by Thomas Wakley in 1823 specifically to report on metropolitan hospital lectures, and thus traditionally at the forefront of medical advancements.

Journal of Psychology: probably fictitious. There is a *Journal of Psychology*, though it was not founded until 1935. *The Psychological Review*, an American journal based in Princeton, was founded in 1894. *The British Journal of Psychology* was founded in 1904.

6 *Thorsley, and High Barrow*: fictitious Dartmoor parishes, though there is a Two Barrows near Widecombe, and a Three Barrows Tor near Shipley Bridge in South Dartmoor.

7 '*Mister . . . humble MRCS*': this might again imply that Mortimer is a surgeon rather than a doctor (see note to p. 3), though as 'a man of precise mind' (p. 7), Mortimer may rather be drawing attention to the fact that he does not have an MD degree, and thus is addressed as 'Doctor' as a matter of convention rather than qualification. ACD was acutely aware of the distinction, having chosen to write his own MD thesis (on syphilis) in 1885; as Lycett notes, 'He was proud to append these two letters [MD] to his name in the church register' (110). *A Study in Scarlet* is largely narrated by 'John H. Watson MD', and opens with the words 'In the year 1878 I took my degree of Doctor of Medicine from the University of London' (*SHCLS*, 3, 5).

a picker up . . . unknown ocean: Frayling, Klinger, O'Gorman, and Robson all agree that this is an allusion to a quotation from Isaac Newton: 'I do not know what I may appear to the world, but to myself I seem to have been only like a boy playing on the sea-shore, and diverting myself in now and then finding a smoother pebble or a prettier shell, whilst the great ocean of truth lay all undiscovered before me.' ACD likely encountered this in David Brewster, *Memoirs of the Life, Writings, and Discoveries of Sir Isaac Newton*, 2 vols (Edinburgh: Constable, 1855), vol. 2, p. 407. Brewster was the Principal of Edinburgh University, ACD's alma mater.

dolichocephalic . . . supra-orbital development . . . parietal fissure?: 'dolicocephalic' = 'long-headed'; 'supra-orbital development' = development above the eye-socket. That is, Holmes has an unusually high forehead. The parietal fissure, or sagittal suture, runs from back to front along the top of the skull, and separates the two parietal bones which join to make the cranium. ACD's writing shows a recurring interest in craniometry and phrenology (the study of the measurement and the shape of skulls). In *The Lost World* (1912), Professor Challenger sums up the narrator, Malone, as 'Round-headed . . . Bracycephalic, grey-eyed, black-haired, with a suggestion of the negroid. Celtic, I presume?' In turn, Malone remarks of Challenger, 'His head was enormous, the largest I have ever seen upon a human being.' ACD, *The Lost World* (London: Hodder and Stoughton, 1912), 45, 32.

anthropological museum: the discipline of anthropology—the scientific study of humanity—developed across the nineteenth century in part as a consequence of imperial expansion, with foundational works such as Edward Burnett Tylor's *Primitive Culture* (1871). The most famous British anthropological museum is the Pitt-Rivers Museum in Oxford, founded in 1884, which contains numerous human skulls, and (notoriously) a collection of shrunken heads.

8 *Monsieur Bertillon*: Alphonse Bertillon (1853–1914), chief of criminal identification for the Paris police from 1880; inventor of the 'Bertillon

System' of anthropometric criminal profiling, which included the development of the mugshot.

9 *the long s and the short*: as both Frayling and O'Gorman note, it is in practice impossible to date a manuscript with certainty using this method. While the long ∫ is certainly often associated with eighteenth-century typography, its use was inconsistent, and continued into the Victorian period.

10 *Great Rebellion . . . Lord Clarendon*: the Great Rebellion is the English Civil War (1642–51). The historian is Edward Hyde, 1st Earl of Clarendon (1609–74), author of *The History of the Rebellion and Civil Wars in England* (1702–4). As a testimony to Clarendon's influence, the term 'Great Rebellion' was a historiographical commonplace to describe the English Civil War until well into the twentieth century.

The West: the South-west of England.

Michaelmas: the feast of St Michael the Archangel, 29 September.

three leagues: a league is roughly the distance one could walk in an hour; the exact measurement of a league differed from country to country, but is generally reckoned at around 3 miles.

flagons and trenchers: wine containers and wooden plates.

11 *swung them to the line*: drove them all in the right direction.

a sound of galloping: *Strand* has 'a galloping'.

goyal: goyle; 'A deep trench, a ravine' (*OED*).

starting hackles: hair on the neck, back, or shoulders standing on end.

great stones: a Dartmoor feature. 'It is remarkable how greatly the set stones vary in size. Some are quite insignificant, and could be planted by a boy, while others require the united efforts of three, four, or even many men, with modern appliances of three legs and a block, to lift and place them in position. . . . There is no district so rich in stone rows as Dartmoor. As many as fifty have been observed' (BD, 60).

12 *Holy Writ*: 'I the LORD thy God *am* a jealous God, visiting the iniquity of the fathers upon the children unto the third and fourth *generation* of them that hate me' (Deuteronomy 5:9). ACD wrote a story entitled 'The Third Generation' (1894), in which a doctor is visited by a young nobleman who has contracted hereditary syphilis from his dissolute grandfather. Likewise, the Curse of the Baskervilles visits Hugo's iniquity upon his descendants.

'*To a collector of fairy-tales*': the collection of folklore was a significant Victorian endeavour. See Introduction, pp. xxxii–xxxiv.

Devon County Chronicle: fictitious, though there have been a number of similarly named newspapers in the region.

June 14th: 'May 14th' in *Strand*.

13 *probable Liberal candidate for Mid-Devon*: around the time of the publications of *Baskervilles*, ACD himself twice stood for parliament (1900, 1905)

as a Liberal Unionist candidate for Scottish constituencies; he was unsuccessful both times. (In 1886, the Liberal Party had split over the question of Irish Home Rule.) Currently, Dartmoor is shared between the parliamentary constituencies of Central Devon, and Torridge and West Devon. From 1330 to 1974, much of Dartmoor fell into the constituency of Tavistock. The dating of the action of *Baskervilles* is the subject of much discussion (see Klinger, 626–7), but if, as is commonly suggested, the novel takes place in 1888 or 1889, then the MP was the Liberal (and then Liberal Unionist) Viscount Ebrington. In 1902, the MP was the Liberal Unionist John Ward Spear. In the actual 1892 general election, in which Sir Charles would 'probably' have stood, Tavistock was indeed won by a 'Liberal candidate', Hugh Luttrell. Traditionally, the Liberal Party have performed strongly in Devon constituencies. Sir Charles Seale-Hayne, a family friend of the Robinsons, was MP for the nearby Devon constituency of Ashburton from 1885 to 1903.

13 *nouveaux riches*: the newly wealthy, who tended to be associated with vulgarity. Ironically, Sir Charles himself appears to be one of the *nouveaux riches*: see next note.

South African speculation: Sir Charles has made his fortune in South African gold. As the South African goldfields opened in the Transvaal in 1869, Sir Charles himself is *nouveau riche* (see previous note), in money if not in lineage.

14 *4th of June*: '4th of May' in *Strand*.

dyspnoea: difficulty of breathing.

coroner's jury: the coroner is in charge of an inquest in cases of unlawful or mysterious death. In English and Welsh law, a coroner's jury of 12 lay people traditionally adjudicated on cause of death at an inquest, though these were rarely convened after the 1920s, and according to the *Coroners Act* of 1988 are generally only to be summoned in cases of deaths in custody.

a tenant for Baskerville Hall: that is, an occupant; a 'tenant' does not, in this case, imply rented property.

15 *Vatican cameos . . . Pope*: the Pope from 1878 to 1903 was Leo XIII. There is no Holmes story of the Vatican cameos, though Holmes does 'oblige the Pope' by investigating the death of a cardinal in 'Black Peter' (1904). Cameos are engraved gems.

Lafter Hall: there is a Laughter Hole Farm (now derelict) on Dartmoor, near Postbridge.

Bushman and the Hottentot: more examples of Dr Mortimer's interest in racial science and other forms of human taxonomy. The Bushmen are the San, the aboriginal people of South Africa. The Hottentots are the Khokhoe, a nomadic Southern African people.

16 *gig*: 'A light, two-wheeled, one-horse carriage' (*OED*).

chimerical: imagined or fanciful.

17 *a gigantic hound!*: this was the end of the first instalment (April 1901) in *Strand*. O'Gorman persuasively argues for the influence of Francis Thompson's popular Victorian religious allegory 'The Hound of Heaven' on this passage, and also notes, 'By an amusing irony—perhaps Newnes's joke as he organized the layout of the edition in the first instalment of *The Hound of the Baskervilles* ended on p. 132 and facing it on p. 133 was the beginning of Lenore Van der Veer's "A School of Animal Painting" and a photograph of the artist with his very large but amiable dog at his feet' (69).

18 *wicket-gate*: 'any small gate for foot passengers, as at the entrance of a field or other enclosure' (*OED*). In this case, 'about four feet high'.

19 *after our own heart*: Holmes is an expert on the identification and meaning of tobacco ash. In *The Sign of the Four* (1890), he tells Watson, 'I have been guilty of several monographs. They are all upon technical subjects. Here, for example, is one "Upon the Distinction Between the Ashes of Various Tobaccos". In it I enumerate a hundred and forty forms of cigar, cigarette, and pipe tobacco, with coloured plates illustrating the difference in the ash. It is a point which is continually turning up in criminal trials, and which is sometimes of supreme importance as a clue' (*SHCLS*, 147). In *A Study in Scarlet*, Holmes observes that the murderer 'smoked a Trichinopoly cigar' (*SHCLS*, 36). More generally, smoking and tobacco is a frequently recurring motif throughout the Holmes stories; one of the first things he asks Watson when they meet, in *A Study in Scarlet*, is 'You don't mind the smell of strong tobacco, I hope?' (*SHCLS*, 12).

farrier: a blacksmith; specifically, one who shoes horses.

20 *Waterloo Station*: major London railway terminus on the south bank of the Thames. Waterloo was opened in 1848 by the London and South-Western Railway Company. Waterloo was the London terminus for trains from Southampton, the major transatlantic passenger port, where Sir Henry Baskerville has just docked.

trustee and executor: a trustee is a person into whose possession assets or property are placed for the benefit of another; an executor carries out the provisions of a will.

yellow fever: tropical disease, spread by mosquito bites.

wire: telegram.

21 *depends upon his presence*: since at least as far back as Maria Edgeworth's *The Absentee* (1812), the practice of absentee landlordism had been criticized in fiction, and in public discourse more generally; being a local squire carries local responsibilities.

parish vestry: a meeting of parishioners to decide upon parish matters.

22 *Bradley's . . . shag tobacco*: Bradley's is a fictitious tobacconist, later identified as being on Oxford Street (see note to p. 32); shag tobacco is 'A strong tobacco cut into fine shreds' (*OED*).

23 *'In spirit?'*: see Introduction p. xxv for a discussion of the meaning of this passage.

Stanford's . . . Ordnance map: *Strand* has 'Stamford's'. Stanford's is a celebrated London map and travel shop, established by Edward Stanford on the Strand in 1853, and then moving to a shop in Cockspur Lane, near Charing Cross. In 1901, Stanford's moved to its current address on Long Acre, Covent Garden. Established in 1791, the Ordnance Survey is the official British mapping agency, famous for its detailed and accurate maps.

large scale map: the Ordnance Survey's most detailed maps; traditionally, these were at a scale of six inches to the mile, or 1:10,560, but were metricized to 1:10,000 in 1969.

High Tor and Foulmire: both fictitious, though there is a Higher Tor on Dartmoor, as well as a Hound Tor, described in BD (175) as 'a noble mass of rocks. It derives its name from the shape assumed by the blocks on the summit, that have been weathered into forms resembling the heads of dogs peering over the natural battlements, and listening to hear the merry call of the horn.' Tors are rocks or piles of rocks on the top of a hill, often resembling human structures, and are very characteristic of Dartmoor topography.

24 *fourteen miles . . . Princetown*: Dartmoor Prison is in the remote village of Princetown, high on the moor, and is one of Britain's most famous prisons. It was established in 1809 to hold French prisoners in the Napoleonic Wars. Rebuilt as a criminal prison in 1850, Dartmoor housed some of Britain's worst criminals, as well as political prisoners and conscientious objectors. Dartmoor features regularly in ACD's work: for example, in the Napoleonic Brigadier Gerard story 'How the King Held the Brigadier' (1895), Gerard is imprisoned 'in the dreadful prison of Dartmoor': ACD, *The Exploits of Brigadier Gerard*, in *Historical Romances*, vol. 2 (London: John Murray, 1932), 508. In *The Sign of the Four*, the criminal Jonathan Small predicts that he will spend the rest of his life 'digging drains at Dartmoor' (*SHCLS*, 238). As Frayling notes, 'If the prison was *fourteen* miles away from Baskerville Hall, though, it would not be on the moor at all! This could well be an uncorrected printer's error for *four* miles, or one of Conan Doyle's slips of the pen' (173). Weller (26) notes that in his *The Book of the West*, Sabine Baring-Gould discusses the Devon habit of using the phrase 'fourteen miles' to signify any long distance.

25 *Baronet*: the lowest-ranked British hereditary title, and not formally a part of the peerage; created by King James I in 1611.

a ruddy-tinted tweed suit: Sir Henry's tweed suit, which is to play a significant role later in the novel, when it is worn by the escaped criminal Selden (see p. 110), was a last-minute addition to the novel by ACD, who wrote to *The Strand*'s editor Herbert Greenough Smith on 17 July 1901 (from the Esplanade Hotel, Southsea), requesting a change to this passage: 'I should like to convey that Sir Henry Baskerville wore "a ruddy-tinted tweed suit" ' (Frayling, xxx).

26 *Northumberland Hotel*: fictitious, though there is a Northumberland Street and a Northumberland Avenue in Central London: both are near Charing Cross. The Northumberland Arms public house on Northumberland Street has been suggested as the location: see Michael Harrison, *The London of Sherlock Holmes* (Newton Abbot: David and Charles, 1972), 204–5. The Northumberland Arms has been renamed the Sherlock Holmes, and contains a collection of Holmes memorabilia gathered together for the Festival of Britain in 1951, including the stuffed and mounted head of the Hound of the Baskervilles. In 'The Noble Bachelor' (1892), Francis Hay Moulton stays in 'one of the most expensive hotels . . . in London' (*SHCSS*, 247), which is in Northumberland Avenue. This is most likely the celebrated Hotel Metropole, opened in 1885, and a favourite haunt of King Edward VII, though *Baedeker's London and its Evirons 1900* (Leipzig: Karl Beideker, 1900), 8, recommends the Hotel Metropole, the Hotel Victoria, and the Grand Hotel as 'three large and handsomely furnished hotels in Northumberland Avenue'.

foolscap: standard-sized writing paper, 17 × 13.5 inches, so called because of the jester's cap formerly used as a watermark on such paper.

27 *Times*: major London newspaper, founded in 1785, initially as *The Daily Universal Register*.

Free Trade: the debate on free trade vs the imposition of 'a protective tariff' on foreign goods was a long and divisive one in British politics, most particularly exemplified in the Victorian period by the 1846 repeal of the Corn Laws, which had imposed tariffs on imported grain. From the 1840s, free trade was established as an economic principle across the British Empire. The issue of free trade was certainly on ACD's mind around the time of the publication of *Baskervilles*: in 1903–5, he wrote a series of letters to the press advocating trade protectionism: see ACD, *The Unknown Conan Doyle: Letters to the Press*, ed. John Michael Gibson and Roger Lancelyn Green (London: Secker & Warburg, 1986), 94–114. This was a debate which had split the Liberal Unionist Party following Joseph Chamberlain's support for the Tariff Reform League in 1903, and which led to the landslide victory of the free trade Liberals in the 1906 General Election.

28 *Esquimaux*: Eskimo; the indigenous population of the Arctic north.

supra-orbital crest . . . maxillary curve: the ridge above the eye socket, and the curve of the upper jaw.

leaded bourgeois type: bourgeois (pronounced 'bur-joyce' in this context) is a size of typeface; 'leaded' means that the lines of type were separated by metal strips, thus producing a higher-quality print than 'the slovenly print of an evening halfpenny paper'. Frayling (175) observes that '*The Times* was set in small Bourgeois, 9 point, 2 point leaded, a type-face known as "the modern face".'

The detection of types: typefaces, but also an allusion to the prevailing criminological theory, following the ideas of Cesare Lombroso (1835–1909), that there were distinct physiognomic criminal 'types' of facial and bodily feature.

28 *Leeds Mercury . . . Western Evening News*: the *Leeds Mercury* was initially founded in 1718, and was amalgamated with the *Yorkshire Post* (still a major regional newspaper) in 1939; the *Western Morning News* (also still in print) is a regional daily newspaper, founded in 1860, and published in Plymouth (where ACD lived for a time in 1882). As many commentators have noted, it is not easy to confuse these papers as they used significantly different typefaces. Robson (176) wonders whether ACD had in mind here not the *Leeds Mercury* but the *Western Daily Mercury*, another Plymouth-based newspaper.

29 *water-mark*: manufacturer's mark set into paper, visible when held up against the light.

30 *dime-novel*: a cheap and sensational American novel.

Strand: major Central London thoroughfare, running from Trafalgar Square to Fleet Street. Frayling (175) suggests that Sir Henry has been shopping for boots at G. H. Harris, 418 Strand, founded in 1865.

I must dress the part: the 'ruddy-tinted tweed suit' (p. 25) and tan boots are characteristic components of a gentleman's country attire.

31 *the pet story of the family*: that is, the favourite or special story, not (or not primarily) a story about pets.

32 *Oxford Street*: major Central London shopping street; Baker Street runs from north to south between Marylebone Road and Oxford Street.

Regent Street: major Central London shopping street, completed in 1825, and largely built to the designs of the architect John Nash (1752–1835). Regent Street intersects with Oxford Street (see previous note) at Oxford Circus.

hansom cab: 'A low-hung two-wheeled cabriolet holding two persons inside, the driver being mounted on a dickey or elevated seat behind, and the reins going over the roof' (*OED*).

34 *district messenger offices*: the District Messenger Service Company and other similar organizations were private companies for the sending and delivery of messages, telegrams, and parcels, generally by a body of 'messenger boys'.

Hotel Directory: there were numerous publications of this kind. Klinger (445) suggests either *The Official Hotel Directory and the Official Hotel Tariffs, Etc.* (London: J. P. Segg & Co., 1894), or *The XYZ Through Route Railway Guide and Hotel Directory* (London, 1884–6).

35 *Bond Street picture-galleries*: Bond Street is a high-end shopping street in Central London, running between Oxford Street and Piccadilly. The most celebrated of Bond Street's galleries was the Grosvenor Gallery, closely associated with progressive tendencies in Victorian painting, and particularly the works of Pre-Raphaelite painters such as John Everett Millais and Edward Burne-Jones, and of Whistler and the Aesthetic Movement.

due at the hotel: this was the end of the second instalment (September 1901) in *Strand*.

modern Belgian masters: most likely a group of modern Belgian painters known as *Les XX* (*Les Vingt*; 'The Twenty'), associated with the Neo-Impressionist and Symbolist movements, and including Félicien Rops and James Ensor. The group was brought together by the critic Octave Maus, and had links with the journal *L'Art Moderne*. In other words, the 'modern Belgian masters' were at the extreme of fin-de-siècle art, in keeping with the anti-establishment reputation of the Grosvenor Gallery (see note to *Bond Street picture galleries*).

the crudest ideas: from the beginning of *A Study in Scarlet*, Watson is keen to emphasize Holmes's philistinism: 'Knowledge of Literature.—Nil. . . . [Knowledge of] Philosophy.—Nil' (*SHCLS*, 17). And yet throughout the stories, Holmes quotes from often abstruse works of literature in the original languages, and in *Baskervilles* is able instantly to identify portraits by Kneller and Reynolds (p. 118). In 'The Greek Interpreter' (1893), Holmes tells Watson that 'my grandmother . . . was the sister of Vernet, the French artist. Art in the blood is liable to take the strangest forms' (*SHCSS*, 478). The Vernets were a dynasty of three generations of celebrated French artists, but given the dates, Holmes is most likely referring to Horace Vernet (1789–1863), a prominent painter of sporting and martial subjects. (ACD himself, from several generations of painters and illustrators, also had 'art in the blood'.) It is likely that 'the crudest ideas' here signify an aesthetic disagreement—that Holmes and Watson have different opinions about modern art.

36 *Newcastle . . . Alton*: Newcastle-upon-Tyne is a major industrial city in the North-east of England, with particular associations with coalmining. Alton here is probably a market town in Hampshire, though there are in fact several other Altons in England (in Derbyshire, Leicestershire, Staffordshire, and Wiltshire), though these are mostly small villages.

Gloucester: cathedral city in South-west England, on the banks of the River Severn.

Western dialect: that is, the dialect of American West: 'playing me for a sucker'; 'By thunder'. A significant part of *A Study in Scarlet* takes place in the American West, around Salt Lake City.

37 *five hundred cases*: in 'The Final Problem' (1893), which takes place after the events of *Baskervilles*, Holmes says, 'In over a thousand cases I am not aware that I have ever used my powers upon the wrong side' (*SHCSS*, 551).

38 *dogged in London . . . the millions of this great city*: the canine pun on 'dogged' here (one of many throughout the novel) draws attention to the novel's counterpointing of the city with the country, and the supernatural with the rational: see Introduction. By the end of the nineteenth century, London had 6.58 million inhabitants, making it 'incomparably the largest city the

world had ever seen': Jerry White, *London in the Nineteenth Century: A Human Awful Wonder of God* (London: Jonathan Cape, 2007), 4.

39 *securities . . . close on to a million*: securities are share certificates. On the value of money in the nineteenth century, the London historian Jerry White writes: 'I believe readers will not go far wrong if they think of a nineteenth-century pound as equivalent to £100 now. That holds broadly true for the century as a whole': *London in the Nineteenth Century*, xvi.

Westmorland: historically, a county in the North-west of England; a part of Cumbria since 1974.

entailed: an entailed estate passes on by law to a hereditary successor; that is, it cannot be bequeathed away by the current holder.

41 *10.30 train from Paddington*: Paddington is a major Central London railway terminus, originally opened in 1838 and redesigned in 1854 by Isambard Kingdom Brunel for the Great Western Railway, which linked London with the South-west and Wales. Klinger (454) notes that the 10.30 from Paddington would have arrived at Exeter at 2.28 pm.

42 *3, Turpey Street, the Borough . . . Waterloo Station*: Turpey Street is fictitious. The Borough was a traditional name for Southwark, a district of Central London just south of the Thames. Waterloo is a major London railway station on the south bank of the Thames, built in 1848 as the terminus for the London and South Western Railway.

43 *A touch . . . a foil . . . He got home*: a fencing metaphor. Holmes begins by quoting Laertes in *Hamlet* V.ii.285: 'A touch, a touch, I do confess.' A foil is a light and flexible ('quick and supple') fencing sword. In this context 'got home' means scored a point: that is, hit or cut his opponent.

two guineas: a guinea was 21 shillings, or a pound and a shilling (that is, a pound and five pennies). Two guineas was a substantial fee: see note to *securities*, above.

two or three inches shorter than you: in *A Study in Scarlet*, Watson says of Holmes: 'In height he was rather over six feet, and so excessively lean that he seemed to be considerably taller' (*SHCLS*, 15).

a toff: slang for an upper-class person.

44 *a foeman who is worthy of our steel*: Sir Walter Scott, *The Lady of the Lake* (1810): 'Sir Roderick mark'd, and in his eyes | Respect was mingled with surprise, | And the stern joy which warriors feel | In foemen worthy of their steel.' This is a continuation of Holmes's fencing metaphor from p. 43.

45 *Museum of the College of Surgeons*: the Hunterian Museum of the Royal College of Surgeons, Lincoln's Inn Fields, London. The museum was originally established in 1799 to house the collection of the pioneering anatomist John Hunter (1728–93), and contains many anatomical specimens, most famously the skeleton of the 'Irish Giant', Charles Byrne (1761–83).

46 *the rounded head of the Celt . . . power of attachment*: nineteenth-century racial theory, of which Mortimer is a devotee, was particularly preoccupied with craniometry and phrenology (see note to p. 7), following the pioneering work of Samuel Morton (1799–1851), and of Nott and Gliddon's *Types of Mankind* (1854). These figures established the theory of polygeny—the separate origin of the distinct human races—which was used as a justification for slavery and colonialism, and which was criticized by Charles Darwin in *The Descent of Man* (1871). George Combe's influential *A System of Phrenology* (1830) actually draws attention to 'The long head of the Celt', and argues that 'the Celtic race . . . remains far behind the Teutonic . . . in its attainment in arts, science, philosophy, and civilization': George Combe, *A System of Phrenology*, 2 vols (Edinburgh: Maclachlan, Stewart, & Co., 1853), ii, 359, 329. Ideas of Celtic emotionalism and supernaturalism—'the Celtic enthusiasm and power of attachment'—were a nineteenth-century commonplace, given their most celebrated articulation in Matthew Arnold's *On the Study of Celtic Literature* (1867).

half Gaelic, half Ivernian: half Scottish, half Irish (Hibernian)—rather like ACD himself.

47 *a wagonette with a pair of cobs*: a wagonette is a four-wheeled carriage with an open or removable cover; a cob is 'A short-legged, stout variety of horse, usually ridden by heavy persons' (*OED*).

The coachman . . . Baskerville: when ACD visited Dartmoor with Bertram Fletcher Robinson in April 1901, they were driven around by Fletcher Robinson's coachman, Harry Baskerville.

hart's-tongue ferns: the fern *Scolopendrium vulgare*, so called because their undivided fronds were thought to resemble the tongue of a hart (a male red deer).

48 *Notting Hill murderer*: Notting Hill is a district of West London, in the Borough of Kensington and Chelsea. *The Notting Hill Mystery* (1862–3), by the pseudonymous 'Charles Felix', is a contender for the earliest English detective novel.

cairns: piles of stones, 'abundant' on Dartmoor, and frequently 'of considerable size', according to BD (71), and often marking a Neolithic burial-chamber.

darkling: darkening. Robson (180) detects an echo of Matthew Arnold's 'Dover Beach' (1867): 'And we are here as on a darkling plain'. Thomas Hardy's 'The Darkling Thrush' was first published in 1900, and appeared in book form the following year.

49 *the boars' heads of the Baskervilles*: the family crest of the actual Baskerville family, who came from the Welsh borders around Herefordshire, was 'a wolf's head erased, or pierced through the mouth in bend sinister point upwards': *Fairbairn's Book of Crests of the Families of Great Britain and Ireland*, 2 vols, 4th edn (London and Edinburgh: T. C. & E. C. Jack, 1905), 38.

49 *Swan and Edison*: the Edison and Swan electric light company was formed in 1883, bringing together the two pioneers of incandescent electric light, Thomas Alva Edison (1847–1931) and Joseph Swan (1828–1914), both of whom had independently patented electric lamps in 1879.

mullioned windows: windows divided by vertical bars, characteristic of Gothic architecture. Sir Henry's remark that this is 'the same hall in which for five hundred years my people have lived' dates the hall, or parts of it, to the fourteenth century.

50 *dogs*: 'a pair of iron or brass devices placed one each side of the fireplace to support burning wood' (*OED*).

51 *balustraded gallery*: a balcony bounded by a row of balusters (short, pear-shaped columns).

minstrels' gallery: a balcony originally designed as a space for musicians to perform.

buck of the Regency: in this context, a buck is a dandy or a 'dashing fellow' (*OED*); strictly, the Regency is the period from 1811 to 1820, in which Prince George was regent in place of his father, King George III, though it is sometimes taken to refer to the early nineteenth century, up to the accession of Queen Victoria in 1837.

52 *rustle of ivy on the wall*: this was the end of the third instalment (October 1901) in *Strand*.

MERRIPIT HOUSE: there are houses or farms called Higher, Middle, and Lower Merripit near Postbridge on Dartmoor, though Weller suggests that this Merripit is based on Nun's Cross Cottage near Fox Tor Mires.

55 *our mutual friend*: Frayling, O'Gorman, and Robson all detect a conscious allusion to Charles Dickens's *Our Mutual Friend* (1864–5), perhaps as Stapleton's way of signalling his education and cultural status.

56 *The records . . . reached us here*: a knowing allusion to the outrageous success of the Holmes stories, which is what brought ACD to Dartmoor and *The Hound of the Baskervilles*: see Introduction, pp. xiv–xv.

57 *great Grimpen Mire*: while ACD probably got the name from Grimspound Bog, the location is more likely based on Fox Tor Mires, a few miles from Princetown. Bogs and mires are a feature of Dartmoor: BD's opening chapter is entitled 'Bogs', and notes that 'Fox Tor Mire once bore a very bad name. The only convict who really got away from Princetown and was not recaptured was last seen taking a bee-line for Fox Tor Mire' (6). Dartmoor's mires were thought to be home to 'large, glaring-eyed monsters' (BD). See Introduction, pp. xxvii–xxxii.

58 *moor ponies . . . it sucked him down at last*: BD records of Dartmoor's bogs: 'It is a difficult matter to extricate horses when they flounder in, as is not infrequently the case in hunting. Every plunge sends the poor beasts in deeper' (3).

59 *the last of the bitterns*: the bittern is a large wading bird; the inhabitant of reed-beds and marshes, the bittern is a rare and threatened species, and all

the more elusive because of its secretive nature. The bittern is character-
ized by its unearthly sounding, far-carrying booming cry, sometimes
interpreted in folklore as an omen of death.

Prehistoric man . . . wigwams with the roofs off: Dartmoor is full of prehistoric sites; this is a close description of Grimspound (see note to p. 6).

'Neolithic man—no date': the Neolithic Period, or 'New Stone Age', char-
acterized by the use of ground stone implements and the development of
agriculture. In Britain, the Neolithic period lasted from *c*.4000–*c*.2000 BC.
Grimspound is actually a Bronze Age settlement, thought to date from
c.1300 BC.

Cyclopides: a genus of the skipper butterfly. Depending on which specific
species of *Cyclopides* is being referred to here, this may be a native South
African butterfly; certainly, no Cyclopides has ever been recorded on
Dartmoor: see Klinger, 615–16, for an overview of this subject. Like the
Great Grimpen Mire, the Neolithic settlements, the bittern (see note
above), the orchid (see next note), and indeed the Hound itself, it
seems likely that this is an element of the novel's phantasmagoric,
semi-supernatural representation of the moor.

60 *orchid . . . mare's-tails*: the orchid is probably a marsh orchid, common on
Dartmoor, though the heath spotted orchid and the greater butterfly
orchid also grow on the moor: http://www.dartmoor.gov.uk/wildlife-
and-heritage/wildlife/plants. Robson (181) suggests that Beryl Stapleton
has in mind the more exotic orchids of her native country, Costa Rica; in
which case this orchid would be another instance of the moor's fantastical
flora and fauna (see previous note). 'Mare's-tails' are *Hippuris vulgaris*,
a common wetland plant growing with its roots in water.

61 *commoner*: strictly speaking, Sir Henry, as a Baronet and therefore not
a peer, is also a commoner.

grazier: 'One who grazes or feeds cattle for the market' (*OED*).

62 *Lepidoptera*: an order of insects including butterflies and moths.

64 *One page is missing*: reading Watson's account, it is difficult to tell which
page, if any, is missing.

monoliths: prehistoric stone pillars; these are abundant on Dartmoor, often
in stone circles or rows.

65 *earth round the sun*: a reference to *A Study in Scarlet*, in which Watson
discovers that Holmes 'was ignorant of the Copernican Theory and of the
composition of the Solar System. That any civilized human being in this
nineteenth century should not be aware that the earth travelled around the
sun appeared to me to be such an extraordinary fact that I could hardly
realize it' (*SHCLS*, 16).

66 *the spot . . . had its origin*: Hound Tor (see note to p. 23), between
Widecombe-on-the-Moor and Bovey Tracey, seems a likely candidate for
this location.

66 *cotton grass*: *Eriophorum*, a variety of grass found throughout the Northern Hemisphere, and common in boggy soil; so-called because of its heads of long, white silky hairs.

67 *a barrow at Long Down*: a barrow is an ancient grave-mound. There is a village of Longdown on the edge of Dartmoor, though this particular Long Down may well be fictitious.

68 *Fernworthy*: 'Fernworthy [is] a substantial farm in a singularly lone spot. . . . At Fernworthy itself is a circle of upright stones and the remains of several stone rows' (BD, 163). Fernworthy, a few miles from Postbridge, was drowned in the construction of the Fernworthy Reservoir, opened in 1942.

on the escaped convict: *Strand*, Newnes, McClure, *SHCLS*, Baring-Gould, Klinger, and O'Gorman all have 'in the escaped convict'; Robson and Frayling correct this to 'on'.

70 *interesting reading*: this is the end of the fourth instalment (November 1901) in *Strand*.

[Second Report of Dr Watson]: *Strand*, Newnes, McClure, and O'Gorman have the chapter title '[Second Report of Dr Watson] / The Light Upon the Moor'; *SHCLS*, Baring-Gould, and Klinger have 'Second Report of Dr Watson / The Light Upon the Moor'. Robson and Frayling have 'The Light Upon the Moor / [Second Report of Dr Watson]'.

budget: a week's news in one instalment; a bundle of news. This is a term from newspaper and periodical publishing: the publishers of *The Pall Mall Gazette*, for example, also produced a weekly *Pall Mall Budget*.

72 *Plymouth*: city on the South Devon coast. ACD lived and practised medicine there for a time in 1882.

76 *tangled skein*: *A Tangled Skein* was ACD's original title for *A Study in Scarlet*.

lattice-window: a window made of small, diamond-shaped panes set in lead-work.

80 *Cleft Tor*: there is no Cleft Tor on Dartmoor, but there is a Cleft Rock above Holne Chase; BD reproduces a striking photograph of the Cleft Rock.

81 *hunting-crop*: 'A short straight whipstock with a handle and a short leather lop in place of a lash, used in the hunting field' (*OED*).

82 *'The folk on the country-side'*: *SHCLS*, Baring-Gould, Klinger, and Frayling all have 'countryside'.

83 *an evil yellow face, a terrible animal face . . . one of those old savages*: like Dr Mortimer, Watson here uses the language of racial theory and physiognomy (the scientific study of facial features) to represent Selden as a characteristically atavistic 'criminal type'.

84 *We were both fair runners and in good condition*: for its American audience, McClure changes this to 'We were both swift runners and in fairly good training'.

85 *come down to us*: this is the end of the fifth instalment (December 1901) in *Strand*.

[In any case . . . next few days.]: This sentence appears in McClure, but not in *Strand* or Newnes. *SHCLS*, Frayling, and O'Gorman omit it; Baring-Gould and Klinger include it; Robson includes it in square brackets, as here.

there are: *Strand* has 'there is'; corrected for Newnes.

86 *a mere fiend-dog*: MS has 'a mere spectral hound', probably corrected to avoid the repetition of the phrase 'spectral hound' from a few lines earlier: New York Public Library Berg Collection: Sir Arthur Conan Doyle Collection of Papers.

where did it get its food: Frayling (xxvii) recounts that T. S. Eliot, an admirer of *Baskervilles* whose poetry alludes to the novel, asked the same question: 'He had always wondered . . . how the hound had been supplied with so much food without arousing the suspicions of the local butchers!'

distrait: 'Distracted in mind; excessively perplexed or troubled' (*OED*).

87 *And*: *Strand* has 'But he will never trouble...'; changed to 'And' for Newnes, though McClure retains 'But'. Robson and Frayling both speculate that the phrasing here implies a missing sentence, though there is no evidence for this.

88 *Coombe Tracey*: the name 'Coombe Tracey' most likely derives from Bovey Tracey, on the eastern fringes of Dartmoor—there are also two Coombes in Devon, and many more villages beginning with Combe. It is likely that ACD had a number of places in mind here.

89 *my report of the morning's conversation for Holmes*: Robson and Frayling both wonder whether this is the 'missing page' to which Watson refers on p. 64.

90 *Black Tor*: there are four Black Tors on Dartmoor, though this is most likely the one between Princetown and Walkhampton. This is the only Black Tor which BD discusses, noting that it is 'Within an easy stroll of Princetown . . . Black Tor, that looks down on these remains ['hut circles'], is also above a blowing-house and miners' hut' (270)—that is, a hut belonging to the nearby Whiteworks tin mine: see note to p. 131.

dog-cart: 'A cart with a box under the seat for a hunter's dogs. In later use: an open carriage with two transverse seats back to back, the rear seat originally converting into a box for dogs' (*OED*).

91 *his own affairs are considerably involved*: that is, he spends large sums on legal bills.

craniology: the science of the measurement of skulls. See note to p. 7.

92 *écarté*: a French card game for two people. *Écarté* plays a prominent role in ACD's Brigadier Gerard story 'How the Brigadier Held the King' (1895).

a week ago: that is, Holmes has been on the moor since at least October 9th; he arrived there shortly after Watson and Sir Henry.

93 *some lay of his own*: some score of his own; some private purpose.

of Coombe Tracey: here and elsewhere in the chapter, the original manuscript reads 'of Newton Abbott', though this has then been crossed out:
New York Public Library, Berg Collection: Arthur Conan Doyle Papers.
Newton Abbot [*sic*] is a town in Devon, on the eastern fringes of Dartmoor,
not far from Bertram Fletcher Robinson's home in Ipplepen.

94 *without ceremony*: that is, without announcing him. The implication is that
Laura Lyons initially thinks the visitor is Stapleton: 'Her face fell, however, when she saw that I was a stranger.'

Remington typewriter: E. Remington and Sons of New York, founded in
1816, was best known as a firearms manufacturer, but also made sewing
machines and typewriters. The Remington Type-Writer, first produced in
1873, was the first commercially available typewriter, and introduced the
QWERTY keyboard; the Remington Model 2, produced from 1878,
introduced the shift key, thus enabling typing in lower case and capitals.

sulphur rose: *Rosa hemisphaerica*, a yellow, double-flowered variety of rose,
initially native to Asia, but popular in European gardens. So called because
of its unpleasant smell.

something subtly wrong with the face . . . looseness of lip: again, Watson holds
to nineteenth-century theories of physiognomy: see note to p. 83.

95 *stops*: keys.

almoner: 'a person appointed to distribute the donations, bequests, etc., of
another' (*OED*).

96 *a passage of your letter*: manuscript reads 'a postscript of your letter'.

that you wrote it?: manuscript originally read 'that you read it'.

97 *the law is upon his side . . . he may force me to live with him*: the Matrimonial
Causes Act of 1857 established civil Divorce Courts (divorce had previ-
ously been an ecclesiastical issue); its practice discriminated strongly
against women seeking divorce. The Matrimonial Causes Act of 1884
enforced conjugal rights, effectively forcing separated women to return to
their husbands. This was contested in the high profile case of 'Regina v.
Jackson' in 1891, otherwise known as the 'Clitheroe Case' (after the
Lancashire town in which the events took place), which adjudicated that
a husband had no right to confine his wife in the name of conjugal rights:
see Ginger Frost, 'A Shock to Marriage?: The Clitheroe Case and the
Victorians', in George Robb and Nancy Erber, eds, *Disorder in the Court:
Trials and Sexual Conflict at the Turn of the Century* (London: Palgrave
Macmillan, 1999), 100–18. ACD himself became a prominent advocate of
divorce reform, and became President of the Divorce Law Reform
Association in 1909. In 1912, he wrote to the *Daily Mail* that 'English
divorce laws are the most conservative and, from a reformer's point of
view, reactionary in Europe': *Letters to the Press*, 160.

if certain expenses could be met: manuscript reads 'if a certain sum of money
could be found for his expenses my husband was willing to leave the country'.

But the published novel goes on to make it clear that this is money 'for the legal expenses connected with divorce'.

98 *a trap*: a small, two-wheeled carriage on springs.

among the stone huts upon the moor: the original manuscript stops here, before reaching the end of the page, and then continues on a new page, which contains a passage which ACD later discarded: 'Either she was an accomplished actor and a deep conspirator, or Barrymore had misread the letter, or the letter was a forgery—unless there could by some extraordinary coincidence be a second lady writing from Newton Abbot whose initials were L.L. For the time my clue had come to nothing and I could only turn back to that other one which lay among the stone huts upon the moor.'

run him to earth: 'track him to his lair'. This is a phrase from fox-hunting, and one of many figurative uses of 'dog' and 'hound' throughout the novel.

99 *red faced*: manuscript has 'choleric'.

wagonette: 'A four-wheeled carriage, made open or with a removable cover and furnished with a seat or bench at each side facing inwards and with one or two seats arranged crosswise in front' (*OED*).

magnates: wealthy, eminent, or influential people.

Sir John Morland: manuscript has 'the Mayor of Plymouth'.

Frankland v. Regina: Frankland versus the Crown; the female 'Regina', here, as opposed to the male 'Rex', clearly dates the action of the novel to the reign of Victoria, who died on 22 January 1901, several months before the first instalment of *Baskervilles* in August 1901.

101 *flat leads of the house*: in this context, the 'leads' are 'The sheets or strips of lead used to cover a roof' (*OED*); Lafter Hall has a portion of flat, lead roof.

102 *Belliver and Vixen Tor*: Belliver (now written as Bellever) Tor is near Postbridge; BD (145) quotes an article from the *Western Daily Mail* asserting that 'Belliver is the most striking of all her sister tors'. Vixen Tor, 'presenting from one point a resemblance to the Sphinx' (BD), lies between Princetown and Tavistock. According to Dartmoor legend, Vixen Tor was the lair of Vixana, an evil witch who lured travellers to their doom in a nearby bog: http://www.dartmoor.gov.uk/learning/dartmoor-legends/the-legend-of-vixen-tor

curlew: a mottled brown wading bird with a characteristic curved beak.

chequered light: 'dim light' in manuscript.

pannikin: a small pan or drinking vessel; originally a term from Australian English.

103 *Spartan habits*: after the ancient Spartans, famous for the simplicity, frugality, and endurance of their lifestyles.

and yet as I looked at them . . . bringing nearer: manuscript reads: 'and yet here I was waiting for some crisis, waiting with my nerves in a quiver, knowing that…'

104 *outside than in*: this is the end of the sixth instalment (January 1902) in *Strand*.

105 *Bradley, Oxford Street*: see note to p. 22.

107 *Sir Henry did not make love to her*: that is, did not court or woo her.

111 *beetling forehead*: overhanging forehead, generally also carrying a reference to scowling, or to bushy eyebrows; a characteristic of criminal physiognomy (see note to p. 28).

112 *death by the laws of his country*: Selden was not sentenced to death, but to life imprisonment, 'due to some doubts as to his complete sanity' (p. 48).

   by all that's wonderful: an allusion to a scene of discovery from Richard Brinsley Sheridan's *The School for Scandal* (1777): 'Lady Teazle, by all that's wonderful!'

115 *a hound does not bite a dead body*: a strange assertion, though one which becomes significant later in the novel (see p. 137). There are in fact innumerable instances of dogs of many breeds biting, chewing, or eating dead bodies, including the bodies of their owners. In 2017, *National Geographic* magazine published an article on this very subject: Erika Engelhaupt, 'Would Your Dog Eat You If You Died? Get the Facts', https://www.nationalgeographic.com/science/article/pets-dogs-cats-eat-dead-owners-forensics-science

   Sufficient for tomorrow is the evil thereof: Matthew 6:34: 'Take therefore no thought for the morrow: for the morrow shall take thought for the things of itself. Sufficient unto the day *is* the evil thereof.'

116 *ready for our suppers*: this is the end of the seventh instalment (February 1902) in *Strand*.

117 *our views upon the subject differ*: see note to p. 155.

118 *steer*: beef cattle; another of Sir Henry's Americanisms.

   Kneller: Sir Godfrey Kneller (1646–1723), painter celebrated for his portraits and his historical scenes. Born Gottfried Kniller in Lübeck, Germany, Kneller moved to England in 1676, and had much success as a painter of society portraits.

   Reynolds: Sir Joshua Reynolds (1723–93), major British artist of the eighteenth century.

   Rodney in the West Indies: Admiral George Bridges Rodney (c.1718–92); British naval commander and politician. Decisively defeated French naval forces at the Battle of the Saintes in the West Indies (9–12 April 1782), thus preventing a military invasion of the islands. As a consequence of this victory, Rodney was ennobled as the first Baron Rodney in 1782.

   Chairman of Committees . . . Pitt: either William Pitt the elder, 1st Earl of Chatham (1708–78), who led the government from 1756 to 1761, but was technically only Prime Minister from 1766 to 1768, or William Pitt the younger (1759–1806), Prime Minister from 1783 to 1801 and 1804 to 1806. (Robson, Frayling, and Klinger all assume it is Pitt the younger.)

There is no one 'Chairman of Committees of the House of Commons': the United Kingdom House of Commons has many committees, each with its own chair. However, the first (1844) edition of *Erskine May*, the definitive guide to British parliamentary procedure, observes, under the heading '*Chairman of committees in the commons*', that 'In the commons the chair is generally taken by the chairman of the committee of ways and means': Thomas Erskine May, *A Treatise upon the Law, Privileges, Proceedings and Usage of Parliament* (London: Charles Knight & Co., 1844), 224. (The Ways and Means Committee makes recommendations for government budgets.)

Cavalier: a member of the Royalist side during the English Civil War (1642–51). Frayling proposes that this portrait is by the Dutch painter Frans Hals (*c*.1582–1666).

roysterer: roisterer: 'A wild or riotous person; a boisterous or noisy reveller' (*OED*).

love-locks: in the seventeenth century, a love-lock was 'a lock of hair worn longer than the rest and arranged so as to hang forward over one shoulder, often tied with a ribbon' (*OED*).

119 *a throw-back*: see note to p. 6. This is a major recurring preoccupation in the novel, and is the area of Dr Mortimer's academic specialization—though he does not seem to have noticed this particular 'throw-back'.

the doctrine of reincarnation: the later ACD was certainly open to the possibilities of reincarnation, writing that 'On the whole, it seems to the author that the balance of evidence shows that reincarnation is a fact, but not necessarily a universal one': *The History of Spiritualism* (London: Cassell, 1926), vol. 2, p. 176.

121 *the best of the professionals*: Holmes's opinion of Lestrade changes significantly over the course of the stories: when he first appears, in *A Study in Scarlet*, Holmes says: 'Gregson is the smartest of the Scotland Yarders, . . . he and Lestrade are the pick of a bad lot. They are both quick and energetic, but conventional—shockingly so' (*SHCLS*, 31, 27).

122 *York*: cathedral city in North Yorkshire, in the North of England. This is the location of St Oliver's, Stapleton's ill-fated school 'in the north country' (p. 61).

124 *Grodno, in Little Russia*: Grodno, or Hrodna, is a city in the west of modern-day Belarus, near the border with Poland and Lithuania. In the nineteenth century, 'Little Russia' was effectively coterminous with modern-day Ukraine. Although these terms and borders were imprecise, technically Grodno would not have been in Little Russia but in White Russia ('Byelorussia', or Belarus, is a translation of White Russia).

small, wiry bulldog of a man: Lestrade is 'lean and ferret-like' when we first encounter him in *A Study in Scarlet* (*SHCLS*, 31), though this description is in keeping with *Baskervilles*' recurring canine imagery.

I could well remember the scorn . . . practical man: all the Scotland Yard detectives he encounters are initially sceptical of Holmes, though it is Athelney Jones in *The Sign of the Four* who refers to him contemptuously as 'Mr Theorist' (*SHCLS*, 190).

125 *Coombe Tracey*: Strand has 'Temple Coombe', an obvious error, and probably due to ACD's decision to use Coombe Tracey instead of Newton Abbot as a location: see note to p. 93. (There is a Templecombe in west Somerset, but this is many miles from the action of the novel.)

128 *Thank God*: 'Thank Heaven' in *Strand* and Newnes; changed to 'Thank God' in McClure. *SHCLS*, Baring-Gould, and Klinger have 'Thank heaven'; O'Gorman has 'Thank Heaven'; Robson and Frayling have 'Thank God'. The manuscript for this page is lost.

dewlap: the fold of skin hanging from the throat.

the wall of fog: this is the end of the eighth and penultimate instalment (March 1902) in *Strand*.

129 *five barrels*: more properly, five chambers—although small, multi-barrelled 'pepperpot' Derringer pistols, designed for easy concealment, were produced well into the twentieth century. The Holmes stories make frequent reference to Watson carrying his army service revolver (most likely a Beaumont-Adams or a Webley Mk I). Frayling (193) identifies Holmes's revolver, small enough to conceal in his dressing-gown pocket in 'The Final Problem' (1893, but set after *Baskervilles*), as a short-barrelled Webley Metropolitan Police revolver: see also H. T. Webster, 'Observations on Sherlock Holmes as a Sportsman and Athlete', in Philip A. Shreffler, ed., *Sherlock Holmes by Gas-Lamp: Highlights from the First Four Decades of 'The Baker Street Journal'* (New York: Fordham University Press, 1989), 81.

a combination of the two: the exact breed or cross of the Hound is the cause for very much speculation. Robson asserts that breeding a mastiff and a bloodhound is 'said by experts to be impossible' (187). Frayling and O'Gorman both wonder how such a cross could produce this gigantic dog (mastiffs are enormous, but bloodhounds are much smaller). Klinger (591) surveys the various suggestions that have been put forward, from Irish Wolfhound to Great Dane to Doberman Pinscher.

'Phosphorus' . . . 'A cunning preparation of it': phosphorus is a chemical element which glows when in contact with oxygen; its name comes from the Greek for 'light-bearer'. In reality, phosphorus is highly poisonous, and causes severe burning, though there are a number of other phosphorescent substances, such as barium sulphate or zinc sulphate: this 'cunning preparation' could have used these.

131 *an old tin mine*: the Whiteworks tin mine, disused by the 1880s, right next to Fox Tor Mires, a few miles from Princetown. In a letter to his mother, written from the Duchy Hotel in Princetown during his visit to Dartmoor in 1901, ACD wrote, 'Everywhere there are gutted tin mines': Frayling, p. xxii.

132 *miasmatic*: a miasma is a 'Noxious vapour rising from putrescent organic matter, marshland, etc., which pollutes the atmosphere' (*OED*).

134 *Colonel Upwood . . . famous card scandal*: Baring-Gould, Klinger, and Frayling all suggest that this has overtones of the high-profile 'Baccarat Case' of 1891, also known as the Tranby Croft Affair, in which Lieutenant Colonel Sir William Gordon-Cumming, formerly of the Scots Guards, unsuccessfully brought an action of slander against the Wilson family of Tranby Croft, Yorkshire, who had accused him of cheating at cards while staying at their home. The case gained particular attention because the Prince of Wales, who was also a guest at Tranby Croft, was called and cross-examined as a witness.

Since the tragic upshot . . . married in New York: these lines do not appear in *Strand*.

he would never permit cases to overlap: in Chapter 5, Holmes claims that he cannot travel to Dartmoor because 'one of the most revered names in England is being besmirched by a blackmailer, and only I can stop a dangerous scandal' (p. 40). This may be a not-uncharacteristic inconsistency on ACD's part (Watson's first name is both James and John; Watson is variously shot in the shoulder and in the leg in Afghanistan; Professor James Moriarty has a brother called James, etc.), or it may underline the conscious deception which allowed Holmes to visit Dartmoor incognito.

135 *The barrister who has his case . . . the infamous Upwood*: these lines do not appear in *Strand*.

Beryl Garcia, one of the beauties of Costa Rica: Costa Rica is a Central American state, between Panama and Nicaragua. Beryl is not normally a Hispanic name.

a school in the east of Yorkshire: this is St Oliver's (p. 123), Stapleton's school 'in the north country' (p. 62) which 'sank . . . into infamy' (p. 135). Yorkshire was historically divided into three separate Ridings: the East Riding of Yorkshire (formerly Humberside) is now a separate county. The North Yorkshire Moors are also in the north-eastern part of Yorkshire. O'Gorman suggests that the location of St Oliver's carries echoes of Dotheboy's Hall, the school run by the sadistic Wackford Squeers in Dickens's *Nicholas Nickleby* (1838–9), which is in Greta Bridge, on the border of North Yorkshire and County Durham—a remote location for the middle class to send (and forget about) illegitimate, disabled, or otherwise unwanted children.

136 *Ross and Mangles the dealer on the Fulham Road*: the pet shop is fictitious; the Fulham Road is a major thoroughfare in South-west London.

North Devon line: the North Devon line originally ran from Exeter to Bideford on the north coast of Devon, before being amalgamated into the London and South-Western Line, which ran from London to Plymouth. This was primarily a suburban route, rather than the main-line Great Western Railway. Presumably, Stapleton transports the Hound by this longer and slower, but quieter, route in order to avoid attention.

137 *finding him dead, had turned away again*: see note to p. 115 for ACD's erroneous belief that 'a hound does not bite a dead body'.

138 *Mexborough Private Hotel, in Craven Street*: Craven Street, running between Northumberland Avenue and the Strand in Central London, had a number of small hotels, and was very close to Sir Henry's Northumberland Hotel (see note to p. 26). The Mexborough is fictitious, but named after a town in Yorkshire, thus underlining the connection between Stapleton and 'the north country' (see note to p. 135).

139 *boots*: a servant whose job was to clean boots.

outré: spectacularly odd or peculiar.

Folkestone Court: fictitious West Country house.

140 *Anthony is not a common name in England . . . Spanish–American countries*: as Robson notes (188), in England, servants were usually addressed by their surnames, whereas in 'Spanish-American countries' they were addressed by their forenames. While not particularly uncommon, Anthony was a name more frequently associated with the Catholic rather than the Protestant population of Britain.

white jessamine: or white jasmine (*Jasminum officinale*), a sweet-scented plant, common in gardens, and widely used in perfumery.

142 *bogie hound*: a bogey or bogy is a goblin, or a folkloric name for the devil; more generally 'An object of terror or dread' (*OED*). In the North of England, the barguest or barghest is the name of a supernatural black dog (see Introduction, pp. xxxii–xxxiv).

143 *Les Huguenots*: an 1836 grand opera by Giacomo Meyerbeer (1791–1864). Huguenots were French Protestants of the sixteenth and seventeenth centuries, who were often persecuted for their faith. Meyerbeer's opera deals with the events leading up to the St Bartholomew's Day Massacre of August 1572, in which thousands of Huguenots were killed. The repression of the Huguenots was also the subject of ACD's 1893 novel *The Refugees*. *Les Huguenots* was one of the most commonly produced operas in the nineteenth century, performed by the Royal Opera in virtually every season between 1847 and 1902. See Harold Rosenthal, *Two Centuries of Opera at Covent Garden* (London: Putnam, 1958).

the De Reszkes: the Polish siblings Jean de Reszke (Jan Mieczysław Retszké, 1850–1925) and Édouard de Reszke (Edward Retszké, 1853–1917) were both renowned opera singers (a tenor and a bass, respectively). In 1889, both brothers appeared together in the Royal Opera House production of *Les Huguenots* (see previous note) in Covent Garden.

Marcini's: fictitious Italian restaurant.

American Literature

British and Irish Literature

Children's Literature

Classics and Ancient Literature

Colonial Literature

Eastern Literature

European Literature

Gothic Literature

History

Medieval Literature

Oxford English Drama

Philosophy

Poetry

Politics

Religion

The Oxford Shakespeare

A complete list of Oxford World's Classics, including Authors in Context, Oxford English Drama, and the Oxford Shakespeare, is available in the UK from the Marketing Services Department, Oxford University Press, Great Clarendon Street, Oxford OX2 6DP, or visit the website at www.oup.com/uk/worldsclassics.

In the USA, visit www.oup.com/us/owc for a complete title list.

Oxford World's Classics are available from all good bookshops. In case of difficulty, customers in the UK should contact Oxford University Press Bookshop, 116 High Street, Oxford OX1 4BR.

ANTHONY TROLLOPE

The American Senator
An Autobiography
Barchester Towers
Can You Forgive Her?
Cousin Henry
Doctor Thorne
The Duke's Children
The Eustace Diamonds
Framley Parsonage
He Knew He Was Right
Lady Anna
The Last Chronicle of Barset
Orley Farm
Phineas Finn
Phineas Redux
The Prime Minister
Rachel Ray
The Small House at Allington
The Warden
The Way We Live Now